PRAISE FOR *THE SKELETONS IN GOD'S CLOSET*

For a long time many of us have been unsettled with how traditionalists talk about hell. At the heart of the unsettledness is that hell seems to have no large purpose other than vindictiveness, even (as some say it) sadistic punishment. In this book Joshua Ryan Butler beautifully places tough topics, like hell and holy war and final judgment, in the larger mission of God for wedding once again heaven and earth. This, my friends, is a genuinely helpful book and I hope those who struggle with these tough topics will discover here what I have—relief and joy.

—SCOT MCKNIGHT PROFESSOR OF NEW
TESTAMENT, NORTHERN SEMINARY

Profound. Powerful. Paradigm shifting. This is simply the best book I've read from a young author in years. We will be hearing a lot more from Joshua, and I'll be listening to everything he has to say and all that he writes. He writes with the depth of a theologian, the passion of an activist, the mind of a thinker, and the view of a globalist. This book is a book for the 21st century in a pluralistic public square kind of world. We are in desperate need of thinkers and writers like Joshua whether you agree or disagree with him.

—BOB ROBERTS JR.
PASTOR OF NORTHWOOD CHURCH,
AUTHOR OF *BOLD AS LOVE*

Christians need to be a people who, first and foremost, have overflowing love for others, but we also need to be thinkers—not just for ourselves but for those we care about. *The Skeletons in God's Closet* hits some of the bull's-eye topics that frequently come up when we are in dialogue with people about the Bible and our beliefs. I'm thankful for this book: it's theologically trustworthy but stretches your thinking, and you'll come away with more than just powerful ideas on difficult questions—the way Joshua has written truly causes you to worship God all the more.

—DAN KIMBALL
PASTOR OF VINTAGE FAITH CHURCH

I began reading Joshua Ryan Butler's book wondering if his arguments would change my mind about judgment and hell. Instead, as I read deeper and deeper into the book, I found that Joshua's words changed not only my mind, but also my heart, as I began to understand God's pure, unrelenting love for the world.

—SARAH THEBARGE
AUTHOR OF *THE INVISIBLE GIRLS*

Christians find themselves today facing the spiritual equivalents of questions like "Have you stopped beating your children?" The challenge: *you lose no matter how you answer.* Certainly, that's the case with tough topics like hell, judgment and holy war, where those who control the questions often control the debate. In *The Skeletons in God's Closet*, Joshua Ryan Butler undertakes the important work of reframing the questions and putting the emphasis on the right syllables when addressing people's struggles with the God of the Bible. Butler engages these controversial subjects critically, creatively, and constructively. The end result is that Christians will be better able to go from back pedaling to walking with doubters and critics and addressing their questions and challenges in meaningful ways.

—DR. PAUL LOUIS METZGER
DIRECTOR OF THE INSTITUTE FOR THE THEOLOGY
OF CULTURE: NEW WINE, NEW WINESKINS,
AUTHOR OF *CONNECTING CHRIST: HOW TO
DISCUSS JESUS IN A WORLD OF DIVERSE PATHS*

"What if God's not the good and loving Father I thought him to be?" *The Skeletons in God's Closet* doesn't shy away from the awkward subjects most authors avoid at all cost, but charges right into them with theological precision, unexpected biblical insight, and compassionate application. It addresses issues by reframing them within the context of God's historical narrative and demonstrates their relevance by placing them in the context of today's culture. Butler has produced something profoundly unique here: intellectually satisfying and enlightening—as well as entertaining and life-changing—this is a gem!

—KEN WYTSMA
FOUNDER OF THE JUSTICE CONFERENCE, AUTHOR
OF *PURSUING JUSTICE* PRESIDENT OF KILNS
COLLEGE AND PASTOR OF ANTIOCH CHURCH

This book is an anomaly—it talks about dark themes such as holy war and hell in a bold and refreshing way. It is deeply theological but approachable, personal and available. I love that Joshua has the courage to "open the door" to God's skeleton closet and shine a light on what's there. He is a reliable guide.

—JOHN SOWERS
PRESIDENT OF THE MENTORING PROJECT
AND AUTHOR OF *THE HEROIC PATH*

There is a towering stack of books on my desk—many given as gifts by friends. When I received *The Skeletons in God's Closet* I would never have anticipated my inability to put it down. I was challenged and inspired as I read through this book!

—DR. ANDREA COOK
PRESIDENT OF WARNER PACIFIC COLLEGE

The Skeletons in God's Closet is a deeply satisfying read. When referencing Scripture, Joshua mixes equal parts respectful reverence and playful familiarity. He joyfully excavates Christianity's most feared doctrines from the rubble of our modern cultural misunderstanding and restores them to their rightful place as pillars of our faith. Joshua has addressed and dispelled, with unflinching directness, many of my deepest doubts and skepticisms. I am deeply grateful for the faith-strengthening effect this book has had on my life.

—SEBASTIAN ROGERS
PERIPHERAL VISION STUDIOS

The Skeletons in God's Closet comes at such an important time in the Western church. After centuries of nationalism and military violence, a new generation is questioning the status quo. Does violence have any place in Jesus' kingdom? In the life of his followers? If not, how do we reconcile Jesus' teaching on loving our enemies with judgment, hell, and destruction? How do we read the Old Testament texts of genocide and ethnic cleansing? These kinds of questions are paramount. Whether you agree with Joshua's answers or not, I'm just so happy that he's leading the way towards a new kind of conversation. This book is courageous, intelligent, provocative, and sound. Read it.

—JOHN MARK COMER
PASTOR FOR TEACHING AND VISION AT
BRIDGETOWN: A JESUS CHURCH

For more than a decade, I have been dreaming of the day the world would be introduced to the thoughts of Joshua Ryan Butler. Through the pages of *The Skeletons in God's Closet* my dream has come true. This articulate, original, and prayerfully discerned book is a must-read for all Bible-inspired thinkers who have the courage to explore in the lush idea-fields that exist beyond the deep-rutted wagon trails of much religious writing.

—TONY "THE BEAT POET" KRIZ
AUTHOR OF *NEIGHBORS AND WISE MEN* AND *ALOOF*

This is a profound book, a vital antidote to some of our most malicious misunderstandings of God's good news. With compelling stories, careful exegesis, and wise theological grounding, Joshua Ryan Butler invites us not only into a clearer way of understanding, but also into *a different way of being in the world*. Dive into this book and you'll find yourself caught up in the surprisingly hopeful story of how the Creating, Sustaining, and Redeeming God is at work to bring life in all its fullness where skeletons—both imagined and real—have for too long endured.

—MICHAEL YANKOSKI
AUTHOR OF *THE SACRED YEAR* AND
UNDER THE OVERPASS

With sensitivity to those for whom the Christian story is seen as coercive and cruel, Joshua Ryan Butler deftly navigates between biblical narratives and real life experiences to show that God is good and gracious and will put right injustice. Calling for the abandonment of popular typologies of hell, judgment, and holy war, Butler constantly pushes back to the overall arc of the biblical story, that God is at work to reconcile and contain evil, pride, and abuse, not to mete it out in some underground prison or on a battleground. This is a fine book for the postmodern skeptic or bruised reed in our ruthless world, as well as a church needing to reclaim her story of a good King inviting all his beleaguered people into his just kingdom of shalom.

—MICHAEL ANDRES, NORTHWESTERN COLLEGE
MARVIN AND JERENE DEWITT PROFESSOR OF RELIGION

I have taught graduate theology classes for twenty years and have read countless books on apologetics, salvation, world religions, hell, sin, and genocide. *The Skeletons in God's Closet* stands out as one of the most stimulating books I have read on these subjects. It gave me new insights which blessed and challenged me. Josh has an uncanny ability to connect biblical truth with real world issues in an incredibly creative manner. This book won't answer all your questions but it will stimulate paradigm shifts in your thinking. That is its genius. I will be recommending this book to my students and friends. It is truly a must-read work.

—Steve Tracy
Professor of Theology and Ethics
at Phoenix Seminary Executive
Director of Mending the Soul

The
Skeletons
in
God's
Closet

The Mercy of Hell, The Surprise of
Judgment, The Hope of Holy War

The Skeletons in God's Closet

JOSHUA RYAN BUTLER

W PUBLISHING GROUP

AN IMPRINT OF THOMAS NELSON

Published in Nashville, Tennessee, by Thomas Nelson. Thomas Nelson is a trademark of Thomas Nelson, Inc.

Published in association with literary agent Blair Jacobson of D.C. Jacobson & Associates, LLC, an Author Management Company, www.dcjacobson.com.

Thomas Nelson, Inc., titles may be purchased in bulk for educational, business, fund-raising, or sales promotional use. For information, please e-mail SpecialMarkets@ThomasNelson.com.

Unless otherwise indicated, Scripture quotations are taken from the Holy Bible, New International Version®, NIV®. Copyright © 1973, 1978, 1984, 2011 by Biblica, Inc.™ Used by permission of Zondervan. All rights reserved worldwide. www.zondervan.com

Scripture quotations marked ESV are taken from the ENGLISH STANDARD VERSION. © 2001 by Crossway Bibles, a division of Good News Publishers.

Scripture quotations marked KJV are taken from the King James Version (public domain).

Scripture quotations marked NASB are taken from NEW AMERICAN STANDARD BIBLE®, © The Lockman Foundation 1960, 1962, 1963, 1968, 1971, 1972, 1973, 1975, 1977, 1995. Used by permission.

Scripture quotations marked NLT are taken from the *Holy Bible*, New Living Translation. © 1996, 2004, 2007. Used by permission of Tyndale House Publishers, Inc., Carol Stream, Illinois 60188. All rights reserved.

While the author has made every effort to provide accurate website information at the time of publication, neither the publisher nor the author assumes any responsibility for errors or for changes that occur after publication. Further, the publisher does not have any control over and does not assume any responsibility for author or third-party websites or their content.

Certain names and details have been changed to protect privacy. Permission has been granted for use of real names, stories, and correspondence with some individuals.

Library of Congress Control Number: 2014942542

Printed in the United States of America

14 15 16 17 18 19 RRD 6 5 4 3 2 1

For
Holly Beth Butler
Union unto glory

They will neither harm nor destroy
on all my holy mountain,
for the earth will be filled with the knowledge of the LORD
as the waters cover the sea.

—Isaiah 11:9

SKELETAL STRUCTURE

FOREWORD

"Is God good? If he allows people to be tortured by flames for eternity? If he only lets religious folks into his kingdom? If he commands the Israelites to kill innocent children in holy war? There's no way a God who does that is good."

These questions are on the lips and minds of people living in our post-Christian world, and this is the world in which we are called to preach and live the gospel. A God who is not good is a God most of us would rather not exist . . . including myself.

Most of us dodge these questions. We may not like to admit it, but we treat these tough subjects like the title of this book suggests: as if God's hiding skeletons in his closet, showing us a smiling face of love but holding a whip behind his back in case we don't do as we're told.

Jesus' people often seem to be given only two options: capitulate your faith in the bible and swoop everyone up in a universal "love is god" type of pop-theology, or bang your bible on the pulpit and preach about how "those people" out there on the other side of the church doors are all on a highway headed to hell.

I don't like either option.

That's why I'm so grateful Joshua Ryan Butler has given us a refreshing and thoroughly orthodox view of hell, judgment, and holy war. Most of us think of hell more like Dante's inferno than Jesus' warning to those who might miss the kingdom. Joshua turns our assumptions on their head and helps us see these topics clearly through the lens of a God whose motives are love.

I've known Joshua for fourteen years. He's played a large part in shaping our life as a church here in the heart of Portland. He has the mind of a theologian, the heart of a poet, and the hands of a missionary. These three gifts make him a very unique and profound voice to speak on these topics.

As a theologian, he doesn't side-step the issues or dance around the text. He deals with it accurately and with care. But as a poet, he takes notice of things like metaphor and imagery—things often lost on those of us who tend to read the Bible more like an instruction manual. Rather than dismiss the imagery, he lets it spark our imagination the way good literature does.

And he is also a missionary here in our twenty-first century post-everything city with skeptics and cynics and good-hearted humanists. It is this missionary reading of the Bible that I fear we have lost in North America. Joshua helps us learn what it means to read the Bible from its context and translate it into ours. To let it be the acting subject that critiques our assumptions and our fears. And most importantly, to read it afresh as though the God who has spoken still speaks to us today right where we live.

I'm proud to know Joshua: he's blessed my life and lives the message he preaches in humble love for Jesus Christ our King. I hope you'll be blessed by the hope you find in these pages, and equipped to share that hope with your neighbors, friends, and the world around you—a world that God so outrageously loves.

Rick McKinley
Lead Pastor of Imago Dei Community
Portland, OR

INTRODUCTION

SKELETONS IN THE CLOSET

God has some skeletons in the closet. At least, that's what many of us fear. Bones the size of tree trunks. Clothed in cobwebs. Decaying in the darkness. God's skeletons are big.

We say someone has skeletons in the closet when they're hiding deep, dark secrets that, if discovered, would drastically change the way we feel about them. "Growing up, we all thought Uncle Joe was such a great, fun-loving guy . . . until one day we learned he'd embezzled millions, had a string of affairs, and killed his business partner." Uncle Joe had some skeletons in his closet.

God's skeletons are those deep, dark doctrines we'd rather avoid. Hell. Judgment. Holy war. Those parts of God's story that, if we really took a close look at, we're afraid would radically change the way we feel about him. "We all thought Father God was so kind and good . . . until one day we learned he had slaughtered millions in his holy wars, damned those at judgment who'd never heard his name, and carted most of humanity off to his hellish concentration camp for vengeance without end."

Yep, God's definitely got some skeletons in his closet—or at least we think so.

The closet door is heavy. Stone-cold concrete. Six feet thick. Rusted, creaky hinges. Opening the door can be intimidating. We are faced with a dilemma: if we open the closet door, we might not like what we find. The God we thought good might be a fraud. The

Father we thought trustworthy, a felon. The Jesus to whom we gave our lives, a facade. If we pull these bones out of the closet and take a cold, hard look, the God we have come to love and serve might not be found worth loving and serving.

And deep down we know our faith couldn't handle the betrayal.

Best keep the door shut.

And yet, with the door closed we're left wondering whether God's goodness can really be trusted. Refusing to look boldly at the parts of God's story we fear intimidates us from following Christ without reservation and placing full confidence in his gospel. Our faith grows lukewarm and stale as we go through the motions of church services and verbal assent, while our hearts stay distant and unengaged.

The irony of our dilemma? If we open the closet door, we might not like what we find out about God. If we leave it closed, we might not like what we find out about ourselves.

Regardless, God's closet door won't seem to stay shut. Our culture is asking questions, from the latest Amazon best seller denouncing the brutality of God, to the most recent *New York Times* editorial lamenting the inherent violence of religion, to one of many conversations overheard at the local coffee shop on "why I could just never believe." This conversation is on our culture's lips.

And this conversation is on lips more intimate than just our culture's. Our family and friends are asking these questions. From that son who walked away from the faith, to that mentor who one day realized she no longer believed, to the spouse who can no longer join us at church without feeling hypocritical, and that friend in our small group who doesn't come around anymore. Our preference may be to keep the closet door shut, but there are many around us who seem less than willing to respect our decision.

And then, for some of us, there's that suspicion that surfaces as we lie awake at night, curious about the closet door. And what lies on the other side. Our culture, our loved ones, and even we ourselves are asking questions . . . and we're often left unsure how to respond.

Perhaps most surprisingly, God seems to *want* the closet door open. He doesn't accept our comfortable religion; he keeps sending prophets to churn things up. Jesus doesn't skirt the tough issues; he confronts us with them head-on. Scripture doesn't hide the challenging parts; it proclaims them boldly. We don't need a secret access code or crowbar to pry the closet door open; God himself keeps flinging it wide open and inviting us to look inside . . . as much as we may keep trying to swing it back shut.

We want that door shut . . . but God doesn't. Not only is he big enough to handle our questions, he wants us to bring them. God opens the door and invites us to look inside.

MY SKELETONS

I found God inviting me to open the closet door on topics like these early in my Christian walk. During my sophomore year in university, I had a radical encounter with God that turned my life upside down (or perhaps better yet, right side up). Soon after, I found myself excitedly sharing with a close friend in my dorm how Jesus' grace had transformed me and expected him to share in my joy, but was surprised when his first response was, "So, do you think I'm going to hell now?"

I wasn't sure how to respond. I hadn't even brought up hell; it wasn't something that was really on my radar. Taken aback, I blurted out something like, "I don't know. I guess that's God's territory. You'll have to take that up with him."

While in retrospect I think that was a pretty good answer (for reasons we'll explore later in this book), at the time I felt uneasy and insecure. Had I failed my test as a Christian? Was I *supposed* to tell him he was going to hell, in hopes of scaring him into the kingdom? What *did* the Bible say about hell? Would God roast my friend like a kālua pig over a burning spit forever? I didn't want that. And if that really was the way God worked, how did this mesh with the radical grace and undeserved mercy of the cross I had encountered in Christ?

The Skeleton of Holy War

Next came holy war. I worked for a few months on a Navajo reservation, supporting a traditional community of impoverished indigenous shepherds fighting a land-rights case against a multibillion-dollar international mineral corporation. While there, I began learning more about the many injustices my country had perpetrated against the Navajo and other native peoples: the unending string of broken treaties, the massacres and forced migrations, the manipulation and coercion frequently used to get what we wanted for as little as possible in return.

And like a black eye in the middle of it all was Manifest Destiny, a prominent ideology of the nineteenth century that drew upon Old Testament imagery of Israel conquering Canaan to justify US expansion throughout North America. This gave a sense of God's redemptive blessing, even mandate, to the atmosphere that fueled the broken treaties, the massacres, and the expulsion of native peoples to the barren, unwanted, and isolated islands of the reservations.

It's bad enough to say, "We knocked you down." Something much more to say, "God gave us the punch." Talk about adding insult to injury: America's historic declaration that God was driving the train that ran over native peoples.

As I lived with the Navajo families, I wondered about the spiritual impact this ideological blow had left on their communities. How many struggled to receive the love of Christ, or even see it clearly, in light of the historic failures of our witness? How many, when even considering Christianity, lived under a crushing sense that the Christian God was against them *as* native people? And all this led me to wonder: What the heck *was* going on with holy war in the Old Testament? Why *did* God tell Israel to take out Canaan? Did I really want to follow a God who commanded his people to conquer and destroy the indigenous inhabitants of the land?

My gut was telling me I'd rather side with the Navajo.

The Skeleton of Judgment

And finally, there was judgment. During my junior year, I had a summer internship on the border of Burma and Thailand. I was working with a Thai organization fighting the trafficking of young girls into the sex trade. Hundreds of girls in the community had been trafficked—and local leaders had decided enough was enough.

They established a successful alternative school for at-risk girls, with rescue-rehabilitation services and community development initiatives to help address the issue. They sacrificially gave their time, energy, and resources, and courageously put their lives on the line to end the tragedy in their community. Death threats and attempts had been made on the lives of some of the leaders. I was proud to call them friends and work alongside them.

On Sundays, I would walk an hour to join the only church I could find in the area. The worship, sacrament, and fellowship were extremely powerful and meaningful, but after the services the Thai pastor would repeatedly ask me, "Why are you out there working with the Buddhists? You should be here helping me build the church!"

To be honest, I hadn't considered that the people I was working with *were* Buddhist, or at least I hadn't considered it directly. I suppose most of them were, in a cultural default sort of way, not in a blatant evangelistic sort of way, like monks in a temple or something like that. But Buddhist or not, they were my friends. And I admired them. They cared sacrificially and generously for the flourishing of God's world, and even if we saw the world in radically different ways, I was honored to work side by side with them.

I asked the pastor, "Is there anything you are doing to address the trafficking of children in your community that I could come to work alongside?" He answered, "This is a tragedy in our community, but it is more important that we focus on saving souls so that on Judgment Day they can go to heaven."

His words reminded me of a missionary I heard speak earlier that year at a campus group I attended back home. He painted a gruesome picture of billions of lost souls around the world "heading to hell in a handbasket" (his words), unless I and others like me heeded the call to head overseas, like him, and become missionaries to intervene in their impending doom, to get them to "pray to receive Jesus" so they might avoid being found on God's bad side at the great final judgment.

I found myself angry at this depiction of Judgment Day. Was it really so simple as "Christians go to heaven and everyone else goes to hell"? Was my role as a witness to Jesus' sovereign authority and saving mercy really centered around getting people to pray a magic prayer? Was stopping men from raping children really secondary to saving souls? Were all my Buddhist friends (whose generosity, courage, and sacrifice put me to shame) really bound for judgment predominantly because of the time and place into which they were born, while this Thai pastor and visiting missionary (who both came across to me a bit closed-minded, arrogant, and self-righteous) were destined for salvation simply because of the "which religion are you?" box they would check on a questionnaire? Could I really bear the massive weight that the eternal destiny of billions around the world was riding on my wee, tiny shoulders?

I had encountered the grace of Christ in a radical way, but these were the skeletons I was afraid were lurking behind God's closet door: hell looked like a torture chamber; holy war looked like imperial conquest; judgment looked like a racist farce.

But I heard God's voice in the midst of it all, inviting me, beckoning me, challenging me, to open the closet door. To not be afraid to ask the questions. To bring them to him. I had a sense that something special was waiting on the other side of the questions—an intimacy to be found just beyond the apparent darkness.

And gradually, the picture began to change.

I began reading the Bible.

CONFRONTING THE CARICATURES

I had read the Bible before, but I was reading now with new lenses. I had questions. I wanted to know what the Bible had to say about them. And as I read, I found something strange happening: the Bible didn't freak me out. It actually inspired me. It didn't talk about these topics the same way many people, including church people, talked about them.

Jesus talked about hell and judgment in a way that was radically different from not only my atheist friend in the dorms, but the Thai pastor overseas and the visiting missionary on campus. Where they brought confusion, Jesus brought conviction. Where they inspired hubris, Jesus inspired hope. The Bible talked about holy war in a way that didn't justify my country's treatment of native peoples; it systematically critiqued and confronted it. It actually seemed, in a strange way, to offer hope to oppressed and marginalized communities—like those of my indigenous friends—around the world. There was something profoundly different happening here, even if I couldn't yet put my finger on precisely what it was.

In the fifteen years since then, I have come to believe that our culture's popular understanding of these difficult doctrines is often a caricature of what the Bible actually teaches and what mature Christian theology has historically proclaimed.

To Laugh At, To Live By

What do I mean by a *caricature*? A caricature is a cartoonlike drawing of a real person, place, or thing. You've probably seen them at street fairs, drawings of popular figures like President Obama, Marilyn Monroe, or your aunt Cindy. Caricatures exaggerate some features, distort some features, and oversimplify some features. The result is a humorous cartoon.

In one sense, a caricature bears a striking resemblance to the real thing. That picture really *does* look like President Obama, Marilyn Monroe, or your aunt Cindy. Features unique to the real person are included and even emphasized, so you can tell it's a cartoon of that person and not someone else. But in another sense, the caricature looks *nothing* like the real thing. Salient features have been distorted, oversimplified, or blown way out of proportion. President Obama's ears are *way* too big. Aunt Cindy's grin is *way* too wide. And Marilyn Monroe . . . well, you get the picture.

A caricature would never pass for a photograph. If you were to take your driver's license, remove the photo, and replace it with a caricature, the police officer pulling you over would either laugh . . . or arrest you. Placed next to a photograph, a caricature looks like a humorous, or even hideous, distortion of the real thing.

Similarly, our popular caricatures of these tough doctrines do include features of the original. One doesn't have to look too far in the biblical story to find that hell has flames, holy war has fighting, and judgment brings us face-to-face with God. But in the caricatures, these features are severely exaggerated, distorted, and oversimplified, resulting in a not-so-humorous cartoon that looks nothing like the original. All we have to do is start asking questions: Where do the flames come from, and what are they doing? Who is doing the fighting, and how are they winning? Why does God judge the world, and what basis does he use for judgment? Questions like these help us quickly realize that our popular caricatures of tough biblical doctrines are like cartoons: good for us to laugh at, but not to live by.

But the caricature does help us with something important: it draws our attention to parts of God's story where our understanding is off. If the caricature makes God look like a sadistic torturer, a coldhearted judge, or a greedy génocidaire, it probably means there are details we need to take a closer look at. The caricatures can alert us to parts of the picture where our vision is distorted.

One of my hopes for this book is to place the caricature and the photograph side by side, so we can ask which is appropriate to laugh at, and which to live by. To let the comparison between the two drive us deeper into the gospel.

The Bigger Picture

So how do we begin confronting the caricature and reclaiming the photograph? There are two main methods we'll be using. First, we'll be placing these topics back within the storyline in which they make sense. I've found that our caricatures often arise when we as churches are telling central elements of the bigger story wrong, in ways that differ significantly from the Old Testament and New Testament storyline.

Stories are important. They make sense of the people, places, and plots within them. If we get the broader story wrong, we'll be rightfully confused when the people, places, and plots within them don't make sense anymore.

Let me use an analogy. My daughter has a puzzle of children playing in the forest. Within the forest, the smaller puzzle pieces of the children fit smoothly—the pieces are the right shape, size, and color. But she also has a puzzle of sea creatures in the ocean. Now, if she tried to fit the children inside the bigger picture of the ocean, or the sea creatures in the forest, she would be very frustrated. The pieces wouldn't fit; colors would be different, the characters wouldn't make sense, and the edges would need to be trimmed or the pieces crammed on top of each other.

They were made to fit as components in a different bigger picture.

Similarly, I've found that our frustration with tough topics like hell, judgment, and holy war often arises because we try to fit them into the wrong bigger picture. If our bigger picture of heaven and earth's relationship is significantly off, then we are going to have a hard time making sense of how a smaller subtopic, like hell, fits into it. If our storyline of salvation is severely distorted, we are going to be confused understanding the appropriate place of judgment. If we miss God's radical critique of our world's empires and their unholy wars, we will have a hard time recognizing the radical distinction of why and when God goes to battle.

So, in the chapters that follow, we will spend time framing these topics back within their bigger pictures. When we reclaim the biblical story of God's reconciliation of heaven and earth, the subtopic of hell starts to fall naturally into place again. When we reclaim the biblical story of God's purpose to bless, reconcile, and heal the nations through his international, multiethnic kingdom, the subtopic of judgment against those forces that stand opposed to this kingdom begins to come into clearer focus. When we reclaim the biblical story of God's identification with the weak against the oppression of the strong, the subtopic of holy war begins, again, to make more sense.

So we will spend time reclaiming the biblical story from its distortions, reframing these topics back within that story, and demonstrating the difference this makes. The beauty of this method is that dealing with these topics can give us fresh insights on not only these questions, but our faith as a whole. It can provoke paradigm shifts that help us look afresh from new angles at the bigger picture where our vision has been distorted.

Pulling out the skeletons can be more than just an exercise in cleaning closets; it can give us a fresh appreciation for the house as a whole.

In the Trenches

The second way we will be confronting the caricatures is by demonstrating the practical relevance of these topics today. Often, we think of these matters as more relevant to a fairy-tale world, with dragons and monsters, kings and magic trees, fiery furnaces and epic battles. Fairy tales are fun, but for another world, right? As I will seek to demonstrate, these topics are much more at home in our everyday world than we might think. They speak powerfully and profoundly to day-to-day life in our modern society, with all of its most pressing needs and wildest hopes.

In the chapters that follow, we will explore issues as wide-ranging as sex trafficking and genocide, American democracy and Third World dictatorships, modern suburbs and social media. We will travel to places as diverse as Nigeria, China, and my hometown of Portland, Oregon; from Boston high-rises and the heights of the global economy, to Brazilian cardboard shanties and displaced slums in the developing world. We will explore the cultural longings embodied in our fairy tales, and the historical longings embodied in our war stories. We will have respectful conversations with Buddhism, Islam, and atheism. We will visit history from World War II to the European colonization of the Southern Hemisphere to the ancient Roman Empire. And on the way, we'll deal with pedophile priests, cancer surgeries, pub rockers, home makeovers, and unruly wedding crashers.

Buckle your seatbelt; we're in for a ride.

The tough topics we'll explore in this book are, I have found, powerfully and profoundly relevant to life in our contemporary culture. Though the imagery can sometimes look like the stuff of fairy tales, it speaks to the everyday realities, deepest needs, and wildest hopes of life on this ol' spinning rock we call Earth. My conviction is that we approach these topics best when we approach them not as detached observers in ivory towers, looking for complex, mathematical solutions to abstract, intellectual problems, but rather as soldiers in the trenches, searching for meaning in the midst of a war. I hope to demonstrate that, when properly understood, these are not just pieces of the Christian faith we can learn to live with; they are profound plotlines in the story of the whole we (literally) cannot live without.

And when they are properly understood, what central message do they give us?

GOD IS GOOD

God is good. That is the central message and driving theme of this book. Not just a little bit good. Not just partially good. Not just sometimes good and sometimes not. But extravagantly, mercifully, gloriously, better-than-we-can-ask-or-imagine good. There is a refrain one can often hear in churches that proclaims loudly and boldly, "God is good—all the time!" That is the refrain of this book. Even in the tough topics—perhaps especially in the tough topics—all the time, God is good.

In the chapters that follow, I will seek to demonstrate that God's goodness is continuous with, not contradictory to, these tough topics of hell, judgment, and holy war. Indeed, that it is precisely *because of* God's goodness, not in spite of it, that these topics arise. When properly understood, these doctrines can enhance, rather than detract from, our vision of the glorious goodness of God.

As we shall see, not only does God not have skeletons, God himself is good *in his very bones*: not just in what he does, but in who he is; not only in his actions, but in the architecture of his character, the beauty of his being, the depths of his divine affection for the world.

This book is divided into three parts: "The Mercy of Hell," "The Surprise of Judgment," and "The Hope of Holy War." Mercy, surprise, and hope are probably not characteristics most of us today would associate with these doctrines. But I believe strongly, and will argue in the pages ahead, that these are central features, key attributes, and driving characteristics of these topics when placed back within the overarching context of the biblical story.

Though this book is divided into three parts, it is written as a whole. Skipping chapter 1 to jump into chapter 2 or 3 could be confusing. We will be building themes in each section that are picked up and developed further in the following sections. Together, these themes are envisioned as something like a symphony, harmonizing with one another, building upon each other, and rising to a crescendo at the climax that proclaims loudly, boldly, and clearly the one central message of this book: God is good.

While I've written this book for the many people who wrestle with these topics, there is also, in a strange way, one other person I've written this for: myself, fifteen years ago. These are the things I would share with myself if I could go back, the insights I've found powerful, the paradigm shifts these questions have provoked that have revolutionized the way I look now at not only these questions, but my faith as a whole. While writing this, I've often envisioned myself now sitting across the table, talking with myself back then. These are the things I would share. And at the heart is this: God is good.

Does that sound too good to be true? Too farfetched for reality? Then let's grab hold of the handle together, open that old closet door, and find out.

Part 1

THE MERCY OF HELL

Micah set his coffee mug down, leaned across the table, and asked the question he'd really come to talk about: "Do you really think God is going to torture billions of people in a burning barbecue forever?

"I've been following Jesus since I was a kid," he continued, "but the more I think about this image I have of hell, the more God looks like a sadistic torturer.

"Can such a God really be _good_?"

There was a look of sadness on his face. Micah had been following Jesus for years but was unsure he could reconcile this picture of God with his faith and was considering abandoning the faith altogether. Hell was a skeleton in God's closet.

1.

HEAVEN AND EARTH

THE UNDERGROUND TORTURE CHAMBER

I used to hate the doctrine of hell. In my head, it looked something like this: Deep in the cavernous bowels of the earth was a special place where blazing flames roared high. God was at the center of the flames, with an apparent look of glee on his face as he flayed people's skin from their bones. Sorrowfully repentant, the people cried out to God in agony: "We're sorry! We love you! We'll change our ways, do whatever you want us to do!" But God laughed a loud, bellowing laugh, like a dark, sinister Santa Claus, and responded mercilessly, "Too bad! You had your chance! Now it's too late, and I get to punish you forever!"

Hell looked like an underground torture chamber.

While this is an obvious caricature, I'd like to make three observations that I've found are common to many people's popular perceptions of hell. First, it is underground. Beneath layer after geological layer of rock and dirt, God has created a special place deep in the basement of our terrestrial home for the particular purpose of punishment. It looks like a hobby room—as if a father put a punching bag in the basement for when he needs to let off steam. How do they breathe down there underneath all that dirt? Why do the walls not collapse and cave in? God must have installed a special supply of oxygen and given it some profound construction. With all the intentionality God put into making this place happen, he must really want it to work.

Second, its purpose must be torture. God looks like a sadistic monster, capable of a capricious cruelty equivalent to the kid next door who enjoys spending his spare time tormenting cats. This torture serves no positive purpose, makes no constructive contribution to the flourishing of the world. God is not like Jack Bauer, going after information to prevent an imminent terrorist attack. God *is* the terrorist in this picture, looking for a few sadistic kicks, out for pure and simple vengeance.

Third, its construction must be a chamber God locks from the outside. The people want out. They are repentant. They want to love and serve God and change their ol' cheating ways. But God has padlocked and chained the doors. In a strange reversal of the gospel, the people are the ones pursuing God and God is the one unwilling to be found. Jesus apparently loves us enough to die for us, but hates us enough to lock us in a torture chamber, throw away the key, and plug his ears to our cries once the stopwatch runs out.

The skeleton in God's closet? Hell is an underground torture chamber. Its location (underground), purpose (torture), and construction (chamber) all speak to a particular storyline where God is maligned as a vicious and vindictive villain.

Is this the way the Bible talks about hell?

In the next few chapters, we will confront this caricature. As we explore the New Testament, we will find that (a) hell's location is not underground, (b) its purpose is not torture, and (c) its construction is not a chamber. These characteristics are not only a little bit off; they are in many ways completely backward.

So how do we begin confronting the caricature and reclaiming the photograph? A good place to start is to ask, "What is the broader story in which hell is found? What is the bigger picture this puzzle piece fits into? What is the symphony in which its dissonant notes play?"

A PROBLEMATIC STORY

We get hell wrong because we get heaven and earth wrong. Our caricature of hell is rooted, I have come to believe, in the problematic way we tend to talk about heaven and earth today. It is not the way the Bible talks about heaven and earth, and because heaven and earth are parts of the Bible's broader story into which the smaller subplot of hell fits naturally, when we get this broader story wrong, the smaller subplot just doesn't seem to fit right.

So what is this problematic story? The distorted picture in which the puzzle piece won't seem to fit? If you ask most folks today how hell works, they will usually tell you something like this: "Right now I live on earth. One day I will die. When I die, I will stand before God and God will either send me *up* to heaven if I've done the right things, or *down* to hell if I haven't."

Pretty straightforward, right?

Me-Centered vs. God-Centered

The gospel has three major problems with this story. First, this story is me-centered, not God-centered. Notice how many times "I" show up as the main character: "*I* live on earth . . . *I* will die . . . *I* will stand . . . If *I've* been . . ." This story tells us nothing about who God is. It revolves around me, not around God.

The trouble with this story is that there *is* no story: it offers no past or present narrative of God and his world. This is more than just semantics; God appears in a supporting role at the end of a story that is otherwise about me from start to finish. This story is individualistic: it is all about me. God is introduced secondhand as a supporting actor, a mere arbiter to determine my final destiny.

The gospel, in contrast, is God-centered. It starts with God, ends with God, and is filled with God in the middle. God creates a good heaven and a good earth before our rebellion enters his good world. Jesus proclaims and displays God's redemptive kingdom before he challenges those who reject it. The apostles give extravagant declarations of who God is and what he has done, before calling listeners to worship and obedience in response. For example, Paul opens Ephesians declaring, "Praise be to the God and Father of our Lord Jesus Christ, who has . . . ," and goes on for three chapters (half the book!) to describe what God has done before moving on to how our lives as followers of Jesus should respond.[1]

The gospel's story is centered around who God is, not around us.

Works-Centered vs. Grace-Centered

The second problem the gospel has with the prevailing story about hell is that it is works-centered rather than grace-centered. It emphasizes our actions, not God's. This story makes us ask questions like, "Have I been good enough? Have I *done* what I need to *do* for God to send me to heaven?"

The "what I need to do" varies depending on who you talk to: for some we are supposed to pray a prayer, for others we are supposed to feed the homeless, and for still others we're merely supposed to make sure we've got a heavier weight of good works under our belt than bad ones. But either way, the emphasis is on our actions, not God's.

In other words, this story promotes behavior management: trying to put myself together and make myself good enough to get into God's kingdom. This story tells us nothing about God's actions—what God has accomplished and what he is doing in the world today. God only appears at the end, not in the past or present.

The gospel, in contrast, starts with God's actions. God unshackles Israel from Egypt's slavery before he gives her ten commandments to obey. The world first hears that Jesus is Lord, that God is reconciling the world to himself through his death and resurrection, and that forgiveness is freely offered under his reign, and then, only on the heels of this proclamation, the church rises into existence.

In other words, the gospel starts with God and his grace. We enter the story secondarily, not as the primary actors but as those who must stand in relation to the redemptive play God is writing in the world around us. The gospel story revolves around God's redemptive work in the world. The God who calls for our complete submission to his reign is not an abstract, arbitrary, ambiguous god; he is our world's redeeming King. Our obedience is framed as a worshipping response to the experience of God's redemptive love.

Where Is Earth?

The gospel has a third major problem with the conventional heaven-and-hell story. Once we recognize this problem, I believe it will provide our most helpful clue to illuminating the way forward in reclaiming the biblical story. The problem is this: Where is earth? Earth is seen in this story as somewhere we live *now*, but that is irrelevant to our future home. "*Right now* I live on earth . . . *One day* God will send me *up* to heaven or *down* to hell." Earth is here today, gone tomorrow. Nowhere in our future picture with God.

The gospel, in contrast, declares that God's purpose in Christ is to reunite heaven and earth, to reconcile creation to himself, to make our broken-down old world new as our eternal home with him forever.[2] The absence of earth's future in the problematic story leads to a glaring distortion that should alert us to something being seriously wrong: heaven and hell are treated as two coequal counterparts competing for my eternal destiny, one the "yin" to the other's "yang," one the "good" to the other's co-powerful "bad," two sides of the same metaphysical coin.

Why is this problematic? Here is an illuminating experiment you can do to find out: (1) Go to www.biblegateway.com (an online Bible website) and type "heaven hell" into the search feature. (2) Select "New International Version" (a reliable, popular translation) and hit "Search" to see how many verses show up. The results will show you how many times the words *heaven* and *hell* appear together within the same verse.

The answer? Zero.

There are *no* verses where heaven and hell appear together as counterparts in the same verse.[3] Nowhere. Not in the Old Testament. Not in the New Testament. Nowhere from Genesis to Revelation. Heaven shows up in Scripture, and hell shows up in Scripture, and they certainly bear a relation to one another. But they do not show up in the same places.

This is shocking given how prominent we use language like this in modern times. Both in our churches and in our culture at large, we talk about "heaven and hell" as if they are two coequal counterparts competing for our eternal destiny, and we assume this is the way the Bible talks about them too. But this is simply not the way it talks about them. The Bible has a different way of framing their relationship.

So if heaven's primary counterpart is not hell in the biblical story, then what is it? We can use another version of the same experiment to find out: (1) In the search feature, type in "heaven earth." (2) Hit "Search" and see how many verses show up. The answer? You will find around two hundred verses where *heaven* and *earth* appear together.[4] These two hundred or so verses are not clustered in one particular place; they are spread everywhere throughout the Old and New Testaments, showing up all over the place between Genesis and Revelation.

The point? Heaven's primary counterpart in the gospel story is not hell; it is earth. Heaven and earth are threaded throughout the biblical drama of creation, rebellion, and redemption. If we want to confront the caricature of hell and reclaim the photograph, we must reframe it back within this biblical story of heaven and earth. We should first ask, "What is the biblical story of heaven and earth?" And as we shall see in the pages to come, when this broader story is in place, the logic of hell begins to arise as a smaller subplot in a broader story that proclaims loudly and clearly the glorious goodness of God.

RECLAIMING THE STORY

So what is the biblical story of heaven and earth? The story has three major movements: (1) Heaven and earth are created by God. (2) Heaven and earth are torn by sin. (3) Heaven and earth are destined for reconciliation. Let's take a look at each to see the overarching story-line that emerges.

Created by God

Heaven and earth make their debut at the very beginning of the story. The book of Genesis opens with a celebration of God's creative act: "In the beginning God created the heavens and the earth."[5] Introductions are important. Authors tend to open stories with things they want to emphasize and draw our attention to. God's story for the world is no different: heaven and earth are the setting, the context, the stage, in which the ensuing drama of human history is about to unfold.

From just this one verse, we can make three important observations that challenge aspects of the caricature. First, heaven is part of the creation. God made it. It is a mistake when we speak of heaven as only a future place, a home that exists only in eternity. Heaven is here today. It is not absent from the world, waiting to make its entrance only at the end of history. Heaven is a part of God's creation here and now.

Genesis' words for heaven and earth are roughly equivalent to our words for "sky" and "land." Genesis is talking about the ground beneath our feet that we walk on daily; the atmosphere above our heads that surrounds our world: this land, this sky, this world. If there is a difference, it is that we tend to think of land and sky as merely physical places, raw material, with no underlying spiritual substance. In God's story for the world, however, land and sky are spiritually loaded, charged with the presence and purposes of God: heaven and earth.

The second observation is that heaven is created in integral relationship with the earth. They are depicted as counterparts, created with each other and for each other. Heaven does have a counterpart, but it is not hell; it is earth. This counterpart relationship between heaven and earth is threaded throughout the biblical story. Here are a few examples to help illuminate some of the different features of this counterpart relationship:

> In the beginning you laid the foundations of the earth,
> and the heavens are the work of your hands. (Psalm 102:25)

It is I who made the earth
> and created mankind upon it.
My own hands stretched out the heavens;
> I marshaled their starry hosts. (Isaiah 45:12)

To the LORD your God belong the heavens, even the highest heavens, the earth and everything in it. (Deuteronomy 10:14)

You alone are God over all the kingdoms of the earth. You have made heaven and earth. (2 Kings 19:15)

Let the heavens rejoice, let the earth be glad;
> let them say among the nations, "The LORD reigns!"
> (1 Chronicles 16:31)

But God made the earth by his power;
> he founded the world by his wisdom
> and stretched out the heavens by his understanding.
> (Jeremiah 10:12)

These verses declare that God created the heavens and the earth, that everything within them belongs to him, that he rules over the kingdoms of the earth, that this is a cause of rejoicing for the nations, and that heaven and earth are a sign of God's wisdom, power, and care.

Heaven and earth—not heaven and hell—are counterparts, created with and for each other, and bound together in inseparable relationship.

The third and final observation from Genesis' introduction: hell is mentioned nowhere. It is not part of God's creation. Genesis does not say, "God created heaven and earth . . . and hell." God created heaven and earth, a good creation, a glorious world. Hell does not show up on the scene until later. We shall see in later chapters that sin, death, and hell, when they do enter the story, are presented not as good things created by God but rather as invasive intruders into God's good world.

Together, they constitute an "anti-creation" force, not as substantive things in themselves so much as parasites that prey upon the good creation God has made in an attempt to devour it and destroy it, to drag creation back down into the nothingness, the darkness, the void from which it came. But this is jumping ahead.

For now we can say this: heaven and earth are created by God.

Torn by Sin

The second movement in the biblical story's plotline is this: heaven and earth are torn by sin. When Adam and Eve rebel, it impacts everything under their authority. God gives Adam and Eve authority over the earth: "Let them rule over the fish of the sea and the birds of the air, over the livestock, over all the earth."[6] This is a picture of God calling us as the human race to co-reign together with him in his world, to bring forth the flourishing of creation.[7]

But when Adam and Eve sin, their fall disrupts the flourishing of the earth beneath their feet. Where once the earth flourished, now thorns and thistles come up from the cursed ground.[8] The human community plunges into a downward spiral of violence: Adam blames Eve, Cain murders Abel, Lamech is a dangerous killer, and by the days of Noah, the earth is "filled with violence."[9] In only three chapters, the human race moves from a pointing finger to mass destruction, the growth of our violence apparently rising in direct symmetry with the growth of our population.

Sin enters the world like a wicked seed that sprouts quickly into the groaning of our quaking earth in its distance from the face of God.

God's intimacy on the earth is, in some important ways, lost. Before sin, God made the earth his home, walking in the garden with Adam and Eve.[10] But after sin enters the picture, God packs his bags and makes his home in heaven, giving the earth to us. Like the prodigal son in Jesus' most famous parable,[11] we asked the Father for our inheritance (the earth he gave us to rule), not to enjoy it together with him, but to squander it on ourselves in distance from him.

And God generously gives us our wish.

Now like a marriage gone bad, heaven and earth have a ruptured relationship, torn by sin. We find ourselves distant, "east of Eden," in a state of exile from our Creator. Responding to our desire to "be like God," to have autonomy from him, God hands us over to what we want: a world without God. Our rebellion has cosmic consequences: earth is ruptured from heaven.

Heaven is then depicted as the dwelling place of God in the biblical story. God is said to establish his throne in heaven, make his home in heaven, call from heaven, hear from heaven, orchestrate human affairs from heaven, blot out the wicked from under heaven, come down from heaven to judge and redeem. Here are a few examples to help illuminate this torn relationship:

The highest heavens belong to the LORD,
  but the earth he has given to man. (Psalm 115:16)

He sits enthroned above the circle of the earth,
  and its people are like grasshoppers.
He stretches out the heavens like a canopy,
  and spreads them out like a tent to live in. (Isaiah 40:22)

For he views the ends of the earth and sees everything under the heavens. (Job 28:24)

Then hear from heaven, your dwelling place, and do whatever the foreigner asks of you, so that all the peoples of the earth may know your name and fear you. (2 Chronicles 6:33)

Those who oppose the LORD will be shattered.
He will thunder against them from heaven;
  the LORD will judge the ends of the earth. (1 Samuel 2:10)

The LORD has established his throne in heaven,
  and his kingdom rules over all. (Psalm 103:19)

These verses show that heaven and earth still exist in integrated relationship, but this relationship has been torn by sin. Earth rebels against heaven, while God's kingdom continues to reign from heaven over the earth. God's will is not currently done on earth as in heaven, implying a distance in heaven and earth's relationship. The earth exists in a state of exile and alienation from its intended home with God.

So where does the story go from here?

Destined for Reconciliation

This brings us to the third and final movement of the gospel story's plotline: heaven and earth are destined for reconciliation. Jesus went to the cross, Colossians tells us, to reconcile heaven and earth:

> God was pleased to have all his fullness dwell in [Jesus], and through him to reconcile to himself all things, whether things on earth or things in heaven, by making peace through his blood, shed on the cross.[12]

Jesus' cross brings peace to the war we've waged on heaven. His atonement heals the rupture wrought by our rebellion. Jesus' blood reconciles creation to God.

The cross and resurrection may accomplish more than this, but they do not accomplish less.

Jesus is the Savior who reunites heaven and earth.

This theme is central to the gospel: our future hope is for that day when the kingdoms of this world have become the kingdom of our Lord;[13] when God brings all things into subjection under Christ's feet;[14] when the earth is flooded with the glorious presence of God as the waters cover the sea;[15] when creation is delivered from its groaning under the weight of sin into the glorious freedom of the righteous reign of God.[16]

God's purpose is not to get us out of earth and into heaven; it's to reconcile heaven and earth.

God has given Jesus authority, as his resurrected King, to establish this kingdom reality on earth as it is in heaven. Upon his resurrection,

Jesus declares: "All authority in heaven and on earth has been given to me."[17] God's reason for giving Jesus this authority is, in the words of Paul, to "bring all things in heaven and on earth together under one head, even Christ."[18] In Christ, God's purpose is to reunite that which sin has torn asunder, to thread the ripped fabric of creation back together again.

Jesus' resurrection brings the earth back from exile into the glorious, heavenly presence of God.

Jesus reconciles heaven and earth.

Revelation envisions the consummation of world history with God's holy city "coming down out of heaven from God, prepared as a bride beautifully dressed for her husband."[19] Notice the direction of movement. God is not bringing us *up* out of earth into heaven. He is bringing heaven "down" into earth, through his holy city. God's purpose is to redeem the earth, not to abandon it. His goal is to heal the rupture, not to let it win. God's promise is not to whisk us out of earth into heaven, but rather to usher in his heavenly kingdom to reign on earth with us forever.

Notice also the marriage imagery. The holy city is "prepared as a bride beautifully dressed for her husband." Weddings celebrate union, and this wedding celebrates the union of God and humanity, of heaven and earth. And the result of this reconciling union, this marriage of heaven and earth, is that it can be said again, as it was in the garden of Eden so long ago, "Now the dwelling of God is with men, and he will live with them. They will be his people, and God himself will be with them and be their God."[20]

To summarize, in the biblical storyline we've looked at thus far, heaven and earth are created by God, torn by sin, and destined for reconciliation. This provokes the question: What is it heaven and earth need to be reconciled from? It is here that the logic of hell naturally arises, that the puzzle piece starts to fit. For the world to be reconciled *to* God, it must be reconciled *from* the divisive and destructive powers that have caused the problem in the first place. It must be rescued from hell.

To pray Jesus' prayer that God's kingdom would come "on earth, as it is in heaven," is to pray implicitly that all those powers that stand unrepentantly opposed to God's kingdom be sent packing, that sin, death, and hell be banished. To long for the dawning of the light is to long for the casting out of darkness. To hope for the resurrection of life is to hope for the banishment of death. To dream for the healing of the body is to dream for the excising of the disease.

There is a symmetry between hope for the coming of God's kingdom and hope for the casting out of hell. We've now observed two stories: the problematic one and the gospel one. Let's wrap up by comparing them.

COMPARING THE STORIES

God is on a mission to get the hell out of earth. Ironically, this phrase can be applied to both of the stories, but within each story it means something dramatically different. Because of this dissimilarity, this phrase can be a helpful way for us to compare the two stories. In the first story, the problematic one, this phrase means that God is on a mission to abandon the earth, to "get the hell out of Dodge," and take a bunch of us with him. In this construal, Jesus and his followers are on a mission to escape the world, to make a break for our heavenly home and leave this mess behind.

Unfortunately, Christianity has at times—especially in recent times—framed things this way and, in doing so, horribly distorted the gospel story.

But this phrase can also be taken a second way. In the second story, the biblical one, it means that God cares deeply for his world, that the Creator loves his creation, that our heavenly Father has dramatic compassion for the humanity he has brought up from the dust. In this second story, it means that God is grieved by the sin, death, and power of hell that afflicts his world, and is sacrificially involved in the removal of all that destroys and alienates his world from himself.

As we have seen, this is the movement of the gospel story. God's agenda is to get the hell out of earth.

The following two diagrams illustrate how these two different stories give rise to a competing conception of hell. In the problematic story, earth is now; heaven and hell are later. Heaven, when it arrives, is "above"; hell is "below." They are two coequal counterparts competing for my eternal destiny. It is easy to see how the caricature of the "underground torture chamber" can start to arise. Hell begins to look like a place God creates alongside heaven for the primary purpose of torturing sinners for eternity.

But this is the wrong story.

PROBLEMATIC STORY   **GOSPEL STORY**

In the gospel story, heaven and earth are currently torn by sin. Our world is being ravaged by the destructive power of hell. Sin has unleashed it into God's good world, and God is on a mission to get it out, to reconcile heaven and earth *from* hell's evil influence *to* himself *through* the reconciling life of Christ. The time is coming when God's heavenly kingdom will come down to reign on earth forever, when Jesus will cast out the corrosive powers of sin, death, and hell that have tormented his world for so long.

This is the right story.

This gospel story begins to give rise to some radical contrasts with the caricature. As we will see in the coming chapters, God is not the one who unleashes hell's destruction; we are (chapter 2). Hell's location is not "underground" but rather "outside the kingdom" (chapter 3). Hell is not a place God creates to torture people, but a power God excludes to protect the flourishing of the new creation (chapter 4). Its construction is not a chamber God locks from the outside, but a coffin we latch from the inside through our desire for freedom from God (chapters 5 and 6).

We will explore each of these distinctions more fully in the following chapters. But for now, we can simply observe that the gospel story of heaven and earth gives rise to an understanding of hell that is poles apart from the caricature. Heaven and earth are the bigger picture into which hell's little puzzle piece starts to fit naturally, the broader storyline in which its subplot begins to make sense. Heaven and earth are major movements in God's symphony for the world, a symphony in which hell's dissonant notes can begin to be heard properly in a way that contributes to the beauty of the whole.

If God's purpose is to reconcile heaven and earth, the questions that now start to arise are:

- Where has the power of hell come from?
- When God reconciles heaven and earth, where is it going?
- Does understanding it provide a powerful, relevant, and meaningful resource for everyday living in our world today?

It is to these questions that we now turn.

CHAPTER 1 KEY IDEA

WHAT IS THE BIGGER STORY HELL FITS INTO?

God's mission is not to get us out of earth and into heaven or hell, but rather to reconcile heaven and earth *from* the destructive power of sin, death, and hell. This gives rise to a radically different understanding of hell from the caricature.

2.

THE WICKED ROOT

THE POWER OF HELL

The power of hell is alive and well in our world. My own realization of this began with things more obvious, things most of us would agree look like hell on earth today—like kids getting enslaved and raped so others can make money. As I shared in the Introduction, during my junior year in university, I had the opportunity to work on the borders of Burma and Thailand with an indigenous organization fighting the trafficking of their community's children into the sex trade. In some of their villages, as many as 90 percent of girls older than ten had been trafficked into the cities.

This was devastating.

Slave traders preyed on poor families in desperate circumstances. Families were often deceived, told their daughters would have good jobs in a restaurant or a small business in the city. At first, the girls were excited to leave small-town life for the glamour of the big city. The parents were given a loan that their daughter would pay off easily at her new job. Once in the city, however, it was too late. By the time the girls realized where they were, they were locked in small rooms, held against their will, and forced to see as many as fifteen to thirty brothel clients a day.

It was heart-crushing to meet some of these girls who had been rescued and imagine what they had been through. The horror of the trauma inflicted upon them still haunts me today. And they were but a few survivors affected by a much bigger problem: the United Nations estimates nearly two million children are enslaved in the sex trade today.[1]

The power of hell is indeed alive and well in our world.

Tree and Root

At that point in my life, I still had a hard time with the doctrine of hell. I was a new Christian and there were some parts of the faith I was still trying to make sense of. But the seed of a realization was growing inside me: there are some things I want out of God's world forever.

I would soon find out there are some things God wants out of his world forever too. Reading through the Gospels one day, I came across Jesus talking about the power of hell in relation to lust. Here is what he has to say:

> You have heard that it was said, "Do not commit adultery." But I tell you that anyone who looks at a woman lustfully has already committed adultery with her in his heart. If your right eye causes you to sin, gouge it out and throw it away. It is better for you to lose one part of your body than for your whole body to be thrown into hell. And if your right hand causes you to sin, cut it off and throw it away. It is better for you to lose one part of your body than for your whole body to go into hell.[2]

Suddenly, I had a problem. Jesus wants to get rid of sex trafficking too, only he takes it a lot more seriously than I do. I want to get rid of sex trafficking; Jesus wants to get rid of lust. I want to prune back the wicked tree; he wants to dig out the root.

And that wicked root is in me.

I may not be a sex trafficker, a pedophile tourist, or a greedy madam—but I have lust. I can be one lusty animal. Jesus says if you even look lustfully at one of God's daughters, demeaningly commodifying her as an object for your own self-centered gratification, then the power of hell has its roots in you, and when God arrives to establish his kingdom, you are in danger of being cast outside the kingdom with it.

I was no longer simply part of the solution; I was part of the problem. The enemy was no longer simply "out there," but "in here." In the famous words of Pogo, "We have met the enemy, and he is us."[3] There is a wicked tree that has grown to monstrous proportions in our world, damaging and destroying the lives of tens of millions of young girls beneath its dark and disastrous shade, and the root of that wicked tree lives in me.

More on that in a minute.

Wildfire and Spark

Soon after, I discovered another thing I wanted out of God's world forever: genocide. Human rights journals were sprawled across my dorm room floor. I would read Amnesty International reports for hours. Stories of torture from around the world canvassed across my imagination. It was almost an obsession. I remember having trouble sleeping some nights; it was as if I could hear screams erupting from around the world, knowing that somewhere right then, something was happening that could be in one of those journals next month.

Then I got the opportunity to work in Rwanda and Cambodia, both home to some of the worst genocides of the twentieth century. In Rwanda, in a hundred days, an estimated eight hundred thousand people were killed—more than 10 percent of the population![4] How were they killed? Not with guns or bombs from a distance, but with machetes and garden tools up close. They were butchered not by invaders from a distant land, but by their neighbors and trusted friends.

The picture is brutal.

In Cambodia, an estimated 20 to 25 percent of the population was wiped off the face of the earth over the course of five years.[5] The Khmer Rouge regime targeted the country's leadership and educated professionals: journalists and judges, teachers and bankers, doctors and lawyers, monks and police officers. The Khmer Rouge did more than systematically exterminate a substantial portion of the country's population; they decimated the country's leadership, leaving no one to rebuild in their wake.

Like Abel's field of long ago, the blood of many butchered brothers cries up from the horror of Cambodia's killing fields, screaming into the ears of God.

Rwanda and Cambodia are not alone; they are simply extreme cases. The twentieth century was the most violent century the earth has ever seen, and there is no clear indication that the fate of the twenty-first will be markedly different. These events are complex. International pressures, historic forces, and evolving local antagonisms are involved. But at the end of the day, we are left with the traumatic horror of the dramatic outcome.

I wanted genocide out of God's world. And as I continued reading through the Gospels, I found that Jesus did too. Jesus talks about the power of hell in relation to violence:

> You have heard that it was said to the people long ago, "Do not murder, and anyone who murders will be subject to judgment." But I tell you that anyone who is angry with his brother will be subject to judgment. Again, anyone who says to his brother "Raca" [a term of contempt], is answerable to the Sanhedrin. But anyone who says, "You fool!" will be in danger of the fire of hell.[6]

Once again, I had a problem. Jesus wants genocide out of God's world too, only he takes it a lot more seriously than I do. I want to get rid of genocide; Jesus wants to get rid of rage. I want to put boundaries on the wicked wildfire; he wants to snuff out the spark.

And that wicked spark is in me.

I may not be a Third World dictator, a genocidal soldier, or an interrogation torturer. But I have anger, and it's most often not the righteous kind. I can be a vindictive beast. Jesus says if you are nice to folks on the outside but rage against them in your heart, you are in danger of the fire of hell.

Once again, before Jesus I find that the enemy is no longer simply "out there," but "in here." As Solzhenitsyn famously observed, the line separating good and evil passes not between countries, nor between classes, nor between political parties, but right through the middle of every human heart.[7]

As much as I may like to think of myself as part of the exalted solution to the world's issues, I am first and foremost a part of the problem.

Fire as Metaphor

We are the ones, not God, who unleash the destructive power of hell in the world. Fire is used as a metaphor in the biblical story for the damaging nature of our sin. There are other ways that fire is used, and we will look at these in future chapters. But this is a good place to start. Isaiah says that "wickedness burns like a fire," unleashing destruction in the community like the burning down of a forest.[8]

The community is like a forest; sin is like a fire.

Hosea says similarly that the hearts of wicked rulers burn "like an oven whose fire the baker need not stir." As they plot their wicked plans for the community, "their passion smolders all night; in the morning it blazes like a flaming fire. All of them are hot as an oven."[9] And the community is reduced to ashes.

Our red-hot sin leaves a trail of devastation in its wake.

James makes the same point in a passage that is particularly illuminating for our purposes here:

> The tongue is a small part of the body, but it makes great boasts. Consider what a great forest is set on fire by a small spark. The tongue also is a fire, a world of evil among the parts of the body. It corrupts the whole person, sets the whole course of his life on fire, and is itself set on fire by hell.[10]

James says the same way a small spark can burn down a forest, so our little tongue can unleash destruction. And when it does, notice where James says its destructive power comes from: it is *itself set on fire by hell.*

Hell's destructive power is unleashed through us.

When my coworker gossips in the neighboring cubicle, she is more than being annoying, she is *breathing hell* into the office. The reason fire is such a fitting metaphor for human sinfulness is its amazing ability to spread. Light a match, and watch your house go up in flames. Roast marshmallows around a campfire, and see a wildfire burn through an entire state. It's not hard to see why fire so adequately portrays sin and its resulting ruin. Our sin, if left unchecked, can burn up the world.

And James tells us the origin of this fire is hell.

Hell gains entrance into God's good world through us. *We* are the agents of destruction, the architects of demolition. God is not the architect of hell, the creator of its soul-destroying power; we are. We unleash its wildfire flame into God's good world.

But there is good news: God is coming as King to establish his redemptive kingdom. He will kick out the destructive power of sin that has raged like a wildfire in his world for far too long. And there is more good news: God loves us all, rebels that we are, and wants to forgive us. Even though the power of hell has its roots in our wicked hearts, God wants to heal us and get it out.

LEVELING THE PLAYING FIELD

Jesus' doctrine of hell levels the playing field. This is one of the things I have come to love about it. It does not elevate me above the world; rather, it humbles me before the world. As a man, I need to come to grips with the fact that lust is not allowed in the city where all God's daughters are treated honorably, with respect, and lifted high. As an American, I need to understand that nationalist superiority will not be allowed in God's kingdom, where the nations are healed, where Iraqis and Afghans are at the center of the celebration, where we rejoice together in God's presence. As a pastor, I need to accept that self-righteousness and hypocrisy will not be allowed in Jesus' city, where religious folks seem to have a harder time getting in than most.

As I stand before Jesus, the problem I am faced with is this: I am a lusty, violent hypocrite. In the Gospels, Jesus relates the power of hell to three primary issues: lust, violence, and religious hypocrisy.[11] These are not abstract "spiritual" ambiguities that are distant from everyday life. These are global realities that are as close as the news that pops up on the TV screen every evening and as intimate as the person I look at every morning in the mirror. And Jesus is the resurrected King, who wants to send these toxic houseguests packing.

The good news? I want them out too. The bad news? When I really get honest with myself, these things have made their home in me. I need the healing grace of Christ if I am going to have any shot at the kingdom. So do you.

Most folks I know want sex trafficking and genocide eradicated forever. Many give their lives working toward this end. This demonstrates that we are not so far from the Christian doctrine of hell as we might think; there are things we *want* gone, damaging forces we long to be banished so that our world can flourish. An atheist lawyer may protest vociferously on the injustice of hell and simultaneously fight to keep thugs and rapists off the streets. His actions ironically demonstrate the biblical story's logic of hell: that for our world to flourish, there are some harmful powers that must be kept at bay.

And there is good news for our world: God is going to kick sex trafficking and genocide out of it. But there is a rub: he is more serious about it than we are. The spark that sets the wildfire lives in us; the root of the wicked tree is in our hearts; the poisoned spring from which the deadly waters flow is not just "out there," it is "in here." The problem is us.

"Will You Let Me Heal You?"

If I had grown up in Rwanda or Cambodia, under the same international pressures, historic forces, and evolving local antagonisms, I'm not sure I would have avoided murdering my neighbors and perpetrating the same brutal actions these societies did. Knowing the distorted cultural understandings of sex and dysfunctional experiences of abuse that have led so many johns to seek solace and comfort in the arms of a prostitute, I'm not certain I would be immune from their behavior if in their shoes. Knowing Jesus' harshest words of judgment are leveled not at the outsiders, but at the religious leaders, I find myself as a pastor with a target on my chest. I've found self-righteousness and hypocrisy living inside me, masked in religious garb.

Jesus' doctrine of hell does not elevate us over the surrounding world; it humbles us before the surrounding world. It levels the playing field—and it levels it before the cross. This leveling of the playing field is important, because it clears the way for God's grace, not our behavior, to be the basis for entrance into God's kingdom. Pol Pot (the architect of the Cambodian genocide) and my sweet grandmother (who wouldn't hurt a fly) stand together before the Great Physician, and his question is not, "Which one of you was better?" but rather, "Will you let me heal you?"

In leveling the playing field, Jesus makes way for grace.

Grace has the power to trump behavior. And if grace trumps behavior, the implications are radical. In God's kingdom, there will be murderers who've committed genocide and slave traders who've trafficked children, while good ol' boys and respectable neighbors will be cast outside. Jesus paints a picture of prodigals, tax collectors, and sinners partying it up in the Father's house while upstanding citizens, elder brothers, and those with the moral high ground cling to their credentials and complaints in the backyard.

By locating the vices of hell in the human heart, Jesus has leveled the playing field and identified our need not first and foremost as better behavior, but rather as reconciliation with God.

Us Under Extraordinary Conditions

We are not as good as we think we are. In the wealthier nations of the world, we often harbor a subtle, unrecognized arrogance that assumes we are somehow immune from complicity in truly evil behavior. But it is much easier to not steal food when you are well fed, to not covet your neighbor's cow when you have two cars, and to maintain the appearance of respectability when you are the beneficiary of a wealthy society that enjoys relative stability.

We should beware of being too self-congratulatory. Our implicit moral applause can mask and cover over the sin that lives inside us. It can deceive us from recognizing the power of hell that has its savage hold on our "civilized" hearts.

We would be shocked at what we are capable of. I've spent a lot of time hanging out with ex–Khmer Rouge soldiers and have been surprised to discover how normal they are. Though responsible for the horror of Cambodia's killing fields, their demeanor reminds me of my peaceful grandfather. Jewish Holocaust survivors recount stepping into postwar courtrooms, expecting to encounter the Nazi soldier on the stand as a demonic monster, but shocked to find in him a neighborly normalcy. This is because these killers are not the "other"; they are *us* under extraordinary conditions.

Raising the Bar

Jesus' doctrine of hell is good news not because he is less serious about sin, but because he is more. Jesus doesn't lower the bar; he raises it—and reveals that despite my résumé, I am a cruel, lascivious con artist. In so doing, Jesus paves the way for grace.

Grace trumps behavior. It levels the playing field. It puts us all without claim or merit before the cross. The criteria for entering the eternal joy of God's kingdom is found not in our résumés, but in his righteousness; not in our goodness but in his grace; not in our qualifications but in the healing power of the kingdom's King.

Everybody wants murder and rape out of the world. I've never met a fan of genocide and sex trafficking. Every beauty pageant queen dreams of world peace. But we are not beauty queens. Even beauty queens are not beauty queens. They—and we—are the very ones who've set God's world aflame. We've unleashed the destructive power of hell in the beautiful place God once called "very good."[12] Our own sin has left a trail of tears through our tragic and traumatized history. We have brought all the horror of hell to planet Earth.

And Jesus is going to kick it out.

GOD OR US

We are now in a position to address a central feature in the caricature of hell: the origin of its destructive power. In the caricature, God creates hell in order to torture sinners. But in the biblical story, we are the authors of hell's fury. God does not create the power of hell; we do. God does not rape kids and murder his neighbors; we do. God is not the one with skeletons in his closet; we are.

So how do we join Jesus' fight against the power of hell in God's good world today?

Personal and Social

Joining Jesus means pushing back the darkness on both the personal and social fronts. In the Introduction, I shared the story of the Thai pastor who told me sex trafficking was "a tragedy in our community, but it is more important that we focus on saving souls so that on Judgment Day they can go to heaven." The Thai pastor was wrong. The enslavement and raping of kids in his church's neighborhood was a major arena where the power of hell was unleashed. And Jesus calls his followers to redemptive engagement.

Like the Thai pastor, we have a tendency to separate the person and the community, to emphasize one and neglect the other. Some streams of Christianity emphasize personal morality: don't sleep around, get wasted, or steal from your boss, and you should be all right. Other streams emphasize social justice: feed the hungry, stop racism, and end poverty. Unfortunately, we often tend to separate these streams and overlook one or the other.

Jesus confronts us by taking both streams and bringing them back together into a larger, rushing, raging river.

There is a husband and wife in our church whom we often tease about being a "super couple." The husband is a police officer who leads our city's task force to rescue sexually enslaved children and prosecute their offenders. His wife is a counselor who leads our city's team that counsels, supports, and wraps their arms around youth who are survivors of the sex trade. Their faith in Jesus motivates their lives and work. They are working on big-scale, structural levels in our society.

They are fighting against the ferocity of hell on a social level, lopping off branches on the wicked tree.

Others are engaging these powers on personal fronts. My friend Tom points out that at its root, sex trafficking is a demand problem. Kids are raped because men want the kids. As long as men want them, and are willing to pay for them, the industry will find new supply. As long as the guillotine is operating upstream, the dead bodies will keep floating down the river. We can and should rescue children, prosecute offenders, and restore survivors. But we also need to find creative ways to address the demand side of the problem.

So Tom's working hard equipping men to create a different culture of manhood—one that lifts up and honors women and children, one that lives into a more redemptive vision of sexuality, and one that uses power and influence to protect the vulnerable rather than exploit them.[13] Tom's faith in Jesus motivates his life and work. Tom is addressing obstacles rooted in people's hearts.

Tom is going toe-to-toe with hell on personal fronts, taking a shovel to the wicked root.

Ben is another friend who is engaging this on yet one more level. He leads a recovery ministry in our church for men dealing with sexual addiction. Ben realizes that the line separating good and evil runs not between people but through us all, and that we all stand as sinners in need of the grace and mercy of Christ. Ben also realizes that Christ calls us to follow him together, not alone. Together, with raw transparency and authentic community, those with the courage to confront their demons are discovering what it means to let Christ heal us. Together, they are fighting the power of hell in their hearts. And in so doing, they are helping to create a more redemptive sexual culture in our world, one that bears the marks of God's kingdom.

The power of hell is alive and well in our world today. Sex trafficking is obviously just one example. We will explore many more examples in the chapters to come. But the point for now is this: if we are going to join Jesus' fight against the power of hell in God's good world, it will mean addressing both the personal and social fronts, engaging both the root and the wicked tree, the spark and the wildfire. So as followers of Jesus, how do we do that? What tools has Christ given us for the task?

Holiness and Justice

Jesus has given us holiness and justice as tools for the task of combatting the evil around us. Once again, we have a strong tendency to focus on one and neglect the other. When some streams of Christianity think of the power of hell, justice is nowhere on the radar. We envision Satan and his demons flying around in the air, trying to get us to use a Ouija board, go to a séance, or join a New Age cult.

Many assume that God only cares about "spiritual" things, and "spiritual" things are assumed to be those that have nothing much to do with everyday, physical life. This assumption is disastrous because it strains out a gnat and swallows a camel; it misses the obvious. It distracts vital time, energy, and resources from the more pressing, concrete, physical arenas of our world where Jesus says the power of hell has been unleashed.

Jesus confronts our tendency to ignore justice and tells us justice is spiritual.

Reclaiming this language can be powerful. Samantha Power, one of the world's leading scholars on genocide, has titled her influential book on the subject *A Problem from Hell*. I don't know whether she merely uses the phrase for its rhetorical power or if she truly believes in the spiritual framework the title suggests. But either way, her terminology is correct. Genocide *is* a problem from hell. There is a spiritual side to the most pressing problems of our world today that Jesus calls his followers to recognize.

And this recognition does have rhetorical power. Reclaiming the language of the power of hell can help the church today to recognize the spiritual side to justice and to hear Christ's call to action. When a child dies for lack of clean water in Africa during the richest and most technologically advanced century in our world's history, it is more than just an unfortunate tragedy.[14] When 27 million people are enslaved, held against their will, and exploited for profit in an industry that generates an estimated $32 billion a year, this is more than just a grievous calamity.[15] When 250-plus major wars kill more than 23 million people and leave tens of millions homeless, this is more than just a traumatic outrage.[16] All of this is the power of hell itself at work in our world.

Jesus also confronts our tendency to ignore holiness. I have met too many Christians who work tirelessly against war, conflict, and genocide in our world on a social level, while being prideful and self-righteous at home. Jesus stands against us. I have met other Christians who are passionately active in ending sex trafficking on a social level while being womanizers and greedy consumers in their personal lives. This does not fly with Jesus. Many in the Christian justice community are rightfully battling the wicked tree while wrongfully ignoring the wicked root in their own hearts.

Jesus raises the bar and calls us to a different kind of discipleship. He calls us to pursue holiness: to the plucking up of the wicked roots that lie inside of us. The classical language of vice can help us here, identifying things like lust, anger, greed, pride, gluttony, laziness, and envy. Like a "vice grip," these are the ways that hell gets its tightening hold on our lives.

These are the sparks that start the wildfires. The poisoned wells that pollute the river. The roots that give rise to the noxious weeds.

These are areas where Jesus wants to heal us. And we don't have to deal with them alone; he has given us himself by his Spirit, and friends for the journey in the body of Christ.

Holiness is another area where reclaiming the language can help us hear the urgency of Christ's call to action more clearly. When a husband cheats on his wife and tears at the threads of his marriage and family, this is more than just a "mistake"—it is lust at work. When a mother relies too heavily on wine and narcotics to escape her frustrations with life, and neglects or lashes out at her children, this is more than just a sad state of affairs—it is gluttony at work. When a depressed high school student gives in to the cultural pressure to become a consumer, identifying himself primarily through the clothes he wears, music he listens to, and latest technology he owns, this is more than just an unfortunate reality of modern society—it is greed at work.

Lust, gluttony, greed—all powers of hell, working to unravel our world.

Jesus calls us to holiness and justice. Holiness involves dealing with the spark, the poisoned well, the root in our own hearts. Justice involves dealing with the wildfires, the raging rivers, the wicked trees in our world. Holiness and justice are the tools Jesus has given us to join his fight against the power of hell. These are the inseparable pathways through which he calls us to follow him. Together, they are means by which the church proclaims its resurrected King and bears witness to his good kingdom that is coming soon to reconcile heaven and earth and redeem the world.

We must now ask: when God's justice reigns, where will genocide and sex trafficking flee? When God's presence dwells in power and intimacy, where will religious hypocrisy and idolatry hide? In short, where is the destructive power of hell going? It is to this question that we now turn.

CHAPTER 2 KEY IDEA

WHERE DOES THE POWER OF HELL COME FROM?
We are the ones, not God, who unleash the
destructive power of hell in the world.

3.

OUTSIDE THE CITY

THE CHEAP HOTEL

Jesus is going to kick the hell out of earth. The King is coming to establish his kingdom—and when he does, sin's destructive power will be cast outside. Like a good homeowner, Jesus longs for his house to be perfect. But like an unwelcome houseguest, sin has made a mess of things—for far too long. So Jesus is coming to kick out the vandals and put his house back in order through his resurrecting reign. This is the hope of the gospel.

But when hell gets kicked out, where does it go? The popular caricature, as we have seen, says "underground." But this is not where Jesus tells us it is going. Rather, the New Testament tells us that the power of hell is going to get kicked *outside the city*. This is significant, because this location speaks to a different storyline and motive than the caricature—a storyline and a motive that proclaim loudly and boldly the glorious goodness of God for his world.

The Valley of Hinnom

Jesus' word for hell is *Gehenna*. If you're reading through the New Testament and you come across the word *hell*, chances are it's the Greek word *Gehenna* translated into English for our modern ears.[1] For example, in the passages we looked at in the last chapter, where

Jesus relates the power of hell to lust and violence and James to the destructive power of the tongue, they are all using the word *Gehenna*.

The good thing about the English word *hell* is that we don't have to run around speaking in ancient foreign languages all the time. Dads cut off in traffic don't have to shout, "What the Gehenna?!" The danger of our English word, however, is that we can have negative associations not implied by Jesus' word *Gehenna*, and *Gehenna* can have positive associations that we miss with our word *hell*.

So if we want to reclaim a healthy understanding of hell, a good question to ask would be: "What is Gehenna?" Or perhaps better yet, "*Where* is Gehenna?" What may surprise you is to know that Gehenna was an *actual physical place*, a geographical location, just outside Jerusalem's walls. In the Old Testament, it is known as "the Valley of Hinnom."[2] When Jesus talks about Gehenna, or the Valley of Hinnom, he is not referring to a cavernous hole deep in the bowels of the earth, or to some black vortex in a galaxy far, far away. He is talking about a place you could MapQuest, a geographical location you could pinpoint on a map.

Jesus is talking about a place in Jerusalem's backyard.

The Valley of Hinnom had a dark and dangerous history in the Old Testament. What was this history, and why did Jesus make this his central image for where the destructive power of hell is someday going?

Idolatry and Injustice

The Valley of Hinnom had two primary associations. First, it was a place of idolatry. Israel went there to cheat on God with other lovers. God had redeemed Israel from slavery in Egypt and made her his wife, calling her out from under the oppressive gods of Egypt's empire and into a special, covenantal relationship with himself. When she left him to worship the idols of the surrounding empires, she was in essence cheating on her husband with her old, abusive boyfriends. The prophets railed on the valley because it was where Israel went to defile herself with the gods and religious practices of her neighbors.

The Valley of Hinnom was the cheap hotel outside the city where Israel cheated on God with other lovers.

Second, it was a place of injustice. Israel went there to kill her children. The valley was identified frequently with child sacrifice. And it made God angry. This was perhaps Israel's most brutal and detestable form of idolatry. Not only had she forsaken God as husband; she murdered her sons and daughters—who were also *his* sons and daughters!—in the fires she made to other lovers. Israel was killing *God's* children! All in the name of her whole adulterous affair.

The Valley of Hinnom was the woodshed out back where Israel beat God's children.

So God came home to confront his cheating, abusive wife. For the prophets, the Valley of Hinnom became a symbol of the idolatry and injustice that had come to saturate Israel's life as a whole. Consider the following passages:

[King Ahaz] did not do what was right in the eyes of the LORD. He walked in the ways of the kings of Israel and also made cast idols for worshiping the Baals. He burned sacrifices in the Valley of Ben Hinnom and sacrificed his sons in the fire, following the detestable ways of the nations the LORD had driven out before the Israelites. He offered sacrifices and burned incense at the high places, on the hilltops and under every spreading tree. (2 Chronicles 28:1–4)

[King Manasseh] rebuilt the high places his father Hezekiah had demolished; he also erected altars to the Baals and made Asherah poles. He bowed down to all the starry hosts and worshiped them. . . . He sacrificed his sons in the fire in the Valley of Ben Hinnom, practiced sorcery, divination and witchcraft, and consulted mediums and spiritists. . . . Manasseh led Judah and the people of Jerusalem astray, so that they did more evil than the nations the LORD had destroyed before the Israelites. (2 Chronicles 33:3–9)

The people of Israel and Judah have provoked me by all the evil they have done—they, their kings and officials, their priests and prophets, the men of Judah and the people of Jerusalem. . . . They set up their abominable idols in the house that bears my Name and defiled it. They built high places for Baal in the Valley of Ben Hinnom to sacrifice their sons and daughters to Molech, though I never commanded, nor did it enter my mind, that they should do such a detestable thing and so make Judah sin. (Jeremiah 32:32–35)

The Valley of Hinnom was a signpost of Israel's infidelity to God and injustice to one another. It was a place that symbolized the cruelty of the idols and those who bowed down in their service. Talk about skeletons in the closet . . .

Jerusalem had skeletons in her backyard.

The Idols Are Cruel

Idolatry and injustice are interconnected in the Valley of Hinnom, not two separate realities. Forsaking God resulted not in a more peaceful society, but in a more brutal one. As Israel turned away from God, she turned in upon herself. God doesn't just have a problem with the infamous valley because he's personally offended; he has a problem because he loves the world its powers seek to destroy.

In another passage on the Valley of Hinnom, God makes this interconnection crystal clear railing against the idolatry of the valley: "For they have forsaken me and made this a place of foreign gods . . ." and in the very next breath lamenting its injustice, ". . . they have filled this place with the blood of the innocent."[3] Injustice and idolatry are integrally interrelated, and God has a problem with them both.

So if Jesus says the Valley of Hinnom is the *place* of hell, what does this have to teach us about the *nature* of hell?

Three observations: First, the idols there are cruel. God is a faithful, loving husband who cares for his people. The idols are depicted as abusive lovers who seduce with flattering words only to ultimately enslave and destroy. The cruelty of the Valley of Hinnom arises from the idols that there hold sway.

Hell is cruel. Yet to blame the cruelty of hell on God is like an alcoholic blaming sobriety for the pain of his addiction. Sobriety is the cure the alcoholic needs, not the disease that afflicts him. His enslavement arises not from sobriety but from those forces that exist outside sobriety's realm. His problem is rooted in the fact that he ultimately craves sobriety's absence more than its presence; the cruelty is in the craving and its consequence.

The Valley of Hinnom is cruel not because of the good and faithful husband but because of the cheap and adulterous affair and the abusive and vindictive lovers we give ourselves to. Hell's internal logic is cruel not because of God but because of his absence in the attainment of our idolatrous illusions.

A second observation: the fires in the Valley of Hinnom are lit by human hands. Jerusalem's people lit these fires as acts of devotion to their idols. They burned these flames to brutally devour their children. For Israel to blame God for the fires in the Valley of Hinnom would be like an arsonist blaming a good homeowner for the backyard he set aflame; or an abusive babysitter blaming a loving parent for her child's black eye; or a cheating spouse blaming a faithful marriage for the pain of an affair she had herself pursued.

For Jesus to say the King is coming to kick sin out of Jerusalem and into the Valley of Hinnom, is to say in an important respect that the rebellion will be handed over to the destructive mess it has itself made.

There is a tradition that adds to this imagery, a tradition that holds that the Valley of Hinnom was, in Jesus' day, Jerusalem's city dump. Today we are accustomed to modern sanitation services with dump trucks that pick up our trash and transport it to landfills far, far away, outside the city limits. In Bible times, however, ancient cities burned and buried their refuse just outside the city walls. While there was a lot less trash before plastic bottles, newspapers, and the other trappings of an industrial consumer society, a place was still needed to deal with the refuse of ancient life. Given its unpopular history of idolatry, the Valley of Hinnom would have been a likely place outside Jerusalem's walls for trash to be burned.

If so, then inside Jerusalem's walls were light and life; outside the city walls were the smoldering fires of the local dump, burning the rubble as the sun went down into the night. If this tradition is right, then when Jesus says God is coming to cast sin outside his city and into the Valley of Hinnom, he is saying God will take sin out with the rest of the trash. Even if this tradition is not right, however, the same general implications apply from its Old Testament history.

Jerusalem vs. Gehenna

Third, there is one more characteristic of the Valley of Hinnom that is so central, yet perhaps so easily missed, precisely because it is so obvious: it is *outside the city.* Jerusalem was Israel's capital, the center of her national life. Jerusalem is pronounced *Yeru-shalom* in Hebrew and means literally "the *shalom* of God." *Shalom* is the abundant flourishing that results when God, the human community, and creation are in right relationship and intimate communion.

Jerusalem was thus called to be a reversal of the curse. A place where Eden's "very good" state was restored at the center of a fallen world. A signpost of *shalom* in the midst of a sin-struck, war-torn, devastated earth. Every time the city's name passed the lips of an Israelite, it was a reminder that God's *shalom* was to stand at the center of her national life as a people.[4]

This is important for our understanding of hell, because it reveals *why* sin must be cast outside the city walls. Sin wages war on *shalom.* Gehenna opposes Jerusalem. It wants *inside* the city walls. Those who murdered their children in the valley came back into the city to sleep at night. The affair that began at the cheap hotel soon wanted inside the husband's house. The idols in Gehenna were soon brought into Jerusalem and set up in Israel's temple.[5] The mistress soon wanted to lay claim to the marriage bed.

Sin is not content to keep to its own; it covets and seeks after that which belongs to God. The power of hell wants to take its destructive flame inside God's city.

When God shows up, the reason sin is cast *outside* the city is because it stands in opposition to God's good and redemptive purposes for the *inside* of the city. To ask God to redeem Jerusalem but not cast sin outside the city walls is like asking a doctor to heal your body without excising the disease. Like asking the light to arise without casting out the darkness. Like asking for restoration to come and destruction to remain.

It is to ask for a contradiction.

God excludes sin from his kingdom *because* of his goodness, not in opposition to or in spite of it.

THE RETURN OF THE KING

We want this story to be true. This story is, at its core, that of the good king returning to establish his redemptive kingdom and kick out the oppressive, enslaving powers that have hurt and destroyed for far too long. It is a classic story. The stuff of fairy tales, novels, and blockbuster movies. The stuff of hope.

This story is embedded in our cultural longings: the tales we tell ourselves and the dreams we dream for our world. Only, the gospel is not the fairy tale we dream up from earth and project onto heaven. It moves in the other direction. It is God's heavenly dream for the world come to earth: the fairy tale come true.[6]

The Fairy Tale Is True

The gospel fulfills the hopes and dreams embodied in many of our fairy tales. This came to life for me back in the day when reading the classic children's story *The Voyage of the Dawn Treader*.[7] In the story, an island kingdom has long suffered under the unjust power of a corrupt governor who exploits and enslaves the people. Selfishness and greed characterize the culture of the land. And yet, there are many who hold out hope for the return of the good and rightful king.

Eventually, the king returns to the island on his ship. He enters discreetly and is dismayed at the state of affairs in the land. When word spreads that the good king has arrived, a grassroots movement forms around his reign. As the king enters the capital, throngs of people burst into celebration and song, flocking into the city to rejoice. Eventually, the good king and his crew take the capital, while those who stood aligned with the old order of things realize the game is up and flee the city.

The kingdom is reestablished in the land.

Those who flee outside the city do so, for the most part, of their own accord. They realize their glory days are over. That life under the new order of things is not for them. Their character stands opposed to the justice and righteousness that mark the life of the new kingdom. Yet there are some who try to stay. The unjust governor and his cohorts seek to work out a bargain, a compromise, with the good king.

The good king offers his pardon if they will repent and receive the new order of things, but he will hear nothing of compromise with the old, corrupt order. When the king realizes the crooked governor is set in his ways, the only remaining question is "whether you and the rest of the rabble will leave without a flogging or with one. You may choose which you prefer."[8] The corrupt governor and his crew of injustice slink away, following the others who've fled outside the city.

When we hear this storyline in the context of a children's fairy tale, the king does not strike us as malicious or vindictive or cruel. He seems good and right and true. We are hopeful that when he returns he is unwilling to compromise with the old order of things. We want injustice cast outside the city. We hope for the coming of the righteous king, and our hope is not separate from, but rather coincides with, the hope for the banishment of those unrighteous powers that stand opposed to his kingdom.

We want this story to be true. We want the good prince to come and take Cinderella to the ball, and we do not find it surprising when the wicked stepsisters, who've been trying throughout the story to keep this from happening, slink bitterly away at the end, outside the story's dramatic center. We want Luke Skywalker to lead the rebels' strike against the empire, and we have no problem rejoicing in the final victory party as the emperor's forces fade out of center view into the sidelines. Fairy tales bear witness to our hope in this dramatic narrative structure.

Jesus' return bears this same dramatic narrative structure: the King is returning to establish his matchless kingdom, and all those forces that stand opposed to that kingdom, though they currently dominate our world, will fade from center view and slink to the sidelines, never again to hurt or destroy the flourishing peace of God's new creation.

The difference, of course, is that when we tell our fairy tales, we tend to envision ourselves in the role of the heroes. But in the gospel, we find ourselves first revealed in the role of the villain: the enemies of the abundant kingdom. But there is hope. Jesus is the hero and, like the prince in the Cinderella story, he wants to make us his bride.

Jesus' return to establish his good kingdom and banish from it the destructive power of hell is, in its dramatic narrative structure, not so far from our cultural imagination as we might think. The good news is: the fairy tale is true.

Liberating the Capital

Fairy tales are not the only cultural witnesses to this overarching storyline. The liberated-capital motif can also be found in the concrete blood and dirt of actual history. In Cambodia, for example, the Khmer Rouge's genocidal regime was toppled when the Vietnamese army liberated the capital of Phnom Penh. The Khmer Rouge had been responsible for the deaths of roughly one-fifth of the population and the wholesale destruction of the country. When the Vietnamese liberated the capital from the oppressive regime, the defeated soldiers fled outside the city. They knew the game was up once the capital had been taken, so they fled far to the peripheries of the country.

From these borderlands, they requested that, rather than being hunted down and killed, the new regime simply allow them to live out their days in these isolated areas, far from the influence and power they once had. Their authority had been taken away and they would no longer have the ability to kill and destroy. The new regime granted this request, going after only the top level of Khmer Rouge leadership and allowing these defeated soldiers to live out their days on the outskirts of the empire.

This is, I would suggest, a metaphor for what is happening in the biblical storyline. God returns to "liberate the capital," Jerusalem, from sin's destructive power and to establish his kingdom in the land. In the biblical story Jerusalem is seen not only as the capital of Israel, but as the center of the earth. So when God comes to liberate it, he will be liberating the very center of our world, so that he can establish his kingdom from there into all the earth.

Once God's capital is liberated, those forces unrepentantly opposed to his kingdom will know the game is up and will be removed from the center of influence, to the outskirts, where they will "live out their days," like the defeated Khmer Rouge soldiers, never again to invade or intrude upon the peace of God's new kingdom.

Cambodia is not alone. Throughout history, when people have been oppressed by foreign invaders, their hope for the liberation of the capital is the hope for the liberation of their country as a whole. This liberation theme is threaded throughout global history and speaks to our longing for the end of all those forces that enslave, oppress, and destroy.

Whereas the fairy tale speaks to a longing for this storyline in our cultural imagination, the liberation of the capital speaks to our longing for this storyline in the blood and dirt of actual history.

The difference, of course, is once again that when we tell our war stories, we depict *ourselves* as the good guys and the hope of the world. In the gospel, however, we are first revealed as the invaders, those God must liberate the earth *from*. We have usurped the Creator's authority over his creation, joined the mutiny, fomented the rebellion, and unleashed the destruction downstream in his world that this entails.

But there is hope. Jesus is the forgiving King who freely offers amnesty to all who will receive his reconciling embrace. He is the merciful victor who longs to pardon us as rebels and bestow citizenship on all who would come. Jesus is the gracious ruler who rejoices to wash us, clothe us, and make us fit for his just and righteous kingdom.

And he is coming to liberate his capital.

The Climactic Finale

Revelation, the final book of the Bible, also presents the hope of world history as God's liberation of the capital from the destructive power of sin. As the biblical story comes to a climactic finale, God brings the New Jerusalem, embodying the *new shalom of God*, down from heaven to earth. From this capital, God's reconciling, restorative power goes out to the world. God's holy city stands at the center of the new creation.

The New Jerusalem holds together an interesting contrast of images. On the one hand, the gates of the city are always open: "On no day will its gates ever be shut, for there will be no night there."[9] The city's open gates speak to its peace, security, and protection. It never has to worry about invasion. It is not protected by military might but rather by the indwelling presence of God.

The open gates also speak to a welcoming posture toward God's world: "The nations will walk by its light, and the kings of the earth will bring their splendor into it. . . . The glory and honor of the nations will be brought into it."[10] This is the fulfillment of the prophetic hope: the nations come streaming to Zion to worship God and glory in his redemption as, through Abraham's people, all the nations of the earth are blessed.

And yet, while the city's posture is one of welcoming embrace, sin and her allies are never allowed to enter inside the city gates: "Nothing impure will ever enter it, nor will anyone who does what is shameful or deceitful."[11] Idolatry, lust, violence, greed, and all the other harmful vices from which we refuse to be healed, will never be allowed to hurt or destroy on all God's holy mountain again.[12] Because God's city embodies his *shalom* for the world, and because sin, by its very nature, wages war on God's *shalom*, it is no longer allowed to invade his kingdom.

Evil is cast outside the city.

Though Revelation never uses the term *Gehenna*, it draws upon the same storyline invoked by Jesus, and the broader New Testament, in their use of the term: the King is returning to liberate the capital, establish his good kingdom, and cast all its stubborn opponents into the distance. Revelation's New Jerusalem imagery confirms what we've seen throughout this chapter: hell's location is not *underground* but *outside the city*, even if this location is understood metaphorically.

So what difference does this location make?

UNDERGROUND OR OUTSIDE

"Outside the city" is a very different location from "underground," and it speaks to a fundamentally different motive on God's part: protection, not torture. To speak of hell's location as outside the city frames it in integral relation to what is happening inside the city. It immediately provokes questions: "What is happening inside the city that precludes the power of hell from being a part? What is the glory and goodness in which evil and injustice may not participate?" A symmetrical relationship arises between God's good, loving, and redemptive purposes for the world embodied in his holy city, and his protection of that city from all those forces that oppose those purposes.

In contrast, the "underground" imagery tends to sever this relationship. The location *down below* bears no obvious relationship to God's broader redemptive purposes *in heaven above*. Once this break from God's redemptive purposes takes place, it becomes easy to twist the purpose of hell. Downstream, hell starts to look like a place God created for the specific purpose of throwing down on sinners. God's primary motive moves from *protection of the good* outside the city, to *torture of the bad* underground. The location has become abstractly disconnected from what God is positively up to in the world.

But God's purpose is protection, not torture. Jesus will protect his city from the destructive power of sin. When his kingdom comes, in the words of Ezekiel:

"Jerusalem will be a city without walls because of the great number of people and animals in it. And I myself will be a wall of fire around it," declares the LORD, "and I will be its glory within."[13]

God wants people in his city: he tears down the walls to let everyone inside. But God's very presence is a fire that protects the city. Like a father protecting his children from the bullies on the prowl. Like a chief protecting his village from hostile invasion. Like a husband protecting his wife from a would-be rapist. God protects his kingdom from the tyrannous onslaught that wants inside.

God fights "fire with fire." He does not need cannons or jets or armies to protect his city: it is protected by the very strength of his presence, indwelling in glory with all who would receive him. God's holy love is experienced *inside the city* as redemptive glory. But to those ill-intentioned powers that want to invade, God's holy love is experienced as protective fire.

God's glorious presence is a boundary that safeguards the city, preventing the destructive power of sin from invading his kingdom. Inside are the fields, mountains, and rivers of the new world; outside is the wildfire that tore apart the old. Inside is intimacy with God given graciously; outside is the self-inflicted darkness of his absence.

The good news of the gospel is this: Jesus invites us into his city. The King wants to pardon. The Lamb desires to forgive. The Great Physician longs to heal. We cannot get him dirty; he can only make us clean. Jesus opens his arms wide on the cross to embrace his sin-sick world. Though we are rebels, his voice calls to us as "Daughter" and "Son." He raises his voice strong and calls to the ends of the earth, beckoning us to receive his reconciling presence and prepare for the resurrection to come.

And when it comes, God's holy love will protect the object of his affection: the new creation. God's holy mountain—Mount Zion, the New Jerusalem—will flourish. Then will come true God's words through Isaiah:

They will neither harm nor destroy
>   on all my holy mountain,
for the earth will be full of the knowledge of the LORD
>   as the waters cover the sea.[14]

CHAPTER 3 KEY IDEA

WHERE IS THE POWER OF HELL GOING?

Jesus will liberate his capital and establish his kingdom in the earth. When he does, the power of hell will be cast "outside the city," away from the seat of power, influence, and authority, where it can no longer hurt or destroy.

INTERLUDE

THE GAME-CHANGER

RESURRECTION AND THE GRAVE

"If hell is not underground, why then does the Old Testament depict it that way?" you may be asking. We have explored the New Testament, but there is a quick problem to be addressed: the Old Testament *does* depict hell's location as underground. Does the Old Testament contradict the storyline we have been exploring? A quick look reveals that the answer is no.

The Old Testament word for hell is *Sheol*. This Hebrew word shows up more than sixty times in the Old Testament and frequently gets translated into English as "hell." Sheol was a very different place, however, from the Valley of Hinnom: it was not a spot on the map near Jerusalem, not a geographical location you could walk to. Rather, it was underground and was our rough equivalent of *the grave*. And yet, though the grave was conceptualized as being beneath the earth, it was very different from our popular caricature of the underground torture chamber.

There were two primary differences between the Hebrew understanding of the grave and our popular caricature of hell. First, the grave was the place where *everyone* went when they died: the good and the bad, the righteous and the wicked, the pagan and the saints. When Jacob, the great father of Israel, heard that his beloved son Joseph had died, he declared, "I shall go down to Sheol to my son, mourning."[1] In the Psalms, the righteous sufferer cries out to God to deliver him from death,

"For in death there is no remembrance of you; in Sheol who will give you praise?"[2] Job declared, "The small and the great are there, and the slave is freed from his master."[3] The grave was home to king and peasant, great and small, righteous and wicked, rich and poor, slave and free.

Everyone went there.

Second, the grave was a place of unconscious death, not of conscious punishment. It was the place you went when your lifeless body was buried in the earth. It is characterized in the Old Testament as: "the pit," a place "dark and deep," the "land of forgetfulness," the abyss beneath the raging floods of the ocean.[4] It was neither a conscious punishment in a bad place nor a release into a good place, but rather an unconscious, negative contrast to the light and life that existed on earth before the face of God.

It was simply a place of death.

Why Underground?

It is not hard to see why the grave was conceptualized beneath the earth. It was then as it is today: when people died, they were buried. Tombs were dug and bodies laid in the graveyard. Gates and bars often protected these graveyards, giving rise to the ancient image of the "gates of hell."[5] Family you once laughed with and mourned with were now six feet under. Your ancestors lay beneath layers of mud, soil, and rock in the family graveyard.

The grave was in the ground.

Genesis enhances this imagery, depicting our death in the grave as our return to the ground from which we came. God raises Adam up from the dust of the earth and breathes life into him: our spirit comes from the very breath of God. When sin enters the world, the consequence is death: our rebellious distance from the Creator of life leads to the absence of life. When Adam dies, God's breath leaves him as his body returns to the dust: "You will . . . return to the ground, since from it you were taken; for dust you are and to dust you will return."[6] Death is a return to the ground from which we came.

Ashes to ashes, dust to dust.

So what happened between the Old and New Testaments to change all this? What was the catalyst that moved hell's location from underground to outside the city? What was the game-changer that shifted our fate from an unconscious death to being raised in life?

The answer: the resurrection of Christ.

All Will Be Raised

A game-changer is that moment when it appears that everything is hopelessly lost, and suddenly something extraordinary and unexpected happens that turns the tide of the game. Jesus' resurrection is like that: it shifts our fate from unconscious death to risen life. It is the game-changer. On the cross, he atoned for our sin—which brought death into the world—and took its punishment with him into the grave. Through his resurrection, he has arisen victorious over its power. Death can no longer hold him.

And death can no longer hold us.

Christ's resurrection does not mean that he will live alone forever and everyone else stays dead. It means that through him all will be raised. Paul calls Jesus the "firstfruits" of the resurrection that is coming:[7] when the first apple appears on the tree in spring, it does not mean we have one apple to eat for the year; it is a sign that the whole orchard is about to burst into bloom. When the cold, dark winter is done and that first bud blossoms, the rest of the garden is about to come bursting at the seams. Christ's resurrection is the beginning, the first blossom, of something that is about to burst upon the world.

All will be raised.

The orchard is the whole human race: about to spring into bloom from the cold, dark winter of death. Paul rejoices, "As in Adam all die, so in Christ all will be made alive."[8] The scope of the resurrection that is coming is Adam's family tree: everyone. God has exalted Jesus as the life-giving King of the human race. Jesus has been grafted in to replace Adam as the new head of the family tree.

Death no longer has the last word.

To limit resurrection to just some people, a few special folks, would be to limit the scope and power of what Jesus has accomplished. The gates of hell have been torn down and its captives released. The road to Sheol has been forever closed. Life underground is no longer an option. Jesus has conquered the grave.

Jesus the Catalyst

Jesus' resurrection is the catalyst that moves hell's location from underground to outside the city. Because he conquered death, the grave can no longer hold us. Jesus laid Death in his grave;[9] it is no longer our eternal home. Christ's resurrection gives hope to a dying humanity that "Death, thou shalt die!"[10] Life has won the victory.

This is not a skeleton in God's closet; this is God's good response to our skeletons in the ground.

Jesus is victorious over the grave.

In light of Jesus' victory, we are all now faced with monumental questions: Where do we stand with respect to the One by whom we are raised? How do our lives stand in relation to the King and his kingdom? Do we turn from ourselves in repentance and enter his embrace? Or do we resist the amnesty of Christ's mercy and cling to ourselves outside the city gates? Do we receive the kingdom's healing power through the life-giving presence of its King? Or do we stubbornly lay claim to our autonomy in the peripheral land of isolation?

In later chapters we will explore this more fully, but for now the point is this: neither the New Testament concept of "outside the city" nor the Old Testament concept of "the grave" look anything like the underground torture chamber. In the Old Testament, the grave was not a place where we went after death to be punished. Death *is* the punishment: the just consequence of our sin, returning to the dust from which we came for our rebellion against the Giver of Life. In the New Testament, "outside the city" involves standing in opposition to Jesus' redemptive kingdom, a resistance to the extravagant and undeserved mercy of the One by whom we are raised.

Jesus' resurrection is the catalyst, the game-changer, that provokes the transition between them.

4.

BOUNDARY OF MERCY

God's purpose is not torture. Earlier, I shared my impressions of God with a sadistic look of delight on his face as he threw down on a crowd of repentant people crying out for mercy. The two passages frequently used to support this caricature are Jesus' parable of Lazarus and the rich man (Luke 16) and Revelation's "lake of fire" (Revelation 20). We will explore these passages in depth in upcoming chapters and find that they do not contradict, but rather powerfully confirm, the paradigm we are developing thus far.

But first, I want to confront this feature of the caricature head-on: hell's purpose is not torture. It is protection.

In my own life, the lightbulb turned on back in my college days, while reading a passage of C. S. Lewis's *The Pilgrim's Regress*. The book is an allegory in which John, the main character, stumbles and fumbles (rather than progresses) his way into the life of the kingdom. He travels through exotic lands and meets interesting characters, each representing different challenges to the life of the faith.

Toward the end of his journey, John has one troubling, lingering question: he wants to know about the Landlord and the black hole. The Landlord is a metaphor for God: "the lord of the land," the ruler of all the places John's travels have brought him thus far. The black hole is a metaphor for hell: a place John has heard rumor of, where unrepentant rebels against the Landlord are banished. John has deep concerns about the Landlord and the black hole, and the ensuing parable is a good place for this chapter's discussion to begin.

THE LANDLORD AND THE BLACK HOLE

John asks his Guide the question that has long been burning within him. If the Landlord allows the existence of a black hole, how can one still say, "The Landlord is 'so kind and good'! . . . At least these poor creatures are unhappy enough: there is no need to add a black hole."[1] John voices the concern many of us have: the fear that hell makes God look cruel.

The Guide seems almost humored by the question's underlying assumptions, but responds with compassion: "I see you have been among the Enemy's people. In these latter days there is no charge against the Landlord which the enemy brings so often as cruelty."[2] The Guide recognizes that at its heart, John's question is about the Landlord's character; it is a question about the goodness of God.

The Guide goes on to explain the nature of the black hole. The following passage is a thick one; it packs many key insights into a short paragraph. Don't worry if some of the words are initially confusing or the images are hard to connect with. We will be unpacking them in the pages ahead. The Guide tells John:

> The Landlord does not make the blackness. The blackness is there wherever the taste of mountain-apple has created the vermiculate will. What do you mean by a hole? Something that ends. A black hole is blackness enclosed, limited. And in that sense the Landlord *has* made the black hole. He has put into the world a Worst Thing. But evil of itself would never reach a worst: for evil is fissiparous and could never in a thousand eternities find any way to arrest its own reproduction. If it could, it would be no longer evil: for Form and Limit belong to the good. The walls of the black hole are the tourniquet on the wound through which the lost soul else would

bleed to a death she never reached. It is the Landlord's last service to those who will let him do nothing better for them.[3]

Like a thick, hearty meal, this passage has a lot to chew on. Let's begin and take it one bite at a time.

The Nature of Evil

John's Guide gives us three important observations on the nature of evil. First, he says evil is "fissiparous": this is a fancy way of saying it is divisive. Sin takes things that are whole and tries to break them up, to put cracks and fissures in them. Sin takes a sledgehammer to God's good world: to divide, devour, and destroy. Adultery divides a marriage; greed devours a resource; murder destroys a body. As we have seen, sin attacks the integrity of God's *shalom* in the world, puts cracks in it, tries to fragment the human community and tear creation apart from the inside out.

Evil's divisive nature is clear in the biblical story. In the early chapters of Genesis, for example, sin's onslaught comes with violence. God creates the human community united: Adam and Eve rejoice in one another and celebrate their union. But when sin enters the world, it immediately divides and fragments the human community. It starts with a broken marriage: Adam blames Eve to detract attention from his own guilt. Next it moves to homicide: their son Cain murders his brother Abel. From there, their great-great-grandson Lamech sings songs about how powerfully violent he is (I envision a Mafia warlord). By the time of Noah, we are told: "the earth is filled with violence."[4]

Filled with violence: earth is like a bowl, humanity like a faucet—violence is what we pour . . . until the earth is full.

Humanity is divided and destroyed.

And God is greatly grieved.[5]

After my time in Rwanda and Cambodia, when I hear of our violence filling the earth, I think of genocide. Sin only takes three chapters, once entering the world, to move from a broken marriage to mass destruction. If we wonder whether this depiction of evil is still relevant today, we only need turn on the evening news or pick up the morning paper. Sin destroys the human community; it is fissiparous.

Evil is like a crack in your windshield: it starts at a point but spreads, working its way throughout the entire glass to shatter it. Similarly, sin spreads cracks through the human community to fracture and shatter us. Augustine envisioned the human community as something like a china doll: created with a unity both beautiful and fragile, yet thrown to the ground by sin and fractured and shattered into millions of scattered pieces that now fill the earth.[6]

Sin wages war on God's *shalom*. As we have seen, its wicked root grows quickly into dark and disastrous trees that tower over the earth. Its spark blazes into a wildfire that threatens to burn down the world. John's Guide is right: evil is fissiparous—a divisive force that aims to destroy the flourishing God intends for the human community.

Evil Is a Parasite

The Guide's second observation on the nature of evil is that it is a parasite: it has no independent existence of its own, but must feed off the good. God creates a good world ("Form and Limit belong to the good") and does not create evil ("The Landlord does not make the blackness"). Evil is, in contrast, an intruder in God's beautiful creation. This mirrors our earlier observation that God does not create "heaven, earth . . . and hell." Rather, God creates heaven and earth—and creates them good. God's world does not need evil to exist, but evil feeds off of God's good world.

Classically, Augustine made this same observation: sin is not a "substance," a physical thing created by God. It is, rather, a "corruption," a distortion of our proper relationship to good created things.[7] Gluttony is not a thing we can put on the lab table to examine and dissect. Food is the thing, and it is a good thing God makes for our flourishing. Gluttony just involves a distorted relationship with it. Sex is another good thing God created; adultery corrupts that good thing. And authority is a good thing, created by God; oppression just happens to corrupt it.[8]

God creates good things so his world will thrive; sin corrupts those good things for its own self-serving ends.

Evil is an adjective, not a noun: a *gluttonous* appetite; an *adulterous* relationship; an *oppressive* authority.[9] Evil is not a person, place, or thing, but rather, a distorted *relationship* with people, places, and things.

Evil is a parasite that wants to tear creation apart from the inside out. In the same way that a healthy body does not require cancer to exist, God's creation does not require evil to exist. But the inverse is not true. Cancer *does* require a living, breathing body to sustain its existence, and evil similarly requires God's good creation to sustain its own existence. Before Satan was a fallen angel, he was just an angel, and that was a good thing created by God.

Like a parasite feeding off a healthy host, evil feeds off the goodness that God provides. So let's review:

God creates good things; he does not corrupt them.

Evil corrupts good things; it cannot create them.

Evil Is Aggressive

The Guide's third and final observation on the nature of evil is that it is aggressive. Sin is not a quiet roommate; it could "never in a thousand eternities find any way to arrest its own reproduction." It is not content to stay in its corner and peacefully coexist with God's kingdom. Gehenna wants inside Jerusalem. Like an addict, the more evil is given, the more its appetite grows.

Sin will not be content until it has destroyed the world. Rage seeks after a person to cut down. Greed hunts for resources to devour. Lust is on the lookout for a body to objectify. Pride is on the prowl for an opportunity at self-exaltation. Imperial ambition preys upon the peace of the neighborhood.

Peace treaties don't work. As was true with Nazi Germany in World World II, attempts at appeasement are doomed by the very logic of evil's imperial intentions. Ground that is given merely feeds its insatiable lust for further dominion. Sin is an aggressor that continually thirsts after more and will deceive to get its way. If hell had its way, it would consume all of heaven and earth; it would devour and destroy until there was nothing left but the chaotic oblivion of its own self-determined annihilation.

Herein lies the chief irony of sin: it wants distance from God, it desires autonomy from the Creator, but in this distance is found its own destruction. When cancer destroys its host, it simultaneously destroys itself. Evil is a cancer out to destroy God's good world, and it doesn't care if it goes down with the ship. Sin seeks to drag creation back into the nihilistic void from which it came. If evil had its way, it would no longer be evil; it would cease to exist.

As sin strives to move away from God, the Source of life, it naturally moves ever closer to the horizon of death. As evil seeks distance from God, the Light of the world, it naturally engrosses itself ever further in the darkness of its own autonomy. Yet even in its self-imposed distance from God, it maintains a relation to God and thus can never fully reach the independence it so desperately craves—it can only sink in upon itself and shrink ever smaller toward, in the Guide's words, "a death she never reached."

Sin is anti-creation. It is an aggressive parasite that preys upon the good to maintain its own consumptive existence. *If* God's good kingdom is to be established upon the earth, a kingdom characterized by holiness, justice, and love; and *if* evil is a divisive, aggressive parasite that seeks to do violence to God's benevolent purposes for his world; *then* something must be done about evil, for it will not be content to coexist in the New Jerusalem as a disgruntled but quiet roommate. If God is to redeem, evil must be expelled and a boundary placed to protect God's holy city from evil's imperial intentions.

This brings us to the nature of the Landlord.

THE LANDLORD'S KINDNESS

John's Guide also makes three important observations on the nature of the Landlord. First, the Landlord does not create evil: "The Landlord does not make the blackness." God is not the author of sin; God is good. God desires the flourishing of his world. Where, then, does evil come from? As we have seen, we are the ones, not God, who unleash its destructive power in the world. We are the architects of autonomy, the engineers of evil, who let loose the blackness that threatens to paint over the vibrant colors of God's universe.

The Guide continues to explain: "The blackness is there wherever the taste of mountain-apple has created the vermiculate will." Lewis is referring here to our fall in the garden of Eden: the "mountain-apple" is a symbolic reference to the Tree of Knowledge of Good and Evil, whose fruit is eaten by Adam and Eve. The word *vermiculate* means "worm-eaten": the Guide is saying that our worm-eaten will, in rebellion against God, is the source of evil in the world; not God.

This is what we saw earlier in Jesus' teaching, that the power of hell is rooted in our distorted desires—the wicked root, the wildfire's spark, the poisoned well—or, in classical language, our corrupted will.

God is not the author of evil; we are. G. K. Chesterton was invited by a London paper in the early 1900s to submit an essay in response to the question, "What's wrong with the world?" He humorously, and wisely, responded with a simple four-word essay: "Dear sirs, I am."[10] One of the problems with the ways we tend to talk about the power of hell is that we shift the blame for the cruelty that is ours in the world away from ourselves and toward the heart of the God who is good.

Our problem is not that we are good and God is evil. The gospel flips this illusion on its head: God is good and we are evil. Our healing begins with our repentant acknowledgment of this fact; then we can fall into the arms of mercy that are waiting to receive us.

But what if we will not repentantly acknowledge this truth? What if we will not fall into mercy? What if we will not receive and be healed?

The Logic of Containment

The Guide's second observation on the nature of the Landlord is that he does set limits to the extent of evil's destruction: "A black hole is blackness enclosed, limited." The Landlord does not create the blackness, but he does contain it. It is in this sense that the Landlord *has* created the boundary of the black hole: to contain its expansion. He has "put into the world a Worst Thing" for the simple reason that "evil of itself would never reach a worst."

God contains the destructive power of evil so that it may not infringe upon the peace of his new creation. Hell is a boundary that says to evil's imperial intent: "You may come this far, and no further." It restrains sin's dark intentions for God's redeemed world. It is a container for evil.

This mirrors what we saw in the last chapter: that at the end of the biblical story, the gates of God's city are always open, yet evil is not allowed inside.[11] God's city is a magnificent gift for the nations of the world who come streaming in, yet those who practice idolatry, murder, sexual immorality, deception, and all those things that would infringe upon the peace of God's new creation are kept outside.[12]

This New Jerusalem imagery illustrates the same point the Guide is making: the Landlord contains the blackness in the black hole so it will no longer be allowed to infringe upon the flourishing of his good world. God contains evil so that it will not be allowed to do violence to the peace of his new creation. When God's kingdom is established, no longer will any evil aggressor be allowed to bring bloodshed to God's planet.

Hell is not a place God creates to torture people, but a power that God contains to protect the overflowing life of his new creation.

The Tourniquet on the Wound

The Guide's third and final observation is this: the Landlord is motivated by mercy. The black hole is "the Landlord's last service to those who will let him do nothing better for them." How is the black hole an act of service, of kindness, of mercy, to the unrepentant rebel?

It is easier to see how God is motivated by mercy in redemption. God does not have to redeem his world, but he does. The Creator is under no obligation or requirement: he could be good in and of himself and leave us to our own devices. But he doesn't. Redemption is an act of glorious goodness, of gracious generosity, of undeserved mercy and kindness. "While we were yet sinners, Christ died for us."[13] God sacrificially redeems our world from the power of evil—and then protects its abundance from that damaging power—because of his mercy.

But the Guide goes further. He declares that the Landlord is motivated by mercy not only toward those who accept it, but also toward those who reject it. How? He explains: the Landlord wants to heal the unrepentant; but if they will not allow it, then he gives them the most merciful option for their self-imposed predicament. The walls of the black hole are "the tourniquet on the wound through which the lost soul else would bleed to a death she never reached."

The imagery is of God as a Great Physician, wrapping a bandage around the wound of sin that we refuse to let him heal. Because our sin grows from the inside out, like a tumor that gets progressively worse the more it grows, God places a boundary that restricts this insatiable growth of the cancer within us. This boundary does more than protect the new creation; it simultaneously protects the rebellious by placing a limit on the harm they can do to themselves. It restricts sin's increase by preventing its ability to feed parasitically off the peace of the new creation.

God is a Great Physician who gives the recalcitrant the best medicine for their situation. If they do not want to be healed, then he will at least restrict the extent to which the cancer inside them can grow. Hell limits the extent of sin's growth as an act of God's mercy toward those "who will let him do nothing better for them."

At the conclusion of the passage, the Guide rejoices in awe at the amazing and unfathomable mercy of God:

> God in His mercy made
> The fixèd pains of Hell.
> That misery might be stayed,
> God in His mercy made
> Eternal bounds and bade
> Its waves no further swell.
> God in His mercy made
> The fixèd pains of Hell.[14]

TORTURE VS. CONTAINMENT

Hell is not a place God creates to torture sinners, but a power God excludes to protect the robust vitality of his kingdom. God's purpose of containment, in radical contrast to the caricature, reveals a motive of mercy. God's mercy redeems the human community and reconciles the broader creation from the destructive power of sin. Perhaps more surprisingly, however, God's mercy is also seen in his treatment of the impenitent: he does not torture or kill them, but rather hands them over to their desire.

God's mercy is revealed through and through: God's mercy toward the human community shattered by the sledgehammer of sin. God's mercy toward his creation groaning under the weight of evil. God's mercy toward the unrepentant rebel who refuses to be healed.

For both God's redemptive kingdom and those who refuse to repent: hell is a boundary of mercy.

But the question arises: "Is this the *most* merciful option?" While this is better than the caricature, are there other alternatives available? So far as I can tell, there are only four options God has for dealing with dissidents if he is going to redeem our world. And of the four, this is not only *a* merciful option; it is the *most* merciful option. Let's explore the alternatives.

"Marry Me and Bring in Your Old Lovers"

God's first option for dealing with unabashed evil is to *ignore* it. But to ignore it or pretend it isn't there would really mean that creation hasn't been redeemed. It would be like a doctor saying he had healed his patient of cancer, and ignoring all the incoming tests and X-rays showing the cancer still there. If children are still crying, nations are still warring, and people are still dying—then it isn't really the new creation.

God ignoring evil in his city would be like him bending down on one knee, pulling out the ring, and saying, "Marry me and bring in all your old lovers."

Let me explain. As we have seen, the gospel is God's invitation to leave sin behind and be united in life with him. The cross is God's marriage proposal: the place where we are invited to turn *from* our autonomy; to turn *to* the One who has borne its curse out of reconciling love for us; to turn *in order that* we might enter into eternal communion in the very life of God.

As we will see in the coming chapters, God's kingdom come is a Wedding Feast at the consummation of world history: the union of heaven and earth and of God with his people forever. This glorious marriage of God and humanity, this consummated union of heaven and earth, *is* the new creation.

To bring sin into God's city is to bring our old lovers into God's honeymoon suite. And our old lovers want to tear that suite apart. Sin is the destructive force that caused the problem in the first place, the power *from which* God redeems creation. Our world is redeemed *from* sin and *to* God. For God to ignore unrepentant sin in the new creation would be to make a farce of redemption; it would say implicitly that creation hadn't truly been redeemed.

It is a sham marriage.

For God to ignore sin is not merciful. If redemption is to be real rather than a farce, it is not really an option at all. It is like God saying, "Marry me, bring your old lovers—and let them tear our new world apart."

"Marry Me or I'll Kill You"

God's second option for dealing with unrepentant evil is to *annihilate* it. Some people have seen annihilation as God's most merciful option: the idea that God would simply kill the rebels, "put them out of their misery," rather than let them live on in their unfortunate condition. I have found, however, that this only *seems* more merciful at first glance because it is responding to the caricature of God torturing people for eternity.

There are a few significant problems with annihilation. First, it is problematic because Christ has conquered death: the grave is no longer an option. Christ has razed Sheol, its gates have been torn down, and its dark road leading down into the depths of the earth has been forever closed. Because of Christ's victory over death, the cessation of existence is no longer possible. Christ's life-giving victory lays life's claim upon even the one who turns away from Christ toward the darkness she can never fully reach.

Annihilation minimizes the scope and power of Jesus' resurrection.

Annihilation is also problematic for a second, more basic reason. At its core, it is like God saying, "Marry me or I'll kill you." If you knew a guy who asked the love of his life to marry him, you would hope he would have the maturity if she rejected the proposal to simply move on and let her go her own way. If he killed her for turning him down, we would think him small, vindictive, and cruel. And we would lock him up as a criminal.

Our everyday etiquette and common sense shows: life "outside the city" is more merciful than annihilation.

God does not shoot us if we refuse to be with him; he simply hands us over to our refusal. As we shall see even more clearly in future chapters, this is punishment enough. If we want independence over communion, if we prefer autonomy to worship, if we desire sin over salvation, then God's most merciful option is simply to let us go our own way, to hand us over to the decision we have made.

For God to annihilate the unrepentant sinner like a spurned lover would be an act not of mercy but of spite on God's part. Hell is the more merciful option.

"Marry Me or I'll Lock You in the Basement"

God's third option for dealing with unrepentant evil is to *redeem* it. The irony, of course, is that redeeming rebels is precisely what God *has* done. In Christ, God has redeemed the human community and the broader creation from sin and its consequence: death. To ask God to redeem us from sin is to ask for what he has already graciously provided on the cross. Hell does not involve God's refusal *to* redeem, but our refusal *to be* redeemed.

God is the object of redemption. We are redeemed *from* sin *to* God. Sin is, by its very nature, opposed to God—this is why we need to be redeemed! To ask God to redeem the *nature* of sin itself is to ask for a contradiction: it is to misunderstand what sin is. It is like asking God to let us accept the marriage proposal and never have to see him again.

Grace and goodness beckon from God's city, but sin must be left at the door.

Along these lines, some have found God's most merciful option to be a universalism in which God sends unrepentant rebels to hell to purge them of their sin until all are eventually redeemed into his kingdom. Once again, however, there is a major common-sense problem with this. It is like God saying, "Marry me or I'll lock you in the basement until you learn to love me." We know from common courtesy and everyday experience that the most mature response to a rejected marriage proposal is not to abduct the unrequited lover and lock her in your basement, but simply to let her go her own way.

And once again, this option is usually responding to the caricature's depiction of torture, and trying to find some constructive use for that torture. Whereas annihilation tries to get rid of torture by simply killing the unrepentant rebel, universalism tries to deal with torture by finding a constructive use for it. Both are problematic because they are responding to a caricature of torture to begin with.

As we have seen, God does not lock unrepentant rebels in his basement until they "learn to love him"; his goal is not to give them a good flogging to try and purge them of their sin. Rather, God lets the marriage-rejecters go their own way, and contains the destructive power of their sin "outside the city" to prevent them from crashing the wedding.

"Marry Me or Go Your Own Way"

This brings us to God's fourth and final option for dealing with unrepentant evil: containment. If God is to redeem creation, there are no other alternatives available as far as I can see, and this is by far the most merciful one around. God invites us into marital union with him, but he creates a space for those who prefer independence to communion, who want autonomy over worship, who desire sin over salvation.

God is good, gloriously good. He has other options: he could lock the unrequited lovers in his basement and beat them senseless until they "learn to love him" and just play along. He could annihilate them on the eternal gallows to show the world once and for all that he's the boss they shouldn't have messed with. But he doesn't. In mercy, he simply hands them over to the life apart from him that they desire.

He hands them over to themselves. The horror of this is, as we shall see, punishment enough.

And God protects his holy city. "No one who does what is shameful or deceitful will enter it."[15] The spark will no longer be allowed to start the wildfire. Our destruction will not be allowed inside. It is God's way of saying, "You can have your sin, but you cannot have it here." God's containment of hell's destructive power outside the city fulfills his promise in Isaiah: "No longer will they hurt or destroy on all my holy mountain."[16] God protects his kingdom from all that stands opposed to its flourishing.

Hell is a boundary of mercy. God hands the unrequited lovers over to the distance they crave, and their adulteries are no longer allowed inside the new home. Jesus banishes those who refuse his amnesty as king, and protects the wedded bliss of his city from all who stand opposed. The Spirit of God, like a Great Physician, wraps the tourniquet on the wound we refuse to let him heal, protecting both the kingdom and the rebel from the insatiable growth of the sickness inside. This is an act of God's goodness toward his new creation: for it secures its redemptive flourishing.

And there is good news for us, the adulterous rebels: God's arms are wide open, inviting us to turn from sin and be healed in his care. The Great Physician beckons. Christ has atoned for our sin and flung wide the gates of his city, calling us to turn to him and be healed.

———

We have now confronted two key features in the caricature of the "underground torture chamber": its location is not *underground*, but rather *outside the city*. And its purpose is not *torture*, but rather *protection*. This leaves one remaining feature to be dealt with: that of the enclosed "chamber." Does God lock us in from the outside against our repentant will? Or is it more like a coffin we latch from the inside through our unrepentant will? It is to this question that we now turn.

CHAPTER 4 KEY IDEA

WHY DOES HELL EXIST?

God's purpose is not *torture*, but *protection*: God contains the destructive power of sin to protect the flourishing of his new creation.

5.

THE GREAT REVERSAL

THE BEGGAR AND THE BILLIONAIRE

Jesus' parable of Lazarus and the rich man is perhaps his most famous teaching on hell. It is also, along with Revelation's "lake of fire," the most popular Bible text used to support the caricature of the underground torture chamber. In a future chapter, we will reclaim the lake of fire from popular abuse.[1] But first, let's start with Lazarus and the rich man. As we shall now see, Jesus' teaching in this parable powerfully confirms, rather than contradicts, the paradigm we've developed thus far.

Jesus opens with a rich man and a homeless guy, a beggar and a billionaire:

> There was a rich man who was dressed in purple and fine linen and lived in luxury every day. At his gate was laid a beggar named Lazarus, covered with sores and longing to eat what fell from the rich man's table. Even the dogs came and licked his sores.[2]

Two observations. First, the rich man's got it good. Purple and linen were the finest, most expensive clothes back in the day, a mark of affluence. Today we might say, "He wore Armani, lived in Bel Air, and drove a Hummer." He's a luxury man. He's also, quite possibly, a political and religious leader: purple was a sign of royalty in ancient times and the priests wore linen. Jesus directs this parable at the political and religious leaders of his day.

The rich man is a picture of the Pharisees. Just before Jesus launches into this parable, we're told the Pharisees are lovers of money.[3] They spend their time chasing after status, wealth, and power. And they don't use their wealth to make friends with the poor and the hurting who need them. The rich man is not a "backslider" or a "pagan," but rather an influential and respected leader among God's people.[4]

The second observation: Lazarus is hurting. He's covered in sores, which means he has a serious disease of some kind. He's disabled: it says he "was laid" at the rich man's gate, meaning he couldn't walk by himself and had to be carried.[5] He's hungry, longing for a few scraps from the rich man's table. Lazarus's only friends are the dogs who, unlike the rich man, take pity on him and come to his aid to lick his sores.

Lazarus is diseased, disabled, and dependent. This isn't a lazy guy who's unwilling to work and trying to mooch off the system. This is a guy who's seriously sick and debilitated. His only hope for survival is in the mercy of others.

In this case, his hope for survival is in the rich man.

THE RICH MAN HAS NO NAME

The most striking feature of the parable's opening is this: the rich man has no name. Lazarus is named, but the rich man is not. Lazarus is the only character in *any* of Jesus' parables who is ever given a personal name. In other parables, Jesus introduces us to farmers, shepherds, and judges, but never to John, Rick, or Mary. Why does Jesus break tradition here and give Lazarus a personal name? And perhaps more importantly, why does he not also give one to the rich man?

Being Known

Lazarus's name humanizes him. He is more than his circumstances. He is not just a beggar. His poverty does not define him.

Lazarus is someone's child: named, known, and loved . . . he is known by God.

Lazarus's name also does something more: it provides a striking contrast with the rich man. In real life, everyone would have known the rich man's name. No one would have known Lazarus. Today, we all know millionaires like Donald Trump and Bill Gates; we cheer for pop stars like Katy Perry and Kanye West; we vote for political leaders like Barack Obama and George Bush. Their names are recognized and known. If you're reading this book, you know my name because it's written on the cover.

But Jesus says God's economy operates on a different basis than ours. In God's economy, I might be a nobody, a fraud trying to make a name for myself off a book deal; while an unknown Brazilian woman scraping by on pennies a day in a slum to feed her children might be, like Lazarus, great in the kingdom of heaven. Donald Trump might have customers, Katy Perry might have fans, and George Bush might have voters who are unknown today, but who will be dancing it up at the center of God's kingdom while the popular and pretty find themselves at the periphery of the party.

Jesus says some people might be close to the limelight but far from God. Right before launching into this parable, Jesus tells the Pharisees they make themselves look good "in the eyes of others, but God knows your hearts."[6] Jesus turns our economy upside down and inverts our world's social structure.

Simply by giving Lazarus a name.

Losing Our Name

The rich man once had a name. And whatever that name was, it represented something: an identity he *received* from his parents, from his community, from God. It was an identity *given* to him that he did not have to create for himself. But now . . . his identity is bound up with his riches. He loves them more than he does Lazarus and, by implication, more than he loves God. He loves his comfort, his prestige, his security. His riches have come to define him.

They have swallowed his identity whole.

The rich man has abandoned who he was created to be. He is identified now not by God's goodness, but by his greed. Not by God's given love, but by his distorted love. What we love is important: it can come to define us, to shape us. This is why Jesus launches into this parable saying, "You cannot serve both God and money."[7] If we love something more than we love God and others, Jesus confronts us by saying our scariest prospect might be God giving us what we want.

The rich man may live in Jerusalem, but his heart is in Babylon—outside the city. It is possible to get ahead in this world by building identities apart from God. Identities that come to define and consume us. We can become famous and well-known while losing ourselves in the process. Conversely, some people are down and out, living in the ghetto and sitting alone at the lunch table—yet God is close to them.

And God is coming for them.

God Will Help

God knows the hurting by name. Tim is the name of a man in our church. Every Wednesday evening, Tim and a group of friends go downtown to spend time with kids who don't have a home. Tim has no agenda, brings no expectations—except the hope that God might show up in the encounter. He just goes to hang out, spend time together, maybe bring a gift of fresh socks for the wet Portland rain. Tim listens to our city's homeless sons and daughters. He wants to know them. Wants to know their story.

Tim doesn't walk by Lazarus; he wants to know his name.

I always admired Tim's faithfulness to youth on the streets. Then one day we had lunch and I learned more of Tim's story. Long ago, Tim's wife had a mental breakdown and, for safety, he had to move her into a care facility. Tim didn't divorce or abandon her. Every week, Tim visits to spend time with her, to listen to her, to know her. And every Sunday, Tim picks her up for church, where they sit together with their son. As family. With the body of Christ.

Tim knows Lazarus's name.

Tim pursues people who are hurting, who are ill, who are dependent. Tim cares for people who don't have a lot to bring to the table. Tim loves them, is faithful to them, wants to know their names. Not many people in our church know Tim's name: he is quiet, humble, and behind the scenes. Most everyone knows my name: I'm up on stage a lot. But in God's economy, things might look different. I might be close to the limelight but far from God. Tim might be sitting with Lazarus outside the rich man's gate and destined for glory.

Sometimes I have a vision where Tim is dancing it up at the center of God's kingdom party, together with Lazarus, and I am looking on from a distance back in the crowd. That vision makes me smile. It makes me happy. Because it means God sees beneath the surface, beyond our facades, to the underlying realities of our world. And God is coming to set things right.

Lazarus's name means, literally, "God has helped."[8] The rich man may be unwilling to help Lazarus, but God is coming and he will.

THE RICH MAN HAS NO RICHES

As Jesus continues his parable, Lazarus dies and goes to be with Abraham, the father of the very faith the rich man proclaimed. The rich man also dies and . . . well, he goes somewhere else:

> The rich man also died and was buried. In Hades [hell], where he was in torment, he looked up and saw Abraham far away, with Lazarus by his side. So he called to him, "Father Abraham, have pity on me and send Lazarus to dip the tip of his finger in water and cool my tongue, because I am in agony in this fire."
>
> But Abraham replied, "Son, remember that in your lifetime you received your good things, while Lazarus received bad things, but now he is comforted here and you are in agony. And besides all this, between us and you a great chasm has been set in place, so

that those who want to go from here to you cannot, nor can anyone cross over from there to us."[9]

This is the part that's often taken to depict torture. We'll deal with that in a second, but before we get there, let's start with three observations.

First, the rich man has no riches. While this is so obvious it can be easy to miss, it is one of the parable's most striking features: that which defines him has been taken away. His status and wealth are gone. His idols have been destroyed. Burned up in the fire. Abraham reminds him, "In your lifetime you received your good things," but now they are gone. God judges the rich man by taking his riches away.

And the agony of the loss is torment.

Protecting Lazarus

Second, notice how the rich man doesn't ask to get into heaven. He asks the opposite: he wants to drag Lazarus down into hell with him. He asks Abraham to "send Lazarus" to serve him. The rich man still wants Lazarus to be beneath him, to order him around: *Hey Lazarus! Get down here, fetch me some water, and cool my tongue.*

The rich man is in denial. He still lives in the old order of things, where he was king and Lazarus was lower on the social ladder. He refuses the Great Reversal that God has accomplished. This is not a penitent sinner saying, "God, I'm sorry! Please forgive me! I want to live with you!" Jesus' parable reveals his heart: he'd rather reign in hell than serve in heaven.

Third, notice heaven's posture toward the rich man: Abraham does not call him "fool," "disappointment," or "idiot," but "son." This is an expression of fatherhood, of filial devotion, of care. This is not a stone-cold heaven shut off to a sorry, penitent sinner trying to come inside. This is the New Jerusalem, with gates wide open and a son who is stuck in the old world, weeping at the toys he wouldn't share that have now been taken away.

Heaven calls him "son," but it does not call him "rich man." God refuses to call him by his riches, to acknowledge his self-chosen name. God instead calls him by his true self, his given name, the identity he has rejected. It is not that we are reaching for God and he refuses to be grasped. It is that God is reaching for us and we are clutching our idols that consume us, clinging to our self-chosen identities and refusing to let go of our sin.

A Great Chasm

But God protects Lazarus. Abraham says, "Between us and you a great chasm has been fixed": the chasm is a boundary that protects Lazarus from the destructive power of the rich man's sin. No longer will God let the rich man treat Lazarus like a dog. No longer will the bully rule the playground, the husband beat his family, the superpower exploit the developing world. When God establishes his new creation, he will protect it from hell's invasion.

The boundary does something more, however, than simply prevent hell from invading the new creation. It also prevents the new creation from being dragged into hell. God will not let the rich man drag Lazarus back down with him. No longer will God let the warlord recruit the child soldier into a living hell, the rapist lure the drunk girl into his burning bed, the terrorist inflict his vindictive flames on innocent families. When God banishes the power of hell from his new creation, his new world is secure.

God protects Lazarus from the rich man's pride. He protects his holy city from the idols the rich man wants to bring inside. He protects the fields of his new creation from the rich man's greed that wants to exploit them. God protects his new world by banishing the tyranny of the old world.

God judges sin's destructive flame by prying creation away from its wildfire-clutching grasp.

Torment vs. Torture

Is God torturing the rich man? The obvious answer from the discussion thus far should be no, but since this passage is frequently used to support the "underground torture chamber," it is worth making a few additional observations that confront this caricature.

First, this is a parable. Jesus uses a lot of images in his parables that we're not supposed to read too literally. Jesus says God is a farmer, but this doesn't mean God spends his days literally shoveling manure. Jesus says we are a lost coin, but this doesn't mean we are made of metal and stuck under a dresser.

We have to ask, "What does this image mean? What is the metaphor for?" The farmer illustrates God generously showering his good news on good and bad folks alike. The coin illustrates our tremendous value in God's sight that causes him to search high and low for us. So in this parable, what do the flames of Hades represent? I would suggest the following three things:

The rich man lives in the rubble of the old world.
The rich man's riches have been burned up in the fire.
The rich man is handed over to the destructive power of his
    unrepentant sin.

Second, Jesus tells us the rich man is "in torment," not that he is being tortured. Torment and torture are two very different things. I can be tormented by a headache, or someone can torture me by hitting me repeatedly over the head with a two-by-four. Both hurt my head, but in radically different ways: torment arises internally; torture is inflicted from the outside. I can be tormented by my sin; and this is something radically different from God torturing me.

Jesus' word choice confirms this. When Jesus says the rich man is "in agony [odunomai] in this flame," the word he uses can also be translated "grief" or "anguish" and conveys a state of emotional turmoil rather than physical pain. For example, this word also shows up two other places in the New Testament. The first is when Mary and Joseph realize their twelve-year-old son, Jesus, is missing and are searching "anxiously" (Luke 2:48); the word describes their emotional distress in realizing something they love—Jesus—has been lost.

The second is when Paul is leaving Ephesus: the church's leaders realize they will never see him again, so they wrap their arms around him, weep, and are "grieved" (Acts 20:38); again, the word describes emotional distress: they are about to lose Paul, whom they love. Both of these passages are pictures not of physical torture but of emotional grief over something being lost; not of pain inflicted from the outside, but of lament arising from the inside.

Similarly, the rich man is in anguish, agony, grief—an emotional distress that arises as he realizes something he loves has been lost . . . his riches.

A third observation: when Jesus says the rich man is "in torment" he uses the word *basanos*, a Greek word for a stone used to test jewelry.[10] You would rub gold or silver on the *basanos*, the touchstone, and it would reveal whether the jewelry was authentic or fake. Touchstones were needed because some jewels look fancy on the outside but are fake on the inside.

Similarly, the rich man looked like a fancy jewel on the outside—he had his riches, reputation, and religion. But God knew that underneath the surface it was a facade—like the Pharisees Jesus confronted just before launching into this parable saying that though they looked good on the outside, "God knows your hearts." While the rich man looks fancy on the outside, when placed under the "touchstone" his veneer comes off. He is being revealed for who he really is . . . and the revelation is agony.

He looks like a jewel on the outside.

But underneath is a fake.

THE RICH MAN HAS NO EXCUSES

Jesus ends his parable with the rich man trying to make excuses . . . and doing so unsuccessfully. First, he implies God didn't give him enough *information*. If God had just given him the right data, a better spreadsheet, all the facts and figures, he wouldn't be in his current predicament. He asks Abraham to "send Lazarus to my family" to warn his five brothers. He's assuming if they just had all the facts, all the information, they could make an appropriate, informed decision. If God had given him this, he could have too.

Abraham responds, however, that this is not where the problem lies: "They have Moses and the Prophets; let them listen to them."[11] They have all the information they need—and he did too. The problem is not a shortage of details or a lack of data. The problem lies somewhere else.

The Problem of the Heart

So the rich man tries again: "But if someone from the dead goes to them, they will repent."[12] Now he is asking for a show of power. If his five brothers just had a miracle, some supernatural fireworks, it would change their heart. The rich man is saying, again by implication, that if God had given him a stronger demonstration of power, he would have believed. God didn't use his power to wake him out of his idolatry (toward money) and injustice (toward Lazarus). He is still blaming God for his predicament.

The rich man believes he is not the problem; God is at fault.

Abraham, however, responds: "They will not be convinced even if someone rises from the dead."[13] If they haven't responded to the witness they already have, a greater show of force won't do the trick. The problem is not a lack of miracle. Not insufficient information.

It is rooted somewhere deeper: in the heart. The rich man's heart is where his love, value, and devotion to his riches are rooted. It is where he worships something other than God and gives his life to something other than his neighbor.

The heart is our problem too. The power of hell resides in our hearts and makes its way into the world through us. Our distorted worship is the root that sprouts the wicked tree. Our corrupted affections are the spark that threatens to set the world aflame. Our vice is the tool that builds Babylon.

The heart of the problem is the problem of the heart.

Our hearts are the place where we worship things other than God; where we love stuff more than our neighbor. Self-centered love is the problem. Love of God and others is the solution.

Love is the answer.

Sin as Compass

Like the rich man's pride and greed, all sin is like a compass. When the direction is first set, things may not look so bad only a few steps down the road. Those first couple miles on a hiking trail into the Grand Canyon, the path may not look so rugged. And our *vice* may not look so bad—for a while.

But the longer we live, the farther we go in the wrong direction. Soon we may find ourselves in difficult terrain at the bottom of the Grand Canyon—and preferring to be there.

In the words of C. S. Lewis:

> It is not a question of God "sending us" to hell. . . . All that are in Hell choose it. Without that self-choice it wouldn't be Hell. . . . Hell begins with a grumbling mood, always complaining, always blaming others . . . but you are still distinct from it. You may even criticize it in yourself and wish you could stop it. But there may come a day when you can no longer. Then there will be no *you* left to criticize the mood or even to enjoy it, but just the grumble itself, going on forever like a machine. . . . In each of us there is something growing, which will BE Hell unless it is nipped in the bud.[14]

Tim Keller observes similarly:

> Hell, then, is the trajectory of a soul, living a self-absorbed, self-centered life, going on and on forever. . . . In short, hell is simply one's freely chosen identity apart from God on a trajectory into infinity.[15]

If sin is "anti-creation," and we are part of creation, then sin wants to tear us down. It wants to consume our very identity. Our sin can do more than hurt the Lazarus in our life; it can rip away at our very souls.

Enter Jesus. Our resurrected King greets us with arms open wide to embrace and heal us if we will receive his life-giving power. Jesus confronts our self-love with the reconciling love of God and invites us with him into his eternal kingdom. To reject this embrace and cling to our sin is to set our compass for the depths of the Grand Canyon. To receive it is to step into the new creation.

Jerusalem Aflame

A strange observation: why does Jesus give the rich man *five* brothers? Why not just "my brothers," or "ten sisters," or "entire family"? Jesus is a masterful storyteller, and his details are intentional. Jesus is giving us, I would suggest, a picture of Jerusalem. Jerusalem was the capital of Judah, who in the Old Testament had five brothers (from his mother Leah; Judah also had six half-brothers from other mothers).[16] These five tribes were, together with Judah, known as the "sons of Leah."

Jesus gives the Pharisees a clue they would have immediately understood: the rich man with five brothers is a picture of Judah's kingdom, with Jerusalem at its center, in all its wealth and glory.

If the rich man is Jerusalem, then Lazarus outside the rich man's gates becomes a picture of the poor and outcast outside the city, who Jesus spent most of his time with. And the dogs who lick Lazarus' sores a picture of the Gentiles ("dogs" were a Jewish image for Gentiles[17])— Jesus implying, as in his famous parable of the Good Samaritan, that the outsiders show more compassion for the hurting of Israel than the elite.

Jesus is, I would suggest, portraying the coming destruction of Jerusalem and downfall of its leadership. Jerusalem's disastrous fate is a prominent theme in Jesus' parables and ministry, *especially* in the Luke narrative leading up to and following this parable.[18] Here is yet one more place where Jesus confronts Jerusalem's leadership with their coming fate—in 70 AD, within a generation of Jesus' rejection and crucifixion, the Temple would be set aflame and Jerusalem torn to the ground by the Romans.

The rich man in Hades is a picture of Jerusalem in flames, her leadership left with only the rubble and ashes of their former prestige and once glorious civilization.[19] (When a city was destroyed, a common Hebrew image was that the city "went to Hades."[20]) Jesus is saying the outsiders (like Lazarus) are about to be welcomed into God's kingdom, and Jerusalem is about to go down in flames.

Jesus' parable is *genius* because it is so multilayered: in its most immediate context, it confronts the Pharisees with whom he is entangled. But the imagery "expands" to encompass the fate of Jerusalem as a whole. And it "contracts" to confront us all with the disastrous fate that awaits us when we give ourselves over to our sin. In all three instances, Jesus' imagery of flame speaks to judgment, not torture.[21]

In conclusion, what is Jesus' primary point in this parable?

THE GREAT REVERSAL

I would suggest Jesus' primary point is resurrection: and the Great Reversal it would accomplish. Jesus does not choose Lazarus's name randomly for this parable. It is reasonable to believe—and some scholars do—that this Lazarus was Jesus' close friend—the same one he raised from the dead.[22] Jesus' resurrection of Lazarus is a signpost, a foreshadowing, pointing to his own death and resurrection. While Lazarus was raised but would one day die again, Jesus was raised and has conquered sin and death forever.

Jesus holds the power to make our world new.

Jesus has conquered the anti-creation.

Jesus is the new creation.

Hades vs. Gehenna

It is worth nothing that Jesus uses the word Hades in this parable, not his usual word Gehenna—that location "outside the city" we looked at earlier. Hades was a different place. It was simply *the grave* (like the Hebrew word Sheol we earlier observed).[23] Lazarus and the rich man are in the ground. Their bodies are six feet under, pushing up daisies, not walking around on earth. Jesus makes clear the timing of this passage is pre-resurrection by giving us the following details:

> The rich man is dead and buried (v. 22).
> The location is Hades, not Gehenna (v. 23).
> Lazarus is not sent back from the dead (v. 31).

The beggar and the billionaire are in the ground. This confirms from yet one more angle that Jesus' primary point is not torture in this passage. The rich man has no body. It's hard to torture someone who doesn't have a body.

Jesus' parable is giving us a conversation between dead people, like Wilder's *Our Town* or Sartre's *No Exit*. Hades was simply the grave. So why does Jesus set the parable pre-resurrection in the ground? I would suggest the following: he is importing the hope of resurrection into the Old Testament concept of the grave. Let me explain.

Turning the Tables

A central question the Jewish faith wrestles with is this: Why do the wicked prosper and the righteous suffer? *Why do bad boys get all the girls and good guys get the shaft? Why is the Roman Empire ruling the world while God's little people get bullied? Why are the Nazis winning while we're in the concentration camps? Why do rich rulers live in luxury while Lazarus weeps outside?*

In Jesus' day, the Jews were having some trouble with "the grave." It was not a sufficient answer. God might redeem my grandkids down the road after I'm dead and gone, but how does that address the suffering I've endured in my lifetime? God might bring an end to Nazi Germany, but how does that vindicate the millions slaughtered in the concentration camps? God might take the tyrants down to the grave, but the masses they've massacred are right there with them.

How will justice be accomplished? "The grave" is not a good-enough response. It poses itself a greater question: How will God deal with the skeletons under our feet?

Resurrection is the answer.

Resurrection arose as the time when God would set things right. When the wicked who prospered would be put in their place and the righteous who suffered would be restored. When the high places would be brought low and the valleys would be lifted up. When the rich man would be humbled and Lazarus exalted. Things would finally be called out as they really are.

God would accomplish the Great Reversal: the setting aright of a world and a history that have gone terribly wrong.

Resurrection was still a speculative hope, however, at the time Jesus told this parable. Remember, Jesus had not yet been resurrected. Some Old Testament passages seemed to strongly indicate a resurrection was coming, but they were ambiguous, not clearly defined. Some powerful parties, like the Pharisees, believed in the resurrection. Others, like the Sadducees, did not.[24]

Jesus has one thing in common with the Pharisees: he believes in resurrection.

And I would suggest that what he is doing in the parable is this: importing the hope of resurrection into the Old Testament concept of the grave. Jesus is proclaiming the coming of God's Great Reversal: the setting of the world aright. The calling of things out as they really are. The undoing of the empire through the coming of the kingdom. The arrogant will be humbled and the humble exalted. The rich man will be brought low and Lazarus lifted high.

Jesus himself is about to make this Great Reversal possible through his death and resurrection. When Jesus says that the rich man's brothers "will not be convinced even if someone rises from the dead," he is giving the Pharisees an ironic setup: he is about to be raised from the dead, and *still* they will not believe. But whether they like it or not, the Great Reversal is coming like a freight train. God's kingdom will be established on the earth through Jesus.

The Embrace of Christ

As Jesus tells this parable, Hades is where the "anti-creation" fire that wants to consume the world is contained. Where the darkness that resists the light and life of God is held at bay. Where the death that undoes creation is imprisoned. But Jesus will conquer Hades: he will take its destructive flame into himself on the cross. He will arise victorious over its consuming darkness in his resurrection. He will liberate the captives from its chains. Jesus will plunder Hades and lay claim to the world in power.

As the resurrected King, Jesus is the beginning of the new creation. He has established his kingdom for the world, "and the gates of Hades will not overcome it."[25] Though Hades's destructive flame may stand opposed to God's kingdom, Jesus has conquered its fire and darkness and will resurrect the world through his life-giving power. When Jesus returns, he will cast Hades itself outside God's holy city.[26]

Jesus, the resurrected King, has overcome the grave.

Jesus is the beginning of the new creation.

Jesus *himself* has issued an invitation to us to join him in the new creation. I've said this before, but it bears repeating: he wants to pardon our countless sins, heal us, and make us fit for his kingdom. And to be made fit for his kingdom is simply to receive his embrace. To exchange our sin for his Spirit. To die to ourselves and receive his life-giving presence. His city gates are wide open. To refuse his embrace is to remain, like the rich man, in the rubble of the old world. To receive his embrace is to enter the new world: made fit by his cleansing power for the glory of the new creation.

CHAPTER 5 KEY IDEA

DOES JESUS' PARABLE OF LAZARUS AND THE RICH MAN DEPICT THE "UNDERGROUND TORTURE CHAMBER"?

No, it depicts God's coming Great Reversal for the world and confronts the destructive power of our sin.

6.

FREEDOM FROM AND FOR

A STRANGE CHOICE

Why would anyone choose hell? If God's city gates are open wide, why would we want independence from God rather than communion with him? Why prefer sin over salvation, autonomy over worship? At first glance, it seems like a strange choice.

The irony is this: we choose hell every day.

While many in the West vociferously protest and lament the Christian doctrine of hell in theory, we simultaneously cling to the Christian logic of hell in our everyday lives. Hell's logic shows up prominently in some of Western civilization's most cherished ideals, our most highly held values, our lifestyle's most salient features. This is seen perhaps nowhere so clearly as in our understanding of freedom, one that is quickly becoming more and more the global understanding.

The gospel gives rise to two distinct understandings of freedom. On the one hand, the gospel is rooted in a freedom *for*: freedom for God, freedom for others, and freedom for the self. On the other hand, sin is rooted in a freedom *from*: freedom from God, from others, and from the self. Like water and oil, these two takes on freedom don't mix well together.

In this chapter, I want to explore our preference for the logic of hell using democracy, the suburbs, and Facebook as metaphors for our understanding of freedom. I should make clear I am using these as metaphors: I am glad to live in a democracy, have had pleasant experiences in the suburbs, and am not against social media. But in the metaphors, we observe something real. Democracy demonstrates our collective desire for freedom from God. The suburbs reveal our personal desire for freedom from each other. Facebook illuminates our existential desire for freedom from ourselves.

Taken together, these images demonstrate that our preference for the logic of hell is not so far from the Western imagination as we might think. They help us see more clearly that hell is not a chamber God locks from the outside against our repentant will, but a coffin we latch from the inside through our unrepentant will.

Hell is the land of the free.

HELL AS DEMOCRACY

I used to think hell was like Guantánamo Bay: a little island offshore of the mainland, where captives are tortured for some supposedly higher purpose. Back home, concerned citizens worry about troubling rumors of what transpires there. Every now and then, the papers get hold of a disturbing photograph and a media blitz ensues.

With Guantánamo Bay, our concern is not just that torture might take place there: that happens all over the world. Our concern is that if torture takes place *there*, then it takes place under the very same authority that protects us. With the exception of Jack Bauer, most of us have a hard time believing that secret torture might be crucially connected to the freedom we experience back on the mainland.

Similarly with God's kingdom, we've heard some disturbing rumors about that little island just offshore of the new creation, where captives are supposedly being tortured. Our culture has gotten hold of some disturbing photographs—the caricatures—and a media blitz has ensued. And our concern is not just that bad things might happen there, but that they might be happening under the very same authority that we've entrusted with our protection. We have a hard time believing that the tortures of hell might somehow be necessary to safeguard the peace of the new creation.

So, as with Guantánamo Bay, the questions of hell arise: Does torture take place there? Have its captives received a fair trial? Is such a place truly necessary? Do we really want to sit quietly under a sovereign authority that is responsible for such a place?

The paradox is, hell is less like Guantánamo Bay and more like America. Less like the secret little prison offshore of the mainland and more like the mainland itself—televised, public, and promoted. Less like the realm where our hands are bound against our will and more like the realm where we are given the collective freedom to do as we please.

Thy Will Be Done

C. S. Lewis's classic *The Great Divorce* paints a helpful picture. The book is a fantasy in which people are not only given the option to leave hell; they are given powerful reasons for why they should leave. People who love them try to convince them to receive God's healing and "enter joy." Tragically, the vast majority refuse the offer, their reasons providing a profound exploration of the psychology of hell. Toward the end, Lewis summarizes the distinction between those who prefer life in the kingdom to life in hell:

There are only two kinds of people in the end: those who say to God, "Thy will be done," and those to whom God says, in the end, "*Thy* will be done."[1]

Hell is that place where God tells its residents: *Thy will be done. Have your way. Live as you want without me.* Hell is a democracy.

Lewis is not inventing something new here. He is simply echoing Augustine's classic thesis in *The City of God*, one of the most influential works in Western civilization:

Two loves built two cities—the earthly which is built by the love of self, even to the contempt of God, and the heavenly which is built by the love of God, even to the contempt of self.[2]

God's city is built by the love of God. It is a place whose residents love God, who love to worship him at the center of their public life, who love one another in the love of God, who are happy to give their lives to the city's glorious King and boldly proclaim, "Thy will be done!"

It is a place of freedom *for*.

God's city has an alternative: a place whose citizens want freedom *from* God, whose residents love themselves more than God, who place the collective self above the glory of God and prefer to hear the King say, "Thy will be done!"

Life outside God's city is built by the love of self.

Two Cities

Let's use an illustration. Imagine God's kingdom comes down and you are invited to live in its capital: we'll call it the New Jerusalem. But let's say you are also given another option. You can reject this offer if you prefer and live in another land, far away in the distance: we'll call it America. You can live in the one you want, but you must respect the governing constitution, the founding documents, the guiding principles of the respective spheres.

To live in the New Jerusalem: you must die to yourself and live unto God; you must repent of your sin and bend your knee before its good King; you must leave behind your autonomy once and for all and enter into union with your Creator. Jesus has freely made your citizenship possible: his atoning work on the cross has flung the city gates wide open. But the cost is a forsaking of your independence, a turning from your self-rule, a repentance of your sin, a death to self.

Or, you can live in America. Here the rules are different: it is a land where everyone is allowed to collectively determine the shape of their public life together, to keep their independence, to live unto themselves as a societal whole. Whereas the New Jerusalem is a place for people who *want* God at the center, this is a place for people who prefer a society without God at the center. And our experience in the West confirms that we collectively prefer a society without God at the center.

Declaring Our Independence

The trajectory of our public life reveals: we want a Declaration of Independence from the kingdom of God. "We the people" want to constitute our lives together around our collective self. Like Pharaoh of long ago, we still want to rule the earth without God rather than with him. We do not need a dictator to tell us God cannot be at the center of our public life; we are happy to vote that way ourselves.

Democracy is not the redemption of authority; it is the dispersal of authority. It is the pulling of authority out of the hand of one big king and placing it in the hands of a million little kings. While this can help prevent corruption, it is limited. As the saying goes, "The problem with democracy is not bad politics so much as bad math: a thousand corrupt minds can be just as bad as one corrupt mind."

The problem is not that it is bad to vote. Voting, checks and balances, popular representation, and constructive avenues for participating in public life are, I believe, great blessings of the modern world. The problem is something much deeper, rooted in the structure of the thing itself: it is our foundational conviction as a society that God does not have the right to rule our public life unless we collectively say he can.

We desire freedom *from* God. And God has given us that freedom. He has handed us over to ourselves. God has given us the logic of hell in the form of democracy. And we prefer it that way.

And yet, God's kingdom lays claim to *this* earth. Jesus is Lord of this world. Jesus' followers look forward to that day when God's will is done here on earth as in heaven. Worshippers lift their gazes in hope, looking toward that day when "the kingdoms of this world have become the kingdoms of our Lord."[3] As King of kings and Lord of lords, Jesus' authority confronts the kings and lords of this world: whether they are lone kings in ivory palaces or all of us in our democratically dispersed authority. The courtly monarch and the collective many are both confronted by God's kingdom claim upon us.

The point is not that people should be coerced to follow God. In fact, it is the exact opposite. God gives us the freedom whether or not to follow him; our society should give that same freedom. But it is precisely here that the logic of hell arises: the handing over of a society that has chosen *not* to follow God, a space created by God for a people who prefer to live *without* him, who desire freedom *from* him.

Hell is the absence of God, found in the presence of our own autonomy.

The point is also not that democracy is a particularly *bad* form of government. That's not the issue at all. Checks and balances are a good thing in a corrupt world. Representation in government is powerful for minority communities who have been excluded, exploited, or oppressed in their countries. I would rather live in a democracy than under a tyrant or dictator. Images of hell could be explored in other forms of government as well—Satan as dictator? As the saying goes, "Democracy is the worst form of Government except all those other forms that have been tried."[4] This side of kingdom come, democracy may be the best form of government in the world.

But there's the catch: "This side of kingdom come . . ." When God's kingdom comes, democracy must go. Jesus' lordship and God's kingdom do not ask for our vote. They invite us to participate with them; they do not ask whether they might squeeze in with us. They lead; we follow. Not the other way around.

While this sounds like good news to me, I have a strong sense there are many who feel revulsion at the thought of a society structured this way; many who want the old America over the New Jerusalem; many who prefer the old creation to the world that is coming. And yet, when God's kingdom comes, democracy must go, for America is hell in the face of the new creation.

HELL AS THE SUBURBS

If democracy demonstrates our collective desire for freedom from God, the suburbs illustrate our personal desire for freedom from each other. We live separated lives. During the day, we work in privatized offices and demarcated cubicles to keep us from interference by others. When work is done, we enter our cars and pull onto the freeway, like isolated atoms in a stream of other steel atoms trying not to bump into each other on the journey home. When we arrive, we pass through the security gate, protected from the intrusive gaze of our neighbors by the six-foot fence, and pull into the garage.

We have entered our personal space: the home.

Surprisingly, once inside, the isolation does not end: we need more and more space from each other. Expansive floor plans separate the family into multiple rooms: a bedroom for each child (who, of course, needs her or his own space); one entertainment room upstairs for the parents and another downstairs for the kids (in case we want to watch something different on TV); a craft room for mom and an office for dad (for when we need some "alone time").

Our houses have gotten bigger and our family and neighbors farther away. It is as if we are fighting for ways to get away from each other.

Cultural Values

If architecture reflects our cultural values, then our architecture leads me to believe we place great value on our privacy, personal space, and autonomy—even from those closest to us. This is not to say there is no healthy place for solitude, but I have many friends who grew up rarely ever seeing their families—even while living in the same house.

Once again, a helpful image can be found in *The Great Divorce*. In Lewis's fantasy, hell keeps expanding in ever-increasing distance from God's city. This happens because people are moving away not only from God, but also from one another. Free building materials are there for the taking, and it only takes imagination for the house to be built. So every time a quarrel breaks out, the neighbors simply pick up and move. A resident explains:

> They've been moving on and on. Getting further apart. . . . There's a bit of rising ground near where I live and a chap has a telescope.

You can see the lights of the inhabited houses, where those old ones live, millions of miles away. Millions of miles from us and from one another. Every now and then they move further still.[5]

Hell's growth is impulsive, expansive, breaking out like a sprawling suburb in ever-increasing distance from God's city.

The resident is disappointed: "I thought you'd meet interesting historical characters. But you don't: they're too far away."[6] Julius Caesar and Genghis Khan live astronomical distances away now in the far-off periphery. Napoleon is said to be the closest: "two chaps made the journey to see him . . . about fifteen thousand years of our time it took them."[7] People want freedom from each other—and are getting farther and farther apart.

Hell is a sprawling suburb.

Atomizing the World

Lewis's fantasy gives us a picture of our desire for freedom from each other, of our inability to live together. In Genesis, Cain had to share space with Abel—and killed him. In hell, one can simply move away. Like Hitler's Germany, hell has an ever-increasing need for lebensraum, living space. Only there is no longer any need to kill for it: land inexhaustible is there for the taking. The result is impulsive, explosive, expansive growth: suburban sprawl.

This is the opposite of *No Exit*, the famous play by Jean-Paul Sartre, in which hell is depicted as being trapped in a room with other people who draw out the worst in you. For Sartre, in the play's classic line: "hell is other people." Hell is being forced to be around other people you want to get away from. In the suburbs, however, hell is the opposite: the absence of other people. The self-imposed logic of isolation witnessed in its inhabitants' ever-increasing need for space in which to retreat: to retreat from others—and ultimately into themselves.

One often hears the complaint today that we feel fragmented, isolated, and lonely. We have access to more wealth, technology, and knowledge than any people in history, yet we simultaneously feel more disconnected and unknown than ever. There is perhaps no greater buzzword than "community": the longing for it and the attempt to re-create it. Yet I wonder if we realize how inevitably intertwined this sense of fragmentation and loss is with the broader cultural fabric we have woven with the thread of our highest cultural value: the autonomy of the individual.

Cities and villages were traditionally centered around the public square, where community life was done: court, church, city hall, market, school. Housing was typically centered around shared space for family life: the Navajo family I lived with raised their eight children in a one-room, three-hundred-square-foot hogan, and the African family I lived with had more than a dozen people living under one roof. Personal space was important but acquired away from the home rather than inside it. And home life was anchored within community life, rather than buoyed apart from it.

One could argue things were traditionally done this way because they didn't have the means we do today to so easily acquire more space. That this was more a by-product of their historical location than a value-laden choice. But this only bolsters the thrust of the broader argument: that this is part of the human condition. As modern wealth and technology advances around the world, architecture and city planning increasingly tend to conform to the Western model. We capitalize on the opportunity we have to create ever-greater levels of privatized personal space in which to retreat further and further from others—and further into ourselves.

If democracy is a picture of our collective desire for freedom from *God*, the suburbs are a picture of our personal desire for freedom from *each other*. Downstream of our corporate rejection of God lies not a liberated collective, but rather an isolated and atomized humanity. Belief in hell does not require an article of faith: we *are* the witness to its social logic.

HELL AS FACEBOOK

We were created to receive our identity from God, but we are caught up with creating identities for ourselves. Facebook is a place where identity can be created rather than received. We can mask who we really are and put forward projections of how we wish to be seen. We can boast a thousand friends and never truly be known. We can follow others we think will make us relevant and all the while fall farther away from our true selves. Our network can be ever expanding, while our identity is ever shrinking.

Facebook illustrates our desire for freedom from ourselves.

The Shrinking Man

Once again, *The Great Divorce* paints a helpful picture. In one scene a husband holds a chain connecting him to a tragic actor. This actor is, like a Facebook profile, a persona the husband has created for himself. He will only speak through the tragic actor and refuses to speak directly himself. It is a mask he hides behind.

As his wife tries to convince him to leave hell, she refuses to speak to the tragic actor and will only address her husband directly. But he refuses the conversation; he will speak only through the tragic actor he has made. Similarly, God addresses us as we really are, like the rich man being called "son," but we often prefer to hide behind our fake IDs.

The tragic actor takes over as the husband's spokesperson: he laments all the ways he has been wronged. He refuses valiantly to let go of the pride that enslaves him. With an ironic mixture of self-righteousness and self-loathing, he refuses to receive eternal joy.

As the actor speaks, something striking happens: the husband shrinks. While the actor accuses others and excuses himself, the husband appears unaware that he himself is gradually getting smaller and smaller.

He is a shrinking man.

Eventually, the husband becomes so small he is no longer visible: "I do not know that I ever saw anything more terrible than the struggle of that Dwarf Ghost against joy."[8] The mask he created to shield himself from God's joy eventually absorbs his identity; it swallows him whole.

We are often like the husband: we hide behind the actor and prefer the false identities we've created. We refuse to repent of our masks, receive our identity as the beloved of God, and live in submission to his kingdom.

Curved Inward

Once again, Lewis is not making up a new idea here. This image of the shrinking man comes from Augustine's classical image of sin as self-love. For Augustine, the idea is that we were created to live "curved outwards," with our gaze upon God and neighbor in selfless love.[9] Life this way has a certain beautiful innocence, a lack of self-awareness, because our awareness is caught up, enraptured, in God and others. Our identity is received from God's overwhelming affection for and affirmation of us.

What sin does, in essence, is pull our gaze from God and others and turns it in upon ourselves, so that we become "curved inward," valuing ourselves over and against God, first and foremost, and the others God has given us to love. The result is a *shrunken* existence: compressed, restricted, and small, in our self-shielded resistance to the source of love and the objects of love for whom we were created.

Self-love shrinks you.

This is seen in Genesis' creation story where, prior to the fall, Adam's attention is turned outward upon God (in worship) and upon Eve (in love). After the fall, however, Adam's first response is to hide from God (in fear) and blame Eve (in self-preservation). His gaze turns inward. God comes looking for his children, while they run, hide, and cover their nakedness with leaves.

Prior to the fall, nakedness was not a problem: Adam's gaze wasn't upon himself; he received his identity from God. He was naked and unashamed, to paraphrase Genesis 2:25. After the fall, however, nakedness is a problem: Adam's gaze has curved inward. He realizes he's naked and is afraid. "Putting on leaves" becomes an image of our attempt to create false identities, while hiding on the run, to cover ourselves before God and others.

The ID Factory

This is not just Adam's story; this is our story. We were created to be enraptured with God and others in love. But our sin alienates us (from God) and isolates us (from others). It curves us in upon ourselves in self-love. Sin takes our outward gaze and turns it inward.

We start to manufacture identities to make us feel valuable, to prove ourselves to others, to justify our existence. We become an ID factory. We search desperately after that romantic relationship—pretending to be who we think our romantic interests will want. We work really hard all week long for success and security—and lose ourselves in our jobs. We get really religious and try to clean up our behavior—and hide behind the tragic actor who laments all we've had to sacrifice. We create a Facebook profile to cover ourselves in twenty-first-century leaves. And it shrinks us.

Our insecurity in the outward search betrays the immaturity of our inward curve.

The point is not that Facebook is the worst thing around. The twenty-first-century ability to stay connected with friends around the world is amazing. So is showing those new baby pictures to everyone you love all at once. So is keeping easily up-to-date on all those upcoming events and opportunities. I am a fan of social media.

But the point is, we were created to receive our identity from God, to know ourselves as his beloved, to live with a healthy lack of self-awareness. We were made to live under our Creator's benevolent rule, to be lost in his rapturous love and caught up with affection for our neighbor.

Yet we have an insatiable, existential desire, witnessed on Facebook, for freedom *from* ourselves as given by God, to create and craft new selves—new identities—that are grounded in our independence and autonomy from our Creator.

And in so doing, we shrink. To retreat from the light is to move toward the darkness. To abandon the campfire is to enter the cold. To walk away from the embrace of the Creator's expansive existence is to walk toward the enclosure of a shrunken, creaturely existence.

Self-love makes us less and less human.

Hell is subhuman.

HELL IS SMALL

We are a culture of freedom *from*. Democracy demonstrates our collective desire for freedom from God. The suburbs illustrate our personal desire for freedom from one another. Facebook displays our existential desire for freedom from ourselves. And the result is an alienated, fragmented, shrunken world.

Hell is the land of the free.

And it is small.

The Grey Town

In a final image from *The Great Divorce*, residents of hell must grow incrementally in size as they journey to the foothills of the kingdom. Because hell is so small, they must get bigger so as to be even visible when they arrive. When asked why this is, the Guide plucks a blade of grass from the earth beneath his feet, points to the miniscule crack left in the ground, and explains that all of hell could fit inside that crack: "All Hell is smaller than one pebble of your earthly world: but it is smaller than one atom of *this* world, the Real World."[10]

A butterfly could swallow all the terrain of hell, he elaborates, without tasting a thing. One could roll all the experiences of hell up into a ball, weigh it against one small experience of joy in heaven, and the ball "would have no weight that could be registered at all."[11]

Hell is microscopically small. Social media is once again a helpful metaphor: where all of one's social interaction feels unbelievably large in the virtual world, but in reality it takes place in a byte of storage in a server rack in a closet somewhere in North Dakota.

When people journey from hell to the foothills of the kingdom, they have a hard time encountering "reality" given the artificial construction in which they've become accustomed to living. Their bodies appear ghostlike and transparent. Their eyes must adjust to the color of the land, after so long inhabiting "the grey town." It hurts to walk on the grass because their feet are not solid enough to handle it. They run from falling rain in fear that it will pierce right through their bodies and destroy them. Like a fabricated existence in a virtual world, hell has become more comfortable than the kingdom.

They are told if they would only receive God's heavenly embrace, it would strengthen them. Their bodies would grow lively and colorful. They could handle the reality of the new creation. But they prefer the smallness and immateriality of their self-enclosed and self-created world.

The Greatness of the Kingdom

Could it be that hell is preferable from the inside for those who live there? I have often found that those who begin to follow Jesus say something like this: "Before, life with God looked small, restrictive, and binding, like a closed-minded straitjacket. Life apart from God felt liberating, free, expansive, the freedom to be who I really am, not defined by another or bound by someone else's claim upon me."

But with their conversion of heart came also a conversion of perspective, and they now find themselves saying something like this: "My life before now looks small, restrictive, and binding. How could I have lived like that? Life with God now feels liberating, free, and expansive. God's affection releases me into who I was created to be. Christ has broken the chains and lifted my gaze to the greatness of the kingdom before me. I no longer have to create an identity for myself; I receive my identity from my Creator's affection; his claim upon me sets me free."

It seems to me quite possible that it is only when we have tasted the greatness of the kingdom that the cruelty of hell is revealed. That self-love seems preferable until we have encountered divine affection.

That the microscopic smallness of our autonomy can only be recognized as such when we begin to receive the expansive embrace of God.

It is when Jesus raises us from the waters of baptism that we realize we would never again want to be submerged in those suffocating floods of sin and rebellion. It is when the Spirit breathes the life of God into our gasping lungs that we realize we would never again want to return to our self-contained life from before. It is when the Father gently removes the scales from our eyes with his gracious presence that our former freedom from God is revealed to be a tyrannical enslavement—in which we were the tyrant.

The Suburb and the Atom

The suburb and the atom: there is a paradox in these images. On the one hand, hell is depicted as a sprawling suburb that is getting bigger and bigger. On the other hand, it is depicted as a microscopic atom that is getting smaller and smaller. This is because, ironically, the more we receive space *from* God and *from* others, the smaller we become. The bigger hell expands on the inside, the smaller it becomes on the outside. For all its internal largesse, hell is infinitesimal: less than an atom in the expansive universe of the new creation.

It is perhaps only from the perspective of the kingdom that hell's giant, sprawling suburb is seen for the microscopic atom it is. It is from this same perspective that my former freedom from God is revealed as enslavement to the narrowness of myself. It is from the expansive vistas of the new creation that my grand, enlightened independence is revealed to be the small, darkened closet in which my heart and mind were enclosed.

Life with God is big. Life without God is small.

Life without God is hell.

———

Hell is not a chamber God locks from the outside against our repentant will; it is a closet we latch from the inside through our unrepentant will. We have now confronted the final feature of the "underground torture chamber": it is not a chamber. It is not a place where our freedom is taken away; it is a place where our freedom is given. A freedom that stands opposed to the God who reconciles the world; a freedom the gospel reveals to be an enslavement to the narrowness of ourselves.

Hell is born of a freedom conceived by sin. If we refuse God's mercy, as he clutches the handle to fling the door wide, then we are the skeletons in God's closet.

CHAPTER 6 KEY IDEA

HOW DOES HELL WORK?

Hell is not a chamber God locks from the outside against our repentant will, but a closet we latch from the inside through our unrepentant will, in our desire for freedom from God, freedom from others, and freedom from the self—the nature of sin.

INTERLUDE

ANCIENT OR NEW?

RECLAIMING THE SYMPHONY

Is this ancient or new? Is the paradigm we've been developing consistent with church tradition, or a lone voice amid a two-thousand-year-old church choir singing a different tune? This is an important question: we should be cautious of anyone who jumps up saying he or she has a "new" interpretation of important doctrine that contradicts the mature historical witness of the church.

Fortunately, this is not the case. We are reclaiming something ancient, not inventing something new. Let's see this through a quick recap of our major themes thus far.

The Reconciliation of Heaven and Earth

God's reconciliation of heaven and earth is one of the hallmarks of the early church's theology and is at the center of our paradigm thus far. One of the earliest challenges the church had to face was Gnosticism, a heresy that said salvation was about Jesus getting us out of earth and into heaven. It derived from an outside philosophy that devalued the created world. Against this, the church proclaimed loudly, boldly, and clearly that God's purpose in Jesus is not to get us out of earth and into heaven, but to reconcile heaven and earth from the destructive power of sin. To redeem creation to himself.

Irenaeus and Athanasius are two of the most prolific authors of the early church, and at the center of their work was the proclamation that God's purpose in Christ is the reconciliation of creation to himself. They confronted the anti-creation heresies head-on, and grounded their work centrally in the incarnation, cross, and resurrection of Christ: Jesus became fully human in our flesh and walked our dust; he lived the life we couldn't live and embodied the kingdom he proclaimed; he took our sin, corruption, and death into himself on the cross and was raised victorious as the beginning of a glorified humanity in a reconciled earth.

Jesus conquered the power of hell to reconcile creation to God.

After Irenaeus and Athanasius, if you read the theology of the early and medieval church, you find a variety of perspectives—but what virtually all of these perspectives have in common is the central belief that Jesus is Lord of *this* world, not another, that his heavenly kingdom reigns *over* the earth in a way that lays claim *upon* all creation.[1] Both emperor and peasant, and everyone in between, are called to bend their knee before the one whom God has exalted as King and through whom God is reconciling creation back to himself.

As we have seen, the caricature is rooted in a bad *storyline*, one that says salvation is about Jesus getting us out of earth and into heaven. It is, essentially, a Gnostic storyline. In terms of historic orthodoxy, the caricature's storyline is heresy. Within it, the caricature's *proclamation* makes Jesus Lord of another world, not this one: also a heresy from the perspective of church orthodoxy.

The caricature of the "underground torture chamber" is grounded in a storyline and a proclamation that are both heresy.

The caricature is heresy itself.

Once we get the storyline and proclamation right, however, the subtopic of hell starts to fall more naturally into place—as we have seen in the preceding chapters. We have not been reinventing church tradition, but reclaiming it from some of its modern distortions.

The Nature of Evil

I have cited Augustine and C. S. Lewis frequently thus far, not only because their insights are helpful, but to demonstrate through these two classic thinkers, one ancient and one modern, our consistency with mainstream tradition.

Let's start with Augustine. On the nature of evil, Augustine can be credited with the key insights we've explored: that it is an aggressive, divisive parasite that shatters the human community. That it is unleashed into the world through us. That it gives rise to a conception of freedom from God and others that is diametrically opposed to the freedom *for* God and others for which we were intended in God. All these insights are central to the chapters thus far.

Augustine is one of the most influential and widely recognized early church fathers in the development of historic orthodoxy, particularly when it comes to the nature of evil. The concept of evil we've been exploring is thoroughly Augustinian and consistent with church orthodoxy.[2]

Now let's look at C. S. Lewis, perhaps the most popular Christian author of the twentieth century. The paradigm we've been outlining shows up not in the margins of his work, but at the center: in the brushstrokes of his children's fairy tales, in the dreaming of his fantasy works, and in the penetrating insights of his nonfiction. Where did Lewis develop such conviction in this paradigm?

Lewis was a Cambridge professor specializing in medieval literature. He was immersed broadly, deeply, and widely in classical, patristic, and medieval literature. He was thus immersed in the context and worldview of Christendom. He seemed to feel more comfortable in ancient Christendom, in some ways, than he did in the twentieth century. And I believe it is precisely this historical immersion that gave him such critical and discerning insights on our modern age.

When Lewis wrote from the perspective of this paradigm, he was not reinventing church tradition, but reclaiming it from some of its modern distortions. Followers of Jesus today are similarly invited to reclaim, rather than feel the need to reinvent, church tradition in order to confront our modern cultural caricatures with the biblical storyline's bold proclamation of God's glorious goodness for his world.

The Victory of God

I've often been asked, "Why, then, are the caricatures so prominent?" My first thought is usually, *Because we don't know our Old Testament.* As we've seen, the Old Testament is central to our exploration thus far. It is in the Old Testament that we see the storyline powerfully arise that God is a good King who is coming to redeem his world from the destructive powers that are tearing it apart, and to kick the rebellion outside his city when he establishes his kingdom in fullness and floods the earth with his glory. The Old Testament lifts our eyes toward the coming victory of God.

Some readers may be saying at this stage, "Yes, this paradigm is refreshing; yes, it fits well within the overarching biblical story, and yes, it has the historical merit of being within mainstream orthodoxy . . . but there are some important biblical passages that have not yet been dealt with, like Revelation's lake of fire. Don't passages like these contradict certain features of what's been said? And while we've reclaimed a healthier understanding of the *nature* of hell, we haven't yet touched the thorny issue of who goes there. And what about the violence of God, prominent in both Old Testament and New—how does this relate to the paradigm developed thus far?"

These are great questions, and no worries: we will be exploring them in-depth in the upcoming chapters. As we shall see, they add powerfully to, rather than detract in any way from, the paradigm we have been developing. For now, I would simply remind you that though this book is divided into three sections, it is written as a whole. We are not now leaving behind this section to begin a brand-new one from scratch; we will be building upon the themes developed so far and integrating new themes from the biblical story.

As we shall see, these upcoming themes shed tremendous light on what are often considered the "difficult" passages. They contribute their voices and movements into the broader symphony as a whole, the symphony we've been listening to thus far: one that sings loudly, boldly, and clearly God's glorious goodness for his world.

Part 2

THE SURPRISE OF JUDGMENT

Jeremiah hated Christianity. As a child, he was molested by a priest and lost a loved one murdered by members of a local church. As a Native American, Jeremiah saw these injustices bound up with a much broader history involving America's encounter as a "Christian nation" with native peoples. Jeremiah's big issue was with judgment:

> Do you really believe God will save all you Christians and judge all us non-Christians?

> Christians have historically been predominantly European and white: Do you realize how racist this picture looks—all the Europeans basking in heaven while the colored masses roast in perdition?

> Don't you think Christianity's belief that God will save Christians and send everyone else to hell makes you arrogant, with a superiority complex over everyone else who doesn't see the world the same way you do?

My friend Jeremiah was astounded anyone could believe the Christian God was good. Judgment was, for Jeremiah, a skeleton in God's closet.

7.

ON PRIESTS AND PEDOPHILES

JESUS JUDGES RELIGION

Shortly after I began following Jesus, a friend explained, "Christians go to heaven; non-Christians go to hell." He wanted to make sure I understood my marching orders: "So our job is to get as many people as possible to become Christians before it's too late." I wanted to be open to new ideas, but I had a few major problems with this one right off the bat.

One of those problems was named Jeremiah.

Jeremiah's Story

Jeremiah was a Native American who was much older than I. He hated Christianity and, as our friendship grew, he let me in on why. As a child, Jeremiah was forcibly removed from his family and taken to a native boarding school for children to be "civilized." As Jeremiah walked through the school's front door, he looked up and saw its motto hanging over the entryway. The motto, as in many such schools of the day, was:

Kill the Indian. Save the man.

They came pretty darn close on the first half.

Jeremiah's school was where he first developed his distaste for

America and its civil religion. First, there was the cutting. They cut Jeremiah's long hair, customary for boys of his tribe, in an attempt to help him assimilate into mainstream society. His hair was not all they cut: he was forcibly circumcised—a confusing experience for a boy of his age separated from his family. Jeremiah was humiliated.

Jeremiah's family was already familiar with cutting: locals cut out his grandfather's tongue for resisting the ban on native languages and continuing to teach youth their native tongue. When intimidation repeatedly failed to silence his voice, they used brute force and went for his throat.

After the cutting, there was the separation. Jeremiah's family was considered a negative influence by school administrators on his assimilation into Western culture. So during the summers, he was to live with a white family in the city while during the school year, his home visits were severely restricted. As a young boy, Jeremiah missed his family and developed a growing sense of shame in his native identity.

Finally, there was the loss. As an altar boy in a local church, Jeremiah was molested by a priest and lost his virginity. This only exacerbated his sense of shame and powerlessness in a culture not his own. The abuse would continue for years to come, but it was not the only loss Jeremiah would experience.

Eventually, Jeremiah fell head over heels in love. When he proposed to his high school sweetheart, she said yes. But, their joy was short-lived. His fiancée was murdered in a racial attack, her car forced off the side of the road by four white boys from the local Catholic high school.

Jeremiah had experienced great loss at the hands of Jesus' ambassadors: his body molested and his fiancée killed.

Jeremiah hated Christianity. And I can't say that I blamed him.

———

So when I was told, "Christians go to heaven; non-Christians go to hell," my question back was: "Does this mean the molesting priest will go running into God's kingdom while Jeremiah is kicked outside, simply because of which box each would check on the 'Which religion are you?' questionnaire?" Will the knife-wielding tongue-cutters, shaming schoolmasters, and racist politicians be dancing around God's throne simply because they sat in the pews of a local church, while the voiceless, shamed, and buried of Jeremiah's community are denied fair trial once again because they found their oppressor's religion hard to swallow?

Is God really that cold-hearted? Are his ways that superficial? Is his justice really that unfair?

I found myself wondering: Had Jeremiah really rejected Jesus, or only a severely distorted witness? Had our horrific muck-ups as Jesus' ambassadors gotten in the way of Jeremiah even encountering Jesus yet? And if so, what does God do with the destructive impact of our witness on his world?

God's judgment is, I would suggest, not the problem in this scenario. It is the solution. We need to redeem it from the caricature.

A Brood of Vipers

Jesus declared to the political and religious leaders of his day that if one of them caused a child to stumble, "it would be better for them to have a large millstone hung around their neck and to be drowned in the depths of the sea"[1] because of God's coming judgment against them. I don't know that I have a firmer picture in my mind of causing a child to stumble than ripping him from his family, forcibly chopping off part of his genitals, cutting out his grandfather's tongue, raping him, and murdering his fiancée.

The Christians in Jeremiah's life may have more to deal with than they bargained for—in the very God they proclaimed.

Religion is not a safe place to hide from God.

Jesus' harshest words are for the religious leaders of his day, not the outsiders. He calls them actors and whitewashed tombs that are shiny and clean on the outside but dirty and dead on the inside.[2] He confronts their missionary endeavors, calling them blind guides who "travel over land and sea to win a single convert, and when you have succeeded, you make them twice as much a child of hell as you are."[3] He calls them a brood of vipers who kill the messengers God sends them and who are in danger of being condemned to hell.[4]

Jesus is not necessarily a friend of the squeaky-clean religious crowd.

Religious hypocrisy is one of the primary things Jesus associates with the power of hell. And God is going to kick it outside his city when he returns.

God raises the bar, rather than lowers it, for those of us who bear his name in the world. James says those who teach the people of God will be judged more strictly.[5] I sometimes wonder when reading passages like these if becoming a pastor was the best career choice I could have made. Being identified with the people of God is not only a gracious gift; it is also a weighty calling.

Jesus takes our sin seriously. In Revelation, as Jesus walks among the churches, his words are primarily words of judgment: we are filled with idolatry, apathy, sexual immorality, a lust for money and power, and our love has grown cold.[6] You don't have to be a rocket scientist to know this is as apt a description of our churches today as it was in the first century.

When people say they are upset about pedophile priests, greedy televangelists, and the multitude of everyday hypocrisies that take place in our churches, I say, "I know, Jesus is too!"

Jesus' warning to Revelation's churches—and to ours—is that if we do not repent, he will remove us from God's presence, fight us with a sword, cause us to suffer intensely, and spit us out of his mouth.[7] No small words. Jesus is prepping for a fight—and it's with his own people. Like the prophets of old, God's words of judgment are directed first and foremost at the "insiders," not at the outsiders.

Why does Jesus take sin so seriously? One main reason, I have come to believe, is that he loves people like Jeremiah. He cares about the picture of God they are given. He wants it to be accurate. And he grieves when we muck it up.

Prodigals and Prostitutes

Jesus says God's judgment will be a surprise. When the King shows up, the prodigals and prostitutes are running into the kingdom while the self-righteous and self-made are weeping outside the party.[8] The sick, poor, blind, and lame are partying it up at God's Wedding Feast while those who thought their own clothes were good enough are cast out into the darkness.[9] Crowds of pagans come streaming from east and west to the Jerusalem banquet while many of those who carried God's name unworthily find themselves outside the city, weeping and gnashing their teeth.[10]

Insiders are weeded out; outsiders are gathered in.

Jesus says God's arrival will be a day of astonishment and reversals.[11] The first become last and the last first.[12] Many who call Jesus "Lord" and did great things in his name are told he never knew them, and many who never recognized him are told that he's known them all along.[13] Many who thought they were in are cast outside, and many who didn't seem to recognize there was an in or an out to begin with are welcomed with open arms.[14]

The name of God's game is shock and awe.

My friend at the beginning of this chapter was wrong. The walls that house our Sunday morning worship services are not the same as the walls that separate the beauty of the New Jerusalem from the brokenness of Gehenna. We cannot look around in our churches today and confidently proclaim that our seats at the Wedding Feast are booked in advance while those outside our walls are destined for destruction simply on the basis of our church membership rolls. In the words of Lesslie Newbigin:

> I am astounded at the arrogance of theologians who seem to think that we are authorized, in our capacity as Christians, to inform the rest of the world about who is to be vindicated and who is to be condemned at the last judgment. . . . I find this way of thinking among Christians astonishing in view of the emphatic warnings of Jesus against these kinds of judgments which claim to preempt the final

judgment of God. It would be tedious to repeat again the innumer-
able warnings of Jesus in this matter, his repeated statements that
the last day will be a day of surprises, of reversals, of astonishment.[15]

Surprise is one of the chief characteristics of Jesus' teaching on
judgment. The gospel tells us who the judge is; it does not tell us the
particularities and details of his judgment's outcome. But it does give
us confidence in this: Jesus is a good judge, and his judgment is good
news for the world.

THE GOOD NEWS OF JUDGMENT

God's judgment may be a surprise, but it is not random. He is not a magi-
cian pulling names out of a hat. Jesus teaches us to expect surprise when
it comes to *who* God judges, but he also teaches us to have confidence
in who the judge is and *why* he judges. Our world is desperately in need
of God to arrive and set things aright. And I believe three features of
Jeremiah's story can help us see why our world is so in need of judgment.

The Deception of Appearances

A first observation from Jeremiah's story is this: appearances can
be deceiving. Things are not always as they seem. To the surrounding
townsfolk, the priest was probably looked up to as a respected leader,
esteemed as an upstanding citizen, regarded as a righteous representative of God. Jeremiah, inversely, was likely viewed as a "troubled
youth," a despairing teenager who just needed to get over his anger
issues and learn to trust in God.

Yet behind closed doors, dark deeds were done that shed light
on the deception of appearances. Fortunately for Jeremiah, God sees
beneath the surface.

We need God to reveal things as they really are, to pull back the curtain on our superficial facades, and call out reality so that it can be healed.

When God arrives in brilliant glory, like the sun rising over the mountains, his presence pushes back the darkness and brings things out into the light. Paul looks forward to God's arrival as a day that "will bring to light what is hidden in darkness and will expose the motives of the heart,"[16] a "day when God judges people's secrets through Jesus Christ."[17] The splendor of God's coming unmasks the deception of appearances and reveals things as they really are.

We need this.

If true healing is to take place, Jeremiah needs the true story told. And whether the priest knows it or not, so does he. His only hope is in repentance before the mercy of Jesus, and you can't repent of something you pretend isn't there. And if the priest prefers the shadows of his pride and lust (a preference his life story would seem to indicate), like the rich man preferred his greed, it is still good that Jesus' arrival in brilliant glory calls his rejection of mercy out on the carpet for what it is.

We need God's judgment because we have a hard time seeing beneath the surface to the way things really are. "People look at the outward appearance, but the LORD looks at the heart."[18] We see what's on top, but God sees deeper. We need God's judgment because it's often hard for us to discern the difference between the outward appearance and the heart.

God's judgment is good news because our judgments are so often wrong . . . because looks can be deceiving . . . because *we've* got skeletons that need to be brought out of the closet.

The Brutality of History

A second observation from Jeremiah's story that can help us is this: history has been brutal. Graveyards of trauma, injustice, and death mark our war-torn world. And they cry out for a response. Jeremiah's fiancée was slaughtered: Who will account for her blood? Jeremiah's tribe was cheated in a trail of broken treaties: Who will weigh their scales of justice? Jeremiah's ancestors have massacred bodies lying in the ground: Who will hear their cry?

And Jeremiah's story is but one of millions whose injustice floods the earth.

The skeletons are wailing in the graveyards for redemption.

We need God to address the brutality of our history.

There is a compelling detail I've always found interesting in the story of Cain and Abel—the world's first murder. While Abel's life slips away, Cain can see the look of fear and trepidation in his brother's eyes. Cain can feel his brother's resistance: struggling back, gasping for air, fighting for life. But once Abel's breath is gone, the resistance is gone. Cain no longer has to sense his brother's struggle, feel his brother's fight, hear his brother's whimpering gasp.

Death steals Abel's cries from Cain's ears. His brother's eyes are closed. And his voice is silent.

But for God, the effect is the opposite. God hears Abel's blood crying out from the ground.[19] Death does not silence Abel's voice, it amplifies it. The same grave that *removes* Abel's cries from Cain's ears, *amplifies* them in the presence of God.

God has big ears. And I think his ears are hurting.

God is a "mighty King, lover of justice,"[20] who hears the cries of injustice arising from our sin-struck, war-torn world. Abel's death, and the death of all history's slaughtered with him, screams into the ears of God. We need God to arrive with justice because the cries erupting from the graveyards of our haunted world are not inconveniences to be forgotten, but injustices to be righted.

God's judgment is good news because the injustices are not forgotten. Death does not have the last word. God hears the cries, and he is coming to set things right.

The Bondage of Creation

A final observation from Jeremiah's story that can help us is this: creation is in bondage. Jeremiah is part of a people whose land has borne the weight of tragedy. Sin continues to tear heaven and earth apart. Our insurrection continues to bring thorns and thistles shooting up from the ground. Rebellion enslaves the world, taking it captive. Creation groans under the weight of sin.

Jeremiah's people have endured a trail of broken treaties, frequently seeing their lands strip-mined, their forests uprooted, and their waters polluted. Practically all nuclear dumping in the United States is done on reservations—with accompanying elevated cancer rates. Native Americans and other minority populations endure the brunt of industrial pollution in impoverished urban neighborhoods, causing asthma, rashes, and the like—especially among children and the elderly.[21]

The groaning of creation goes much deeper, however. An earthquake levels Haiti. A tsunami wipes out Southeast Asia. Hurricanes, volcanoes, and floods reveal a world that was intended to flourish before the face of God, now growing thorns and thistles, erupting and imploding far from the face of its Creator.

Creation is a pregnant mom, Paul tells us, "groaning as in the pains of childbirth . . . wait[ing] in eager expectation" to be "liberated from its bondage" under sin.[22] The universe is a delivery room: the earth is groaning in labor, but about to give birth to something beautiful.

Sin enslaves the world; creation groans toward redemption.

Our distance from the God who is Life bends our world down toward death. Our pulling away from the Light of the World stretches the shadows of darkness across the twilight expanse of our home. We have grabbed hold of the reigns of creation, yanking them away from our Creator and into our own chest. We have commandeered the steering wheel from earth's rightful Captain, and our mutiny drags the world down beneath the waters. Creation is in bondage; but salvation is coming. God's good blessing and sin's destructive pull are the tension we live in today.

Why does God judge the world? We'll explore multiple reasons in the coming chapters, but the first we've seen here is this: God judges the world to heal creation. God's judgment is good news because he cares enough to redeem his universe. His judgment will release the land from captivity. It will reconcile heaven and earth. It will break the bondage of creation.

GOD'S HOME MAKEOVER

God is out to heal the world. The Creator will perform an extreme home makeover on creation, flooding it with his glory and making it fit for us to live in as a home with him forever. God's judgment is central to this renovation project. It is something like the show *Extreme Makeover: Home Edition*, where in every episode, a hurting family that has endured severe hardship gets a knock on the door one day. They are about to receive a total renovation of their dilapidated home.

In God's story, we are the family that has endured extreme hardship. The human community has been torn apart by sin. Jeremiah's story is but one example. And our home is falling apart. Creation is groaning in bondage.

But the gospel knocks on our door.

A total renovation is coming.

Renovating the World

God's arrival is like a construction crew. The first task is to assess which parts of the home are good and should stay, like the foundation, infrastructure, and unique characteristics that once made it such a good home to live in. God does not throw the universe into a cosmic wastebasket and start over; he takes the best of the dilapidated home and builds the renovation around it.

The next task is to assess which parts need to go. Our sin and rebellion are like mold, termites, and decay: they are the reason the house is falling apart. Our sin wants distance from God, and it is our distance from God that is destroying us. Our rebellion against God's love, light, and life has plunged our world into destruction, darkness, and death. God's judgment of sin is the demolition project that precedes the renovation.

Sometimes we say things like, "If God loves the world, why can't he just ignore sin?" But this is to miss the point. God deals with sin *because* he loves the world. Imagine a contractor coming in to renovate a house—and simply painting over the moldy walls, placing a plant in front of the broken window, and building on top of a bad foundation. In time, the mold will begin to work its way through the paint; the chill breeze will sweep past the plant; and the cracked foundation will crumble—bringing the home down on top of the family's head.

We would say they have *deceived* the new home's inhabitants.

We would say they have *jeopardized* the family's safety.

We would say they are a *bad* construction company.

God's love for the world gives rise to his judgment of the world. God deals with sin's destructive power because he cares about people like Jeremiah, because he hears the skeletons wailing in our graveyards, because he wants to renovate our dilapidated home and make it new. Left to ourselves, we would be hopeless. We do not have the power to "fix" our world. But God does.

It is God's love for the world—his extravagant, undeserved, gracious love—that redeems our home from the sin that is tearing it apart.

The Great Architect

Jesus is the Great Architect, the one God has entrusted with this cosmic home makeover. He has been given "all authority in heaven and on earth"[23] to accomplish this renovation. Jesus is the one who "will judge the world with justice;" God has "given proof of this to all men by raising him from the dead."[24]

He's an expert builder, and he knows what he's doing. As the Light of the World, Jesus seeks to cast out our darkness. As the Resurrection and the Life, Jesus stands dynamically opposed to our death. As the Great Architect, Jesus wants to see the world rebuilt and thrive. We need this. Our world needs Jesus.

The gospel tells us who the judge is. It does not tell us the outcome of his judgment in particularity and detail (we are told to expect surprise), but we can take great confidence in knowing that Jesus is a good judge, better than we could ask for or imagine. He loves us sacrificially, generously, and he wants to reconcile us to God. The King who sits on the throne is the crucified Lamb who has atoned for the sin of the world and offers pardon to all who will receive it.

We are invited to relinquish our independence, receive his joy, and prepare for the coming of his kingdom. The Judge offers mercy, if we will accept it. But if we will not, we should be forewarned: Jesus is coming to liberate creation from our bondage. His justice will heal the world.

CHAPTER 7 KEY IDEA

WHY DOES GOD JUDGE THE WORLD?

God judges the world to heal the world. We need God's judgment because of the deception of appearances, the brutality of history, and the bondage of creation.

8.

EAST AND WEST

IS HEAVEN RACIST?

"What about those who've never heard of Jesus?" asked Taketo, an international student from Japan. Taketo struggled to understand this impression of Christianity. "If praying to receive Jesus is the way to get into heaven, what about all the folks who've never heard of him? Are they simply born in the wrong place at the wrong time? Out of luck on a highway to hell? As they approach the pearly gates, will God tell them, 'Sorry, I want to let you in . . . but you didn't pray the prayer'?"

Let's tease out Taketo's question a bit, because it's an important one.

Taketo is not talking about a random exception to the norm, an exotic "lone tribesman" in a remote part of Africa. Taketo is talking about the vast majority of the human race who *could not have* "prayed to receive Jesus" because they never heard of him.

In the last chapter, Jeremiah's story raised the question of how God deals with our *bad* witness. Taketo's question raises the broader question of those who've received *no* witness. As in the last chapter, we will see here once again that God's judgment is not the problem—it is the solution.

The Geographical Problem

Taketo's question raises two problems. First, there is the *geographical* problem. Prior to the fifteenth century, most of the world had little to no access to the gospel. The Mediterranean world where Jesus sailed was distanced from the Americas by the impassable waters of the Atlantic Ocean. The Middle Eastern lands where Peter and Paul walked were separated from much of the African continent by the Sahara desert's intimidating oceans of burning sand. The Roman Empire, where Christ was crucified, looked east to the Ural and Himalayan mountains as nearly impenetrable fortress walls that cut them off from Asia—where Taketo's ancestors are from.

The Roman Empire's *world* maps are revealing: they are of the Mediterranean world. To the east and west, north and south, the early church simply did not know that much of our world existed. Irenaeus, a missionary of the early church, couldn't have moved to Mexico City or Beijing if he'd wanted to. It wasn't that the early church's missionaries were unwilling to go to these places: they didn't know they were there!

And God, presumably, made the Atlantic Ocean, the Sahara desert, and the Ural and Himalayan mountains. He erected the sound barriers that kept these regions effectively out of earshot of the gospel until relatively recently in human history.

The Americas, Asia, and sub-Saharan Africa are massive continents, not minor outposts. Most of the earth has been kept out of earshot of the gospel since the time of Christ by simple virtue of its location. And God appears—as Creator of the mountains, desert, and seas—sovereign over this geographical fact.

The Historical Problem

Taketo's question also raises a *historical* problem. Not only were there fifteen centuries after Jesus in much of the world, but thousands of years *before* Jesus in all the world. What about all those people living BC? Long before Jesus first walked our dust, human history had a track record. Civilizations rising and falling: people making babies, working jobs, laughing and crying, living and dying.

Yes, God was present in Israel, but does this mean his kingdom will be predominantly Jewish from the time of Abraham to Jesus, then expanding after Jesus to include a bunch of Mediterranean folks until the fifteenth century, then finally expanding in only the last few centuries to bring in a more representative diversity from the peoples of the world?

Is heaven racist?

The Country Club

Heaven in this picture looks like an elite country club, ethnically biased and historically lopsided. If God wants the nations in his kingdom, then Taketo's question means either God is a pretty bad planner or some of us have a very reductionistic vision of God's sovereignty. Fortunately, when God arrives to set his world right-side up, this is not the way justice rolls down.

My first clue that this was a caricature came when I realized the New Testament did not talk about Judgment Day this way. The New Testament authors knew full well that thousands of years of human history had gone on before Jesus, but they still saw his coming as good news for the ages that had gone before, the mystery of ages past that had now been fulfilled and revealed.[1] They saw the coming of Jesus not as the annihilation of history, but rather as the purpose of history realized.[2] They believed Jesus could come back at any time, during their lifetime even, yet their picture of God's kingdom was one flooded with every nation, tribe, and tongue from all across the earth, worshipping around the throne of God and his Christ.[3]

The gospel was good news for the nations and for history.

What was different between their understanding of judgment and Taketo's? Jesus' encounter with a Roman centurion is a good place to start. Let's dive in.

A ROMAN CENTURION

A Roman centurion comes to Jesus and asks him to heal his paralyzed servant.[4] Two observations. First: he's Roman. The Roman Empire was an enemy of the people of God. An overtaxing, enslaving empire successfully bent on world domination. His ethnicity was known for privilege and arrogance, an ancient version of something like the "ugly American" complex.

The Roman Empire did not know Israel's God or honor him as God. Rather, they saw themselves as ruling autonomously over the nations through the blessing of their own false gods.

A second observation: he's a centurion. A military officer ordering a bunch of troops around the Holy Land. He is not only identified with the empire, but influentially so. He is a commander in the occupation of the Holy Land, representing and enforcing the structure of Gentile domination that God promised to one day bring to an end.

In both ethnicity and occupation, this is not a good start for someone coming to talk to Jesus, the Jewish Messiah. The Roman centurion is part and parcel of the very nations God is coming to judge and liberate his people from.

Yet in his encounter with Jesus, something dramatic happens: he humbles himself before Jesus, recognizes Jesus' authority as greater than his own and asks Jesus to heal his servant. Jesus responds with amazement, "I tell you the truth, I have not found anyone in Israel with such great faith."[5] This must have come as quite a shock to Jesus' audience. *Within* the people of God, the community that carried God's name in the world, Jesus has not found such great faith as he has found here in this outsider—a Roman centurion identified with the powers and structures of Gentile imperial domination that God has vowed to demolish.

Jesus finds faith in unexpected places.

Weeding Out, Gathering In

Jesus then uses the Roman centurion's faith as an illustration, an example, that foreshadows what will happen when God's kingdom comes:

> I say to you that many will come from the east and the west, and will take their places at the feast with Abraham, Isaac and Jacob in the kingdom of heaven. But the subjects of the kingdom will be

thrown outside, into the darkness, where there will be weeping and gnashing of teeth.[6]

There are two important things I want to point out here. First, God's judgment in this passage is directed primarily at the people of God, not at the outsiders. It is the "subjects of the kingdom" who are thrown outside: those who have heard God's Word, known his promises, and been proximate to his work in history. When God shows up, Israel's leaders are being kicked outside and Roman centurions are streaming in.

The second thing I want to point out is that a *vast multitude* is streaming into God's holy city. Their number is "many": these are not just a few stragglers or isolated exceptions. These are crowds of people rushing into the city of God. A flood of worshippers is coming to feast, to party it up, to join God's people and celebrate God himself. God's kingdom has a posture of welcome and embrace toward the nations.

Note that they come from "east and west": Babylon was to the east of Israel. The Roman Empire to the west. In a similar passage, Jesus says they will also come from "north and south"[7]: Assyria was to the north of Israel and Egypt to the south. A mass assembly is breaking out from the empires and into God's kingdom.

Israel was surrounded by the great empires of the day, at the crossroads of the Mediterranean world, called to be a light to them of God's redemptive presence and kingdom in their midst. Jesus is saying that when God's kingdom comes, Israel's calling is fulfilled: the nations come streaming out from Babylon and Rome, Assyria and Egypt—the imperial powers that formerly held their allegiance—and into God's kingdom.

The Roman centurion's submissive recognition of Jesus' authority is a foreshadowing of this day.

God's judgment is a surprise. It involves a *weeding out* from within the people of God and a *gathering in* from outside the people of God. Many among God's people are being judged while many outside are dancing into Jesus' holy city. God's judgment starts with his people. "The time has come for judgment, and it must begin with God's household."[8] It does not end there, but it starts there.

And Jesus says that *many* will come from outside God's people, not that *all* will come. Jesus does not invert the problem of judgment to say that *only* the people of God will be judged and *all* the outsiders will come in. Judgment is implied here for those who do not join the procession streaming into the kingdom.

The picture is one of sin *inside* the city being cast outside, and sin *outside* the city being restricted from coming in.

God is setting the world right. This is what judgment is all about. And it involves a weeding out and a gathering in. Jesus' rejection by Israel's leaders and the faith of the Roman centurion the weeding out foreshadows gathering and the in that will take place when God's kingdom arrives in fullness.

Every Nation, Tribe, and Tongue

God's kingdom reconciles east and west. Jesus does not pluck a few people from a few nations into an abstract acultural kingdom. Jesus reconciles the nations *from* the fragmentation, devastation, and alienation of sin, *to* the glorious, gracious goodness of his very presence, and *through* himself to one another. God's purpose is to create through his own eternal, holy life a multiethnic, international body from every nation, tribe, and tongue, constituted by worship in relation to himself and communion in relation to one another.

God is on a mission to heal the nations.

This changes the way we see redemption, similar to what we saw earlier: that God's mission is not to pluck us out of earth and into heaven, but rather to reconcile heaven and earth. So also here, God's purpose is not to pluck us out of the nations into an acultural kingdom, but rather to reconcile the nations through himself into his multicultural kingdom. All it takes is a quick look at our war-torn world to see that we are still in desperate need of this today.

This is a lot to pull from Jesus' chat with a Roman centurion. Was this a fluke, a onetime exception in a broader story moving in an otherwise different direction? It's worth zooming out to see this theme's centrality throughout the biblical story: God's purpose has always been to heal the nations.

A SHATTERED CHINA DOLL

God likes nations. Right off the bat, God tells Adam and Eve to go have sex and make babies ("Be fruitful, and multiply"[9]). Babies are like LEGOs: the building blocks that build up the world. Babies make families, families make communities, and communities make nations. In other words, God tells Adam and Eve to go make nations: God wants his world flooded with people.

The context is one of blessing ("God blessed them and said . . ."[10]): as the nations come springing forth from Eve's womb, God wants them to flourish, to experience his *shalom*, his blessing, in the "very good" world he has made.[11] In the words of Paul, "From one man [God] made all the nations, that they should inhabit the whole earth."[12] God blesses the nations.

Right out of the gate, however, the story takes a turn for the worse.

Division and Destruction

Sin fractures the nations. In the early chapters of Genesis, sin is chiefly characterized by brutality: first Cain, then Lamech, and by Noah's day, an earth that is "filled with violence."[13] The nations are a mess. Sin wreaks havoc on God's good purposes. Like weeds in a garden, our evil spreads throughout the human community, leaving us infested with hostility.

As we saw earlier, Augustine compared our predicament to being something like a shattered china doll.[14] God created humanity to be one: with a unity that was beautiful, yet fragile, like a china doll. But the effect of sin has been to throw us to the ground violently, shattering us into a million fragments. And like fragmented shards scattered across the ground, the nations now fill the earth in a state of violent hostility and division toward one another. Sin has shattered the nations.

The Reconciliation Project

So God sets out on a reconciliation project. When God calls Abraham he does not say, "Your nation will go to heaven; all the rest are hosed." God's promise is, rather, that one day, "all peoples on earth will be blessed through you."[15] God reiterates this promise of blessing three times in the early chapters of Genesis—demonstrating its significance at the outset of the biblical story.[16] God calls Abraham out of Babylon, a violent empire that seeks to rule the nations without God, and God's promise is that one day his blessing will make its way back, through Abraham, to the nations trapped in Babylon.[17]

Babylon dominates the nations, but God will reconcile the nations.

God's purpose for his people, Abraham's children, was to bless the nations. God placed Israel at the crossroads of the ancient world and called them to be a "light to the nations," shining the glory of God to the mighty empires that surrounded them.[18] God redeemed Israel from slavery as a beacon of a new world; her privilege was now to "sing the praises of the LORD . . . [and] proclaim among the nations what he has done."[19] God called his children to be a "kingdom of priests," mediating his reconciling presence to the surrounding nations.[20]

God's purpose was to reveal his glory, character, and power through Abraham's children to the world.

Rebellion and Exile

Unfortunately, there was a problem. Israel proved to be more of a mirror to the nations of their own rebellious ways than a window to the glory of God. Her life was clogged and cluttered with sin. With such a horrific witness, how would the nations get a clear picture of God? Frustrated, God declares through Ezekiel the prophet:

> This is Jerusalem, which I have set in the center of the nations, with countries all around her. Yet in her wickedness she has rebelled

against my laws and decrees *more than* the nations and countries around her.[21]

Jerusalem had actually become *even more* wicked than the countries around her!

Like the priest who molested Jeremiah, God's people were a terrible example. And like Jeremiah and his family, the nations received a *very poor* picture of God. Jerusalem had been invaded by the wildfire power of hell—unleashed through the people of God.

And in these kind of circumstances—God gets angry.

So God sent Israel into exile. He left the land and, without his protective presence, the surrounding empires invaded Jerusalem and carried her children outside the city into captivity.[22] Israel's mission to the nations had failed. Abraham's children went back into Babylon, the land from which he'd come.

While in exile, the prophets looked forward to God's return. God would come to establish his kingdom, and his kingdom would be good news not only for Israel, but for the nations as a whole:

> All nations will stream to [Jerusalem]. Many peoples will come and say, "Come, let us go up to the mountain of the LORD . . . so that we may walk in his paths." (Isaiah 2:2–3)

> All nations will gather in Jerusalem to honor the name of the LORD. No longer will they follow the stubbornness of their evil hearts. (Jeremiah 3:17)

> All the nations you have made
>   will come and worship before you, Lord;
>   they will bring glory to your name. (Psalm 86:9)

God's kingdom meant hope for the nations.

———

Jesus' encounter with the Roman centurion draws upon this prophetic tradition. Jesus looks forward to the day when the nations will come streaming from east and west and north and south to worship and feast in the kingdom of God. He looks forward to the day when God will return to judge sin amongst his people and reconcile the nations in his kingdom.

When the King returns, he kicks the rebels outside his city and gathers all who will come to join the celebration of his kingdom.

Jesus will reconcile the nations.

DIVINE SURGERY

God's judgment is like divine surgery: performed to heal the nations. Sin is like cancer: it wants to tear the human social body apart. Sarah is a friend of mine who was diagnosed with cancer at age twenty-seven. She had both breasts removed and went through eight rounds of chemotherapy. If the cancer had its way, it would devour her from the inside out until she had no breath left.

It would consume her life until she was dead.

Similarly, sin wants to tear down humanity. It has fractured the nations, shattering us like a china doll whose shards are scattered across our war-torn world. Since the beginning of the twentieth century, there have been more than 350 wars in the world: violent, bloody eruptions within the human social body.[23] This is just one extreme sign of the shattering of the nations. The human family is currently marked by conquest and competition, aggression and assimilation, war and violence.

But when God's kingdom comes, he will reunite the nations. The tree of life is at the center of his city, whose leaves "are for the healing of the nations."[24] The kings of the earth will bring their splendor in, like the Roman centurion, and the nations will walk by its light.[25] God's judgment is central to this healing, because it extracts the destructive power of unrepentant sin.

The Great Physician

Jesus is the Great Physician, appointed by God to perform the operation. It's a delicate operation, and he's got the right hands for the job. He is a better judge than I am. A better judge than you are. Trusting me to judge the world would be a bad idea—like trusting me to perform heart surgery. You can bet a lot of healthy organs would accidentally be pulled out and a lot of sickness would unfortunately be left inside. But Jesus is a gifted surgeon who knows what he's doing.

Jesus will lay humanity down like a body on the operating table to extricate the rebellion, excise recalcitrant sin, and get rid of the stubborn cancer in order to heal the body. Judgment Day is divine surgery, the day "[God] has set . . . when he will judge the world with justice by the man he has appointed."[26] As the Great Physician, Jesus judges sin in order to heal the nations, to reconcile the world.

Jesus can heal the nations because he is not only the Judge; he has himself borne the judgment. On the cross, Jesus' own body was shattered like a china doll as he bore the fracturing power of sin. With outstretched arms on the cross, Jesus receives the nations' judgment and, simultaneously, receives the nations in mercy. Jesus grabs hold of sin's destructive power that has divided humanity, carries it with him into the grave . . . and buries it there.

Jesus took not only the sin of the ages to come after him into the grave, but also the sin of the ages come before, for he is "the Lamb who was slain from the creation of the world."[27] Jesus is the spotless Lamb, "who takes away the sin of the world!"[28] Though Jesus is crucified late in history, at the end of the ages, his death "works backward" so to speak, taking history and humanity into himself toward both judgment and redemption.

Jesus bears the curse of the nations in order to bring healing to the nations through his reconciling embrace.

Healing Humanity

My friend Sarah beat cancer.[29] She is a survivor. She lives life to the fullest with every breath. If you were to ask me, "Can't she just keep a little of the cancer for old time's sake? Do we really want to get rid of it all?" I would look at you as if you were crazy. Or punch you. Because I care about my friend.

It is because I want her healing that I long for the removal of that which destroys her.

Similarly, it is strange to ask whether Jesus might lighten up a bit and let us keep a little sin in the new humanity, whether he might just look the other way so as to be merciful and all. This misunderstands the nature of the issue: it is *because of* Jesus' mercy that he redeems the nations from sin and excises its destructive power.

For Jesus to leave a little sin in the human social body would not be merciful. It would make him a *bad* surgeon. Malpractice lawsuits would soon come streaming in. Before long, we would be back in the doctor's office for the same predicament he had to heal us from in the first place.

God's goal is not to pluck us *out of* humanity. It is to *heal* humanity. He does not remove a few people from a few nations into a noncultural kingdom. Jesus reconciles the nations *from* the destructive power of sin, *to* himself and *through* himself to one another. God's kingdom is an international, multiethnic body constituted by worship in relation to God and communion in relation to one another. And Jesus is at the center.

Jesus is the Great Physician who brings justice to heal the nations.

CHAPTER 8 KEY IDEA

IS HEAVEN RACIST?

No, God's judgment restores the nations *from* sin's ruin, *to* himself and *through* himself to one another in his multinational, multicultural kingdom. Jesus is the Great Physician who heals the human social body.

9.

WELCOME TO THE WEDDING

COSMIC SECRET

Let me tell you a secret: God's throwing a wedding, and he wants the world to come. It's a wedding he's been dreaming up for the world since the dawn of time. Like an excited wedding planner, the final chapters of Scripture revel in the details of God's coming Wedding Feast. And they let us in on a cosmic surprise: the goal of humanity, the destination of creation, the last pit stop that this whole crazy train of history has been hurtling toward since Eden . . . is a wedding with God.

Weddings are a celebration of union, and this one is no different. God's wedding celebrates the union of *heaven and earth*: when God performs his extreme makeover on this old cosmic rock we call home, to live with us together forever. It celebrates the union of *east and west*, as the nations come streaming into God's holy city to worship the King and be healed. And it celebrates the union of *good folks and bad folks*: in a kingdom where all is given and nothing is earned, whose atmosphere is grace..

So how are God's wedding and judgment related?

Weddings and judgment are not two things we'd usually pair together. But Jesus does. In his parable of the wedding feast, Jesus gives us one of his strongest teachings on judgment. He tells us God's love for the world and judgment of the world are inextricably intertwined: they go together like violin and cello, like wine and hors d'oeuvres, like heaven and earth.

How? Let's take a look and find out.

THE KING JUDGES HIS FRIENDS

As Jesus' story begins, the king's son is getting married, so he's throwing a party. A wedding feast. This is the event of the century. There is no treasure in his kingdom greater than his son. And this will be an all-expenses-paid blowout. A party you don't want to miss. Picture the king: excitedly sending out invitations, welcoming his closest friends to the upcoming wedding. He *wants* them there. The king wants to celebrate together with them over his son and the bride.

Immediately, however, Jesus' story takes an unexpected turn. The king's friends tear up his wedding invite and kill his messengers:

> They paid no attention and went off—one to his field, another to his business. The rest seized his servants, mistreated them and killed them. The king was enraged. He sent his army and destroyed those murderers and burned their city.[1]

What is going on? Wouldn't a simple no have sufficed? People have declined my party invitations, but usually politely—and never was murder involved. Unfortunately for the king's messengers, this was before the days of Evite.

I thought this was a story about a wedding?

Murdering the Messengers

Why does Jesus tell the story this way? For him, this is a picture of Israel: God's friends, his special people, invited to his wedding for the world. But they tore up the invitation: were too busy, had more important things to do. And when God sent prophets with fresh invites . . . they murdered his messengers.

God wanted a wedding and found himself waging a war. When the king's friends kill his messengers, he gets angry (rightly so!) and sends his army to burn down their city. Once again, *overreaction?* It could seem so if we were just talking about a declined party invite. But Jesus is again painting a picture of something bigger: Israel's exile. Hundreds of years before Jesus told this story, God got angry with Jerusalem for murdering his prophets and tearing up the wedding invite. So God sent Babylon's armies (and called them *his* armies) to destroy the city and carry her people into exile.[2]

Jesus is telling Israel why God sent them into exile, why the King judged his friends: because they didn't take his wedding invitation seriously. God wants us at his wedding, but we have to want to come.

Jesus is also painting a picture, I believe, of another event that would occur *after* he told this parable. When the prophets didn't work, God sent his only Son—the Groom himself—as the *ultimate* messenger. And Jesus knew as he told this story that, like the king's messengers who had gone before, the same fate awaited him: he was about to be killed like the prophets of old. The king's friends would murder his son.

So God would again burn down their city: after Jesus' death, the Roman Empire's armies invaded Jerusalem, demolished the temple, and reduced the city to smoldering rubble. All within a generation. God wanted a wedding and found himself waging a war.

When God arrives, it is often those thought to be his closest friends who turn out to be his worst enemies. At Jesus' cross, it is an outcast thief on death row who recognizes Jesus, while the insider politicians are demanding their pound of flesh. It is an outsider Roman centurion who declares Jesus the Son of God while Jerusalem's leaders are kicking him outside the city.[3] At the cross, the central moment of salvation history, the outsiders get it while the insiders don't. The enemies are welcomed in while the king's friends kill his son.

We see from Jesus' teaching once again the same prominent theme from the last few chapters: God's judgment starts not with the outsiders but with his own people.

Preparing for the Wedding

There is a danger when we say things like, "Christians go to heaven; everyone else is hosed." We can miss Jesus' confrontation with those of us who bear God's name. For the Israelites a temptation was to believe that they were exempt from God's coming judgment because they were within God's people: that God would come to vindicate them and judge the pagan outsiders. Yet Jesus paints a picture that starts in the other direction: God is rejected first and foremost amongst his own people, by the religious insiders, those close to his revelation in history.

Today, we have more access to the gospel than any century in history: churches on every street corner, radio stations blasting the airwaves, and Bibles in every hotel nightstand. The wedding invitation has gone out strong. But do we take it seriously? Are we preparing for the wedding, growing in the holiness and justice that mark the life of God's kingdom? Are we allowing God to form us in the image of Jesus?

Unfortunately, like the king's friends, we are often too busy. More important things to do. Going through the motions of church, but not interested in transformation. Not interested in giving our lives away. Not interested in God. Our churches can be filled with the unconverted. God is often rejected by the very community that bears his name.

Jesus teaches us *why* the people of God are judged: because we don't take the wedding seriously.

Starting at Home

Judgment starts with the people of God. There is a famous sermon by Jonathan Edwards called "Sinners in the Hands of an Angry God." I used to hate that sermon. I had never read it, but I hated it. The reason I hated it was the image I had in my head: Edwards as the angry street preacher at the downtown intersection during rush hour, holding up a mean sign with unsavory remarks about communists and homosexuals, yelling at the top of his lungs at all the passersby that they were going to hell unless they became like his self-righteous self.

It was an image of the Christian as the self-confident "insider" shouting at all the non-Christian "outsiders" the omnipotent declaration of their impending doom.

Then I read the sermon. The shocker hit when I realized that Edwards's audience was the church! He spoke not from the street corner but from the pulpit. Not to the passersby outside but to the parishioners inside. The sinners in the hands of an angry God were the people who bore his name! This was judgment for God's people, directed at a church filled with idolatry, apathy, and sin. I began to realize that God's coming judgment is not so much an evangelistic tool used to frighten outsiders into the kingdom as it is a housecleaning tool used to weed out hypocrisy and call insiders back to the faith they proclaim.

It starts at home.

I love Edwards's sermon now. There are a few parts I disagree with, that conflict with aspects of the biblical story we've observed in this book (though brilliant as all get out, he couldn't be right *all* the time).[4] But in the bigger picture, Edwards's sermon is a reminder to me that I cannot slide by on the coattails of calling myself a Christian.

Jesus' words of judgment are spoken first and foremost to those of us who bear his name in the world. We need preaching on judgment in our churches to splash cold water on the face of our lukewarm apathy and wake us out of our self-righteous slumbers. It is God's business to judge those outside the Church, but Jesus has called us in love to spur one another on in the integrity of our witness as a community and the holy love that marks the life of his kingdom.

Jesus has called us to prepare for the wedding.

THE KING WELCOMES GOOD AND BAD

Jesus continues his story. The king still wants a wedding, so he tells his servants:

> "The wedding banquet is ready, but those I invited did not deserve to come. So go to the street corners and invite to the banquet

anyone you find." So the servants went out into the streets and gathered all the people they could find, the bad as well as the good, and the wedding hall was filled with guests.[5]

God's throwing a wedding, and he wants the world to come.

Inviting the World

Two observations. First, the king wants his wedding hall "filled with guests," so he sends his servants out to gather "anyone you can find." God's posture toward his world is one of open invitation and pursuant embrace. We misunderstand God's character if we see God trying desperately to keep us out of the wedding while we try desperately to get in: the movement is in the opposite direction.

God is not a bouncer guarding the kingdom's gates while the repentant try to scale the walls. He does not say, "I'm sorry. I don't think there's any room left; we're full." God wants the world at his wedding, and the cross of Christ is the extravagant sign that he will go to any length—even to hell and back—to get us there.

God is on the hunt to find anyone who will come. In a similar parable, Jesus says that God sends his party messengers into "the streets and alleys . . . roads and country lanes" (everywhere) to bring "the poor, the crippled, the blind and the lame" (everyone), "so that my house will be full."[6] God's kingdom brings together the CEO and the homeless person; the politician and the punk rock kid; the soccer mom and the soldier and the starving artist. God wants his house full.

This is, in an important respect, why God judged Israel in the first place. God called Israel not only to come to the wedding herself but to welcome others. The king wanted his friends not only to receive the invitation but to extend the invitation, to become the messengers, to get caught up in the joy of the party and invite the world. God called Israel to be a light to the nations of his coming wedding for the world.

God has never been about creating a select elite who defensively hole up in retreat from the rest of the world and wait for the end. God has always been about inviting a lost and rebellious world into his kingdom party.[7] God gets frustrated when those of us who bear his name don't share his passion for the coming wedding and invite the world to the party.

This brings us to the next observation.

Good and Bad

The guest book at God's wedding is filled with a lot of signatures you wouldn't expect. The king welcomes "the bad as well as the good." Jesus told this story partly in defense of his unruly friends. Israel's leaders led a smear campaign against Jesus for partying with the "wrong crowd": feasting with tax collectors, prostitutes, and "sinners." But Jesus declares God's kingdom is for the gangsters as much as anybody.

God *wants* them at his wedding.

This means we have a problem if we think of God coming to simply give the good folks their deserved reward and the bad folks their just desserts. We tend to envision God showing up on Judgment Day to welcome the world's shiny, polished citizens into the kingdom and to banish the wicked, debaucherous criminals outside. This assumption is not surprising: it is in many ways the way our world works. You don't go to jail for volunteering in soup kitchens or helping old ladies cross the street. And you don't get awards for robbing banks or taking candy from babies.

Admirable people get shiny gold stars while the naughty are sent to their room without dinner. Citizens get public recognition and criminals get public derision. So it's not surprising that we tend to think of Judgment Day as God showing up to applaud the good folks and kill the bad ones.

The problem is, this is not the way the gospel works.

God does not invite us because we've earned it; he invites us because he *wants* us there. Jesus defiantly declares that the kingdom of God is something dynamically different from the genteel, proprietary insiders running into the wedding feast while the lecherous pagans are kicked outside. Jesus declares it is not our moral behavior that gains us entrance into God's kingdom: it is his mercy.

Pay attention, this is revolutionary: good and bad behaviors are not the basis God uses to judge the world. His mercy is.

God's mercy: there is no other basis for entrance. Too often, we believe and act as if our presence amid God's people is a result of our good behavior, our moral accomplishments, our ethical performance, rather than the sheer grace of Jesus. God does not invite us to his wedding because we've earned it. He invites us because his *affection* is for us, because he *desires* our company, because he *wants* to be with us.

God is not obligated by our accomplishments or required by our merit. He does not *have* to welcome us to his wedding because we prayed a prayer, fed the homeless, or gave our lives in an overseas war zone. God has invited us *in spite of* ourselves, not *because of* ourselves. He doesn't invite us because he *has* to; God invites us because he *wants* to.

The cross is God's wedding invitation, where Jesus levels the playing field before the mercy of God, invites us to be united with him as his bride and reveals some astonishing news about the kingdom: God wants us there.

So if we think God has to let us in because of our good behavior, we're barking up the wrong tree.

The Wrong Tree

Good behavior is often a means of keeping God at bay. Obedience and obligation can erect as much a barrier to life with God as lawless rebellion and wanton destruction. Duty and debauchery have more in common than we might expect. Selfishness and self-righteousness just might be twins separated at birth.

Both good and evil hang from the tree of knowledge of good and evil; the problem is that they are on the wrong tree.

But there is good news. There is another tree: the tree of life. Where life is received from God, rather than sought independently from him. Where all is given, nothing is earned.

At the tree of life, the moralist needs the mercy of God as much as the murderer, the Pharisee as much as the philanderer, the legalist as much as the lawless. Being a good, upstanding citizen who follows all the community's rules and earns the respect of one's peers is not the criterion by which one enters life with God. God's mercy is.

Jesus' cross is the life-giving tree. It is the place where our sin, rebellion, and destruction are absorbed and mercy made the basis for entrance into the life of God. Jesus invites us to let go of our independence and be bound in union with him, to stop eating off the tree of good and evil and start feasting on the tree of life: his life.

Jesus brings us the ultimate wedding invitation: the groom lays down his life in proposal to his bride, welcoming us all, both good and bad, to his wedding for the world. The result is one wild party with a surprising guest list, filled with a lot of folks you wouldn't have expected.

This is a party you don't want to miss.

THE KING JUDGES WEDDING CRASHERS

We've seen that God *weeds out* from his own people and *invites* all who will come, but does this mean *everyone* outside is gathered in? Do all come in? Does Jesus simply invert judgment to mean the moralists, Pharisees, and legalists are out but the murderers, philanderers, and lawless are in? By no means! Jesus addresses this next, as he continues his parable:

> When the king came in to see the guests, he noticed a man there who was not wearing wedding clothes. "Friend," he asked, "how did you get in here without wedding clothes?" The man was speechless.
>
> Then the king told his attendants, "Tie him hand and foot, and throw him outside, into the darkness, where there will be weeping and gnashing of teeth."[8]

Jesus gives us a picture of someone trying to bring his sin in with him, to carry his rebellion into the kingdom.

Navy Seal Bouncer

Notice that the man is "not wearing wedding clothes." Can you imagine being invited by President Obama to attend the formal wedding of his daughter—and showing up at the ceremony in your boxers and a dirty old T-shirt? That would be a royal affront . . . and you'd soon find yourself out in the parking lot.

That's the picture. This is the king's wedding, a regal affair, a presidential occasion: something worth bringing your best, busting out the finest duds, and dressing to the nines for. You would expect the king to be livid.

Yet notice how the king does not call the wedding crasher "jerk," "idiot," or "troublemaker." He calls him "friend," similar to the Lazarus parable, where the rich man is called "son." God's posture is one of friendship, of invitation, of embrace—even to the unrepentant rebel.

God calls the wedding crasher "friend."

But the wedding crasher is silent. Speechless. Dumbstruck. He responds not with repentance but rather as one who's been caught. His silence betrays him: he does not take the wedding seriously.

So the king boots him.

My friend Austin knows about not wanting wedding crashers at his wedding. His bride had an ex-boyfriend who stalked them over the preceding months. There were hostile e-mails, unwelcome phone calls, and even a surprise appearance in person. He wanted her back and Austin out of the picture. Out of concern for their safety, Austin eventually threatened a restraining order if his unwelcome advances continued. As their wedding approached, Austin had visions of his Navy Seal, muscle-bound cousin running point as bouncer to escort him off the premises if he showed up.

Out of love for his bride, Austin wanted to protect their wedding from anyone who would seek to disrupt, disturb, or destroy their celebration and future life together. Similarly, Jesus loves his bride. So when the wedding comes, God boots the wedding crashers who have their own ulterior motive for being at the party.

Our sin is like an ex-boyfriend with an agenda: it wants to tear God's honeymoon suite apart and carry us back to its cheap hotel. But fortunately, God loves us too much to let that happen. So God will not allow our sin to intrude upon the celebration day or the life that follows thereafter. The king loves his bride too much.

So Jesus judges wedding crashers.

Free Wedding Clothes

God wants the world at the wedding of his Son, but sin will not be allowed to crash the party. Though God's posture is one of embrace, sin's destructive power must be checked at the door. It is what has caused the problem in the first place, seeking to disrupt and destroy God's good purposes for the world. If we will not allow God to cast sin out of us, then we must be cast out with sin. You can't bring your sin in with you.

Jesus does not simply invert judgment to mean the religious elite are cast outside and the depraved ol' heathens go running in. Though Jesus spent much of his time with tax collectors, prostitutes, and "sinners," he was continually calling them to repentance, a turning from themselves to God. And it was only through this repentance that many of them were entering the kingdom of God.[9] The philanderers need to be clothed in God's mercy as much as the Pharisees, the murderers as much as the moralists, the lawless as much as the legalist.

There are religious folks who don't want to go to the party, and there are pagans who try to bring their sin in with them. But those who are not made fit for the kingdom will not be allowed inside. God wants us at his wedding, but our dirty old rags of sin must be checked at the door.

There is good news, however: God offers free wedding clothes. We all stand naked before the king, in need of his mercy, but he *asks* to take our filthy rags and give us fresh new clothes in their place— the finest threads for the wedding celebration. God *wants* to clothe us. And what's more, they're free. Jesus has died to clothe us in his righteousness. Those at the wedding are those who "have washed their robes and made them white in the blood of the Lamb."[10]

Jesus wants to give us wedding clothes.

Jesus is happy to clothe us in his righteousness, but this entails repentance: turning from ourselves to God in order to receive his fresh garments in place of our old rags. The king invites all into his wedding, but our sin must be left at the door. We are invited freely into the kingdom, but we must let God make us fit for that kingdom.

Because we can't bring our sin inside.

COSMIC WEDDING

Perhaps the craziest thing about God's wedding is this: he invites us not only to attend, but to *be the bride*. Jesus invites us

> to receive his wedding clothes, letting his hands wash us in his blood and dress us in his righteousness
> to let his Spirit of holy love fill our bodies like a flood and wrap around our hearts like a wedding ring[11]
> to prepare for the wedding day as we hear his voice call us beloved: to pursue holiness and justice, in love and purity, as we prepare for union with our King.

Jesus does much more than invite us to a wedding.

He asks us to become his bride.

Receiving Jesus

Receiving Jesus is, ironically, both the easiest and the hardest thing in the world. It is easy because it is free: he *wants* to embrace us; his affection is *toward* us; his desire is *for* us. Jesus loved us while we stuck the knife in, atoned for our sin while we were his enemies, outstretched his arms on the cross to receive his rebellious world in an invitation of embrace.

And yet, receiving Jesus is the hardest thing in the world, because it costs us everything. To say yes to the wedding proposal is to enter into union with the very life of Jesus. And to enter into union means our old life lived alone must die. "Whoever wants to save their life will lose it, but whoever loses their life for me will find it."[12] To let Jesus fill us with his Spirit is to abandon our freedom *from* God and be filled with his freedom *for* God.

The cost of union with Christ is the death of our independence; the cost of true worship is the exile of our autonomy; if we want salvation, we must leave Egypt—and let him carry us into the promised land.

I still remember my wedding as if it were yesterday. The ambience of music playing, flowers blooming, wine flowing. Surrounded by loved ones gathered round to celebrate us. Above it all, however, my bride was at the center: stunning and radiant. We were about to leave behind our life as two separate individuals and enter into something mystical, something magical: union. Life together as one.

I couldn't wait.

It was one of the greatest days of my life, but its greatness resided in more than simply the joy it brought us. I believe that day held a transcendent joy because it was a picture of the gospel: a signpost of what's to come.

In the End, the Beginning

Jesus wants to marry *us*. And at his wedding, there are no spectators allowed. Weddings celebrate union, and this wedding is no different. Jesus reconciles heaven and earth, east and west, good folks and bad folks (all the major themes we've been developing throughout this book). And at the center is Jesus and his bride—celebrating their consummated union in God, for the world.

Jesus' wedding is *for* the world.

Because Jesus loves the world, he judges all that stands opposed to this reconciling union. God's judgment arises, as we have seen, when we don't take the wedding seriously. The people of God are judged for rejecting the invitation while the outsiders are judged for trying to bring their sin in with them. What both have in common is this: they do not treat the wedding with the honor and respect it deserves.

Jesus' love for the world is holy ground. It is sacred territory. It gives rise to judgment as it comes to make the world new.

In the end is the beginning. Though Jesus' wedding date is on the calendar for the end of history, it is not just a finale, but a fresh start. Not just a closure, but an inauguration. Jesus' wedding inaugurates God's reconciling kingdom come to reign in fullness forever as it brings an end to our sin-struck, war-torn history that has ripped the human community apart. Jesus' wedding celebrates the closure of creation's exile through the consummation of God's glorious presence indwelling the world in intimacy and power forever.

Jesus' love will reconcile the world.

CHAPTER 9 KEY IDEA

HOW ARE GOD'S WEDDING AND JUDGMENT RELATED?

God's throwing a wedding and he wants the world to come. God's judgment arises against those who don't treat the wedding with the honor and respect it deserves: insiders who don't take the invitation seriously and outsiders who try to bring their sin in with them. God's wedding will reconcile the world.

10.

THE SERVANT AT THE CENTER

Does God's judgment meet the deepest needs of our world? Let's return to Jeremiah, the Native boy molested by a priest whose story opened this section. In Jeremiah's story, we saw three major reasons our world is desperately in need of God's judgment: the brutality of history, the deception of appearances, and the bondage of creation. Now that we've cleared some ground, the time has come to ask: Does Jesus address Jeremiah's story? Does judgment meet these dark realities of our world? And if so, how?

Jesus tackles each of these topics head-on in his famous teaching on the sheep and the goats, starting with the brutality of history.

THE BRUTALITY OF HISTORY

Jesus opens with the King arriving "in his glory. . . . All the nations will be gathered before him."[1] It is worth noting that Jesus is not depicted here as simply the leader of Israel or head of the church. He is the King of the world. *All* the nations are gathered before him.

Jesus is a "mighty King, lover of justice,"[2] and he comes to reconcile the nations. Not to weed out Jeremiah's tribe and pat all the white folks on the back, but rather to "bring justice to the nations,"[3] "[to lift] up a banner for the distant nations,"[4] as "the hope of all the ends of the earth."[5] All the beauty pageant queens are finally getting their wish: Jesus is coming to bring world peace.

The King first addresses the brutality of history. Like a shepherd sifting out the goats from the sheep, the King calls the sheep to one side and says to them:

> Come, you who are blessed by my Father; take your inheritance, the kingdom prepared for you since the creation of the world. For I was hungry and you gave me something to eat, I was thirsty and you gave me something to drink, I was a stranger and you invited me in, I needed clothes and you clothed me, I was sick and you looked after me, I was in prison and you came to visit me. . . .
>
> I tell you the truth, whatever you did for one of the least of these brothers of mine, you did for me.[6]

The King goes on to explain to the goats the beef he has with them: they did *not* do these things.

This is *revolutionary*: Jesus says how we treat "the least of these" is how we treat him. When a dictator tortures his people, he tortures *the Son of God*. When a CEO exploits her overseas workers, she exploits *the earth's rightful King*. When the priest raped Jeremiah, he was *raping Jesus*—the Judge of the world. Jesus confronts the brutality of history by identifying with the vulnerable, exploited, and abused.

Where We Find God

The most shocking part is not that Jesus says it's good to help the poor: you could find that teaching anywhere. The shocker is that Jesus *identifies himself* with the poor. He says, "This is where you find God!" This confronts us. Our tendency is to think God is most intimately found on the mountaintop, at the retreat center, in the peace and quiet of a serene vacation. We tend to think if we can just get away from the messiness of people, the distractions of society, the noise of urban chaos, we will find God.

The mountaintop has its place: rest, retreat, and Sabbath are important. God gives them as great gifts for us. But Jesus says this is not where his presence is most intimately found. If you want to find him, go to the slums. Go to the war zones. Go to the prisons. Strap your leg to Mother Teresa's and step with her into the weak, hurting, and ravaged places of our world.

This is where we find God.

I know of a family who moved from a wealthy neighborhood in the suburbs to a slum in the developing world, where the homes have cardboard walls, corrugated tin roofs, and sewage running down the street. When asked why they made such a radical move, they simply laughed and responded, "We just heard where Jesus was living and decided to move in next door!"

Fortunately, you don't have to go overseas to encounter Jesus in this way—Jesus' identification with the vulnerable shows up in a million different faces. My friend Jaime is a mom in our church who loves Jesus radically and has five of the most adorable kids I've ever met. She says she used to feel guilty when she heard this parable: she spent so much time caring for her children she didn't feel there was time left to do the things she thought Jesus was talking about, like feeding the homeless at a soup kitchen.

She was afraid her family was a distraction from God's calling to care for the vulnerable.

Then one day, Jaime had a realization: her kids came bouncing into the kitchen saying, "Mom, we're hungry! Can you make us something to eat?" She suddenly heard the voice of Jesus, crying out to her through her kids; if she didn't feed them, who would? Who else would clothe them from the cold or comfort them in their loneliness?

They were the vulnerable ones in her life; Jesus looked up to her through their faces.

She began to experience the presence of Jesus while caring for her children. She heard him in their voices, asking, "When I'm hungry, will you feed me? When I'm thirsty, will you give me something to drink? When I'm cold, will you clothe me? When I'm sick, will you take care of me? When I'm lonely, will you comfort me?"

Jesus identifies with the vulnerable. How we treat them is how we treat him. But this has a flip side. When a deadbeat dad walks away from his child, he walks away from Jesus. When the cheerleader overlooks the girl sitting alone at lunch, she overlooks the Savior of the world. When the rich man ignores Lazarus, he ignores the presence of God.

Blessing and Curse

Jesus is not teaching something new here. God's identification with the vulnerable is embedded in the foundation of the Old Testament. Out of all the mighty old empires, God chooses to reveal himself to the ancient world not through Egypt, Babylon, or Rome, but through a ragtag nation of weak and outcast slaves. When God calls Israel out of Egypt, they are "the last and the least," getting their butts kicked on the outskirts of the empire.

They are the abandoned child, the girl sitting alone at lunch, the Lazarus of the ancient world.

In the Exodus, God is painting a dramatic picture on an international canvas for the ancient world to see, a picture that says loud and clear: "This is who I am! How you treat them, my weak and wandering people, is how you treat me." As the nations look on, they are supposed to learn something crucial: how they treat the vulnerable matters.

God wants the world to know this is who he is and this is how he judges. When God calls Abraham out of Babylon's empire, he promises to accompany him on the journey and declares that the nations will be judged by how they treat his weak and wandering grandchildren: "I will bless those who bless you, and whoever curses you I will curse."[7] God identifies with the vulnerable, and it is a matter of blessing and of curse. Of judgment and salvation.

Jesus draws on this Old Testament language in the parable. He tells the sheep they are "blessed by my Father" and the goats they are "cursed." This is Abrahamic language: blessing and curse. Jesus is true Israel, and how we treat him is how we treat God. Those who have "blessed Jesus" by feeding the poor, clothing the shivering, and visiting the prisoners are blessed by God. Those who have "cursed Jesus" by ignoring the thirsty, avoiding the stranger, and steering clear of the sick are under the curse. Jesus' identification with the vulnerable of the world becomes central in determining how we stand before God.

How we treat the vulnerable matters. This is not optional. Not a matter of personal preference. It is a matter of blessing and curse. Of judgment and salvation. God wants the world to know this is who he is and this is how he judges.

The Cross of Christ

The cross of Christ is the climax of this revelation. Jesus' identification with the vulnerable is not a Hallmark card sent from a distant heaven, not a pious platitude trumpeted from afar, not a Band-Aid on the gaping wound of our world. The cross is where Jesus' identification with the vulnerable is made concrete. It is where the King of glory is made vulnerable: rejected, neglected, exploited, outcast, weak, and despised. The cross is where Jesus is made hungry, thirsty, lonely, naked, sick, and imprisoned.

The cross is where Jesus *lives* this parable, identified with the vulnerable in the blood and dirt of actual history. Jesus soaks the suffering, shame, and sin of the world into himself and absorbs its destructive power.

At the cross, the one through whom the world was made is himself unmade and God's presence is revealed in the God-forsakenness of our world. It is here that Jesus confronts the brutality of history in order to redeem it.

The cross is where our skeletons in the ground receive the skeleton of God's Son.

The cross becomes a signpost of blessing and of curse. Of judgment and salvation. Jesus has identified with the vulnerable of the world. How we treat him is how we treat God.

THE DECEPTION OF APPEARANCES

Jesus moves on to address the deception of appearances. Overwhelmed at the King's proclamation, the sheep say:

> Lord, when did we see you hungry and feed you, or thirsty and give you something to drink? When did we see you a stranger and invite you in, or needing clothes and clothe you? When did we see you sick or in prison and go to visit you?[8]

The goats are also shocked and similarly say, "When did we see you . . . and did not help you?"[9] Once again, as we've seen throughout the last few chapters, God's judgment is a surprise.

Pulling Back the Curtain

Check out three aspects of what's happening here. First, Jesus is simply calling things out as they really are. He is not turning sheep into goats or goats into sheep. This is not a magic show. Jesus is pulling back the curtain on the deception of appearances and revealing reality.

In the eyes of the community, the priest may look like an upstanding citizen (and maybe even thinks of himself as such), but when Jesus swings the closet door open and *his* skeletons come spilling out, he may very well find himself stammering before Jesus, "Lord, when did I molest you?"

At the ceremonial dinner, the CEO receiving a humanitarian-of-the-year award may look extremely generous (and maybe even thinks of herself as such), while across the ocean children in her Third World factory are working twelve hours a day to build her bank account. When Jesus unlocks the filing cabinet and pulls out the financial statements, she may very well find herself stuttering, "Lord, when did I exploit you?"

The husband may have been hiding the affair for years (and even thinking he was protecting his wife by keeping it a secret), while his faithful spouse wonders why he's been so distant and cold for so long, wondering if she is somehow at fault. When Jesus steps into the bedroom at the cheap hotel, the husband may very well find himself exposed, saying, "Lord, when did I cheat on you?"

The righteous may suffer while the wicked prosper. But not forever. At some point, the curtain comes up.

Tell Us Who We Are

The second thing to check out is this: both the sheep and the goats actually *need Jesus* to tell them who they are . . . and are surprised when he does. It's almost humorous, one of the passage's most striking features. I was once a shepherd and, believe me, telling goats apart from sheep is actually quite easy: The horns. The beards. The bigger size and bullying behavior. These are telltale signs.

It doesn't take a rocket scientist to see the difference.

But the goats don't seem to recognize they are goats and the sheep don't seem to recognize they are sheep until Jesus tells them. If someone were to tell me I was a six-foot-tall American with dark, curly hair, I would simply thank them for pointing out the obvious and move on. It would not be an occasion for surprise. But both the sheep and goats need the King to point out the obvious. They need Jesus to tell them who they are.

We need Jesus to tell us who we are.

Jesus knows us better than we know ourselves. I do not know whether or not Jeremiah will be in the kingdom, but I have hope. Jeremiah considered himself an enemy of Christianity, but he may be shocked to encounter Jesus as one who was with him all along, one who confronts the injustice he experienced at the hands of Jesus' people, one who welcomes him into the kingdom "prepared for [him] since the creation of the world."[10]

In the CEO's factory overseas, the woman whose husband left her on her own to eke out provision for their children in the impoverished Brazilian favela may not have looked like much through the eyes of Wall Street or her neighborhood, or even thought of herself as much. But she might find herself surprised to encounter Jesus and hear his voice call her his beloved, to hear him say, "Well done, my good and faithful servant," and to be welcomed to his feast as he sits her down as a guest of honor at his banqueting table.

The drug-addicted son whose mom brought him into the world strung out on heroin, whose stepdads beat him mercilessly as a kid, and who succumbed to the lie that he was worthless and eventually took his own life, may be surprised to encounter Jesus as the Resurrection and the Life who can raise his body from the grave, the Great Physician who can heal and make him whole, and the Son of God who can call him home to the Father he was made for.

We all need Jesus to tell us who we are.

Stalking Jesus

Finally, check out how Jesus "knowing you" is the basis of his judgment. Jesus welcomes the sheep because he "knew" them. The goats are called on the carpet because he "never knew" them. Somehow, Jesus knowing us is where our salvation is found. Our relation to him judges us.

Jesus is more than the judge. He is, in a strange way, himself the judgment. It is important to note: Jesus knowing you and you claiming to know Jesus are not the same thing. Jesus does not welcome the sheep because "you told everyone you knew me." And the goats seem surprised to find they were not as tight with Jesus as they thought. Elsewhere, Jesus says something similar:

> Many will say to me on that day, "Lord, Lord, did we not prophesy in your name and in your name drive out demons and in your name perform many miracles?" Then I will tell them plainly, "I never knew you. Away from me, you evildoers!"[11]

These many call Jesus "Lord" and can point to amazing things they have done in his name but, like the goats, Jesus says he never knew them.

There are goats hiding in the sheep pen. And some of them look very spiritual. I don't know many who can claim to have driven out demons or performed miracles. Jesus seems to be painting these goats not as apathetic wallflowers hiding on the periphery of his church, but as rock-star Christians and superhero evangelists at the center of the action.

So what does it mean for Jesus to "know" you?

When Jesus talks about *knowing*, he is talking about something much more than an abstract, intellectual, textbook knowledge. He is talking about deep, in-your-bones, relational knowledge. For example, imagine I come to you and say, "I've been dating this amazing girl! Let's grab coffee so I can tell you all about her." And you say, "Great! Tell me all about her."

As we sit down, I start to explain, "Well, every morning she leaves her house around 7:30 a.m. and hits Barista for some coffee. She reads and journals for a little while, then around 8:30 a.m. rides her bike over the bridge to her job at Sincerely Truman. She usually wraps up around 5 p.m. and heads back home, stopping by New Seasons to pick up some groceries for dinner."

"That's great," you tell me. "What's her name?"

"I'm not sure," I respond.

You would probably say, "You're not dating her . . . *you're stalking her!*"[12]

Many people are stalking Jesus. They have *intellectual* knowledge about Jesus, but not *relational* knowledge. They may have theology degrees, know Greek words, and be able to wax eloquent on the "trinitarian perichoresis of the eschatological parousia." But do they *know* Jesus? That is the real question.

There is a difference between being able to point Jesus out from a distance and knowing him up close. Paul says we can give everything we have to the poor, speak powerfully about God, and go to the stake as a martyr, but if we have not love, Jesus-shaped love, then we are simply showing off and bankrupt.[13]

When Jesus talks about "knowing," this is blood-and-guts, relational, in-your-bones knowledge. Jesus wants to know us deeply: Do we want to be known like this?

And it is also important to note: Jesus appears to know many who didn't know him. The sheep are in shock as they say, "Lord, when did we see you?" But apparently Jesus has known them all along. Elsewhere, Jesus tells his disciples something similar:

> I have other sheep that are not of this sheep pen. I must bring them also. They too will listen to my voice, and there shall be one flock and one shepherd.[14]

Jesus says he *has* other sheep: they are his. Even though they apparently haven't met him yet. They are currently outside the pen: outside the visible boundaries that distinguish the people of God from the world-at-large. But he knows them: he *has* them. And they will hear his voice when he calls. Jesus will gather them into the people of God.

Jesus knowing you is more important than you claiming to know Jesus.

THE BONDAGE OF CREATION

Finally, Jesus wraps up addressing the bondage of creation:

> Then the King will say to those on his right, "Come, you who are blessed by my Father; take your inheritance, the kingdom prepared for you since the creation of the world. . . ."
> Then he will say to those on his left, "Depart from me, you who are cursed, into the eternal fire prepared for the devil and his angels."[15]

Notice three features of what Jesus says here. First, he contrasts *when* these places were prepared. While the kingdom has been prepared "since the creation of the world," Jesus gives no such designation for the fire. This reminds us of the point made in chapter 1: God creates heaven and earth—and creates them good. God does not create "heaven, earth . . . and hell." The destructive wildfire of hell is an intruder in God's good world; it holds creation in bondage.

But it does not have the last word. A place has been prepared for it—outside God's kingdom.

God's kingdom exists *for* creation. It's a party that's been planned "since the creation of the world." It's a party that celebrates the world's renovation. God's kingdom reclaims creation from the destructive wildfire of sin and floods it with the glory of God.

Second, Jesus contrasts *who* these places were prepared for. God's kingdom is prepared for "you who are blessed." We might assume, then, that the fire is inversely prepared for those who are cursed; but no such designation is given. Jesus tells us the fire is prepared not for people, but "for the devil and his angels"—the dark spiritual powers that lit the match in the first place . . . and wreak havoc on our world.

This confronts our popular cartoons, where little red devils poke you with pitchforks and laugh at you on into eternity. Jesus tells us this is not a place where Satan reigns; it is a place where he meets his destruction. Where his agenda is contained. Where sin's wildfire is bound with the arsonist who first lit the match.

God's kingdom is made for people. Its city gates are wide open to all who will receive his embrace. But the coming of the kingdom kicks out the destructive powers that want to rule the earth without God. We must choose whom we will serve.

Third, Jesus contrasts *who* blesses and curses. The sheep are blessed "by my Father." We might assume, then, that the goats are inversely cursed by the Father; but no such thing is said. Jesus simply says they are cursed. Like the rich man clutching his greed in the rubble of his riches while heaven calls him "son." Like the wedding crasher refusing wedding clothes while the King calls him "friend." Like the older brother weeping and gnashing his teeth in the backyard while the Father invites him inside to join the prodigal's party.

God blesses; we curse. The Father is good; we want to be left alone. The Light shines brightly; we prefer darkness. Ultimately, we are judged not for our failure to successfully wrap our hands around

God's arm, but rather for our stubborn refusal to be grasped by him, our incessant prying of his fingers from our recalcitrant hearts.

God redeems his world; our destructive power is cast outside.

God's kingdom is established; the wildfire is banished.

God brings an end to the bondage of creation.

LOVE AND JUSTICE

God's love and justice are not opposed to each other; they are integrally intertwined. The Father's love for his world gives rise to his justice for the world. As Jesus shows us in his parable of the sheep and goats, when we abuse and exploit those he loves, we abuse and exploit him. We do violence to God. God gets angry at injustice *because* he loves the world.

This confronts the popular misperception that God's love and justice are *opposed* to each other. Some people think God is bipolar, waking up some days "all about love": a happy hippie spinning through the fields, smelling the flowers and saying, "Isn't life so great! You're all so beautiful!" And then there are his bad days, when he wakes up on the wrong side of the bed "all about justice": a cold and angry warrior who rolls down the street, sword in hand, yelling, "Look out! I'm going to kill you all!"

If we think God's love and justice are schizophrenic, it probably means we have a distorted understanding of both.

Lover of Justice

God loves justice. God is a "mighty King, lover of justice!"[16] He shouts from the rooftops through Isaiah, "I, the LORD, love justice!"[17] Nicholas Wolterstorff observes that God's justice is oriented toward human flourishing. It arises from a vision of God's love permeating the human community and the created order:

> God loves the presence of justice in society not because it makes for
> a society whose excellence God admires, but because God loves the

members of society—loves them . . . with the love of benevolent desire. God desires that each and every human being shall flourish, what the Old Testament writers call *shalom*. That is why God loves justice. God desires the flourishing of each and every one of God's human creatures; justice is indispensable to that. Love and justice are not pitted against each other but intertwined.[18]

As Wolterstorff observes, God's love and justice are not opposites in tension, but two sides of the same coin. They are not discordant chords from separate songs, but harmonious movements within the same symphony.

God loves people. And because God loves people, there are good ways to treat each other and bad ways to treat each other. Because Jesus loves you and wants you to flourish, if I abuse, exploit, or cheat you, I do not treat you in the way you deserve as someone who is loved by Jesus. If I malign, molest, or murder you, I violate you as an object of God's affection. I do violence to the dignity you bear as someone the Creator has created in his image and loves deeply.

I commit an injustice against you.

Do we treat one another as those loved by God? God loves your child—so when you abuse your child, God stands with your child and against you, receiving the blows as your fists rain down. God loves that woman at the party—so when you rape her, God stands with her and against you; as you violate her with your lust, you rape God. God loves your employees—so when you skimp on their pay in order to enrich yourself, God stands with their struggling families and against you; as you enrich yourself you cheat God.

God stands against our injustice because he identifies in love with those we violate.

God's love is more than a comfort; it is a confrontation.

God's love has teeth.

Injustice violates God's love for the world. This is why, in the biblical vision, injustice is not limited to degrading others, but includes degrading ourselves. When we demean ourselves (through degrading behaviors such as sexual promiscuity, gluttonous eating, or drug abuse), we violate ourselves as an object of God's affection. We do violence to God's purposes for our flourishing. Our self-abuse is treason against God—suicide is only its most extreme form.

We live in myriad ways that proclaim our refusal of faith in God's sovereign love for us, that declare our unwillingness to believe that God accepts us in Christ, that do violence loudly against God's purposes for our well-being and flourishing.

This is also why Augustine made the bold claim that there can be no fully just city, no true res publica, where God is not honored as God. Idolatry and religious hypocrisy are injustice against God, a failure to treat God as his worth requires. And to not honor God as God is to attack the center in which the world's *shalom* is grounded, to fly a hijacked plane into the temple where heaven and earth meet, to swing a hammer against the foundation upon which God's city for the world is built.

Injustice is a violation of God's love for the world. *Because* he loves the world, he loves justice.

The Crucified King

The irony is this: we are all both victim and victimizer; abuser and abused; sinner and sinned against. We have all hurt others and been hurt ourselves. Each of us has both wounded and been wounded. None of us can play a trump card. "All have sinned and fall[en] short of the glory of God."[19] I have shared Jeremiah's story to highlight one abused, but I know Jeremiah well enough to know he too has abused and victimized others in his own ways. Just like the rest of us, as sinful as the best of us.

And, for us all, this must be overcome if we are to inherit the kingdom. In our world torn apart by sin, what will we do? Where will we turn to?

Jesus is our crucified King. His cross is the place where love and justice meet. At the cross, we are revealed as *loved sinners*.[20] The Crucified One *bears our sin* as victimizers: as those who have perpetrated injustice against his *shalom* for the world and stand in need of redemption. The Murdered Son *identifies with* us as victims: as those who have been torn apart by our violent, sin-struck, war-torn world. Jesus both reveals the justice of God against our sin and bears that justice on our behalf, revealing God's unsurpassable love for us.

The crucified King reveals on the cross that we are more sinful than we ever could have imagined and more loved than we ever dared dream.[21]

Jesus' arms outstretched on the cross embrace a world immersed in injustice. So we can celebrate together what we saw earlier: his question to us is not, "Are you good enough to get into my kingdom?" but rather, "Will you let me heal you?"

Jesus is the Servant at the center of the world. To love Jesus is to give our lives away sacrificially for the flourishing of his world. As the crucified King, Jesus wants to form those of us who follow him into a community of love and justice. A people who fall in love with the world he loves and in the process, become dramatically enraged alongside him at the injustices that afflict it. To become a community of love that gives rise to justice.

A community of the crucified King.

CHAPTER 10 KEY IDEA

DOES JESUS' JUDGMENT MEET THE DEEPEST NEEDS OF OUR WORLD?

Yes, it addresses the brutality of history, the deception of appearances, and the bondage of creation. Jesus' judgment of the world arises from his love for the world.

INTERLUDE

THE SOVEREIGNTY OF CHRIST

Do we get a second chance? The question often arises: "Can I reject God now but change my mind on the threshold of his kingdom?" To ask the question this way, however, is misleading: it reveals that we probably don't actually *want* the kingdom. If we prefer freedom from God *now*, what makes us think we'll change our mind when his kingdom comes? If we harden our hearts toward his presence today, why would we expect tomorrow to be different?

We are becoming the kind of people we will be for eternity. We are growing into ourselves, so to speak. To live my life for myself today knowing there will always be another chance for grace, another opportunity for mercy, before a God whose generous love is limitless, is to reveal that I *prefer* to live life for myself. To see repentant submission to the kingdom as a chore to be postponed rather than a joy to be entered into is to anticipate in one's decision the decision that is coming. To be a person who, in the face of the radical mercy of Jesus, desires independence from God today, is probably to give myself away as one who will be revealed as such on Judgment Day.

God's judgment is a surprise not because we change our minds, but because Jesus tells us who we are. Not because of our fickleness, but because of his sovereignty.

If sin is like an addiction, then postponing grace but expecting God's city is like injecting more and more of the heroin into your veins as a way to get to rehab—you're moving in the opposite direction of the place you claim to want to get to. If sin is like a compass, then rejecting God now but anticipating his kingdom is like setting out with our sights on the depths of the Grand Canyon, but expecting to arrive at the heights of the Himalaya. The deeper in we go, the harder our hearts become.

God is love, but his love is too magnificent to be mocked. "People look at the outward appearance, but the LORD looks at the heart," we are told in 1 Samuel 16:7. God knows the depths of our hearts, our deepest motives, the inner recesses of our being. We cannot take the gifts without the Giver; the kingdom without receiving the King.

If we think we can win Jesus over with an insincere form of flattery, like a rascal who stops hitting his mother and suddenly changes his tune to, "Mommy, I love you!" when he sees ice cream on the table, we are simply revealing our own duplicity. We have another thing coming.

God's arrival is hope for the world, in part, because he is not manipulated by our showy pretension, deceived by our superficial facades, or mocked by our vain spirituality. God is not so easily duped. His judgment is not a surprise because we are fickle.

God's judgment is a surprise because of the sovereignty of Christ.

11.

RECONCILIATION AS JUDGMENT

THE WORLD RELIGIONS

Does Jesus hate people of other religions? Will Muslims, Hindus, and Buddhists walk up to the pearly gates, eager to worship God, only to hear God say, "Sorry! I want to let you in, but my hands are tied. You checked the wrong box on the 'Which religion are you?' questionnaire. I'm unfortunately unable to let you in"? What does the coming of God's kingdom mean for those of other faiths?

There are two bad answers to this question. First, on one side of the spectrum, some people scandalize the gospel by denigrating the achievements of the world religions and dehumanizing their followers. We make the mistake of pretending we are fully in the light and they are fully in the dark. We dismiss their positive historical contributions to the life of the world and discount their constructive future potential in the shaping of our shared world.

This is wrong.

When we dehumanize them, Jesus himself stands against us. Where we have done this, repentance is called for. Jesus calls us to humble ourselves before followers of other religions as those created in the image of God. They are part of civilizations whose cultural achievements are often monumental and extraordinary. They have frequently stood sacrificially and given generously for justice, mercy, and other movements central to the heart of God.

Jesus is the Light that gives light to the world, and when we see his light reflected in the lives of others, even those who do not know him, we can rejoice. We can celebrate their achievements in areas where we have common ground, like justice and mercy, and work together toward the flourishing of God's world. And we can hold out hope, knowing that God's kingdom is *for* them and that Jesus' judgment will be a surprise that reconciles the nations and gathers all who will come to worship God in his holy city.

In my experience, however, most people today don't struggle with denigrating followers of other religions. Much more prominent is the other swing of the spectrum. On the other side, many today assume that it is, of course, the most devout Muslims, the most ascetic Hindus, and the most compassionate Buddhists who will go running boldly into Christ's kingdom when he arrives. We make the mistake of confidently declaring that the farther down you are on whatever particular path you're on, the greater you are in the eyes of God. We assume the more rigorous you are within your respective religious tradition, the more Jesus loves you and is on your side.

The problem with this is, of course, it is not the way the gospel works.

The most religious folks often have the hardest time with Jesus. When God's kingdom breaks in, it is the prostitutes, prodigals, tax collectors, and "sinners" who are running into the center of the celebration, while the devout Pharisees and older brothers are out sulking in the backyard. When the scandal of grace explodes on the scene, it is the redeemed criminals who are dancing with Jesus at the center of the party, while the moral majority and upstanding citizens are outside weeping and gnashing their teeth.

Religion is not the basis by which Jesus judges the world.

So how does Jesus' judgment relate to the world religions? I would suggest that Jesus' parable of the prodigal son can light our way.

A TALE OF TWO BROTHERS

The parable of the prodigal son is a story of a father and two brothers. As we have seen throughout Jesus' teaching, it is once again a story of surprise. As the parable opens, the younger son takes his father's money, gives him the finger, and runs to a distant land to squander dad's hard-earned cash on liquor and prostitutes in orgiastic binges.

He is a "bad" son: a picture of the immoral outlaw.

He is a "sinner" who's stained the family name.

He is "irreligious."

The older brother, meanwhile, takes the high road. He stays at home, works hard at the family business, and serves his father. He's obedient, respected by his peers, and a constructive contributor to the life of the community. Maybe someday he'll run for office.

He is a "good" son: a picture of the moral, upstanding citizen.

He is "respectable," and everyone looking on knows it.

He is "religious."

If you were to ask the townsfolk which son was destined for reward and which for punishment, the answer would seem obvious. But would be wrong.

Welcome Home

Fast-forward to the end of the story. The younger son leaves his lawless ways behind, receives his father's embrace, and is welcomed home. Dad's been waiting expectantly for him, looking out on the horizon for any sign of his return, and runs to embrace him upon first sight of his coming. Dad welcomes him home, dresses him like royalty, slaughters the fattened calf, and pops open the best bottles of wine to throw the biggest party the town has ever seen, "For this son of mine was dead and is alive again; he was lost and is found."[1]

The "irreligious" son winds up at the center of the celebration.

Jesus told this story partly as a defense of his own ministry, in which the prodigals and prostitutes, the "sinners" and tax collectors, were coming home, receiving the Father's transforming embrace and entering the kingdom. When Jesus shows up, "sinners" become "saints," transformed by the grace of God.

Often to the chagrin of the local religious authorities.

The Backyard

There are two big shockers in Jesus' parable. The first big shocker is this: the *irreligious* outlaw winds up at the center of the kingdom party. This was a scandal to Jesus' original audience and, as we shall see in a minute, is also a scandal to us today.

The second big shocker is, it is the *religious* son, the good, upright, obedient one, respected and admired by the community, who actually winds up weeping and gnashing his teeth outside the party. The father goes out and finds his older son sulking in the backyard, angry at all the attention his irresponsible younger brother is receiving. The father tries to coax him into the house to join the party, but the religious son refuses to enter the festivities:

> His father went out and pleaded with him. But he answered his father, "Look! All these years I've been slaving for you and never disobeyed your orders. Yet you never gave me even a young goat so I could celebrate with my friends. But when this son of yours who has squandered your property with prostitutes comes home, you kill the fattened calf for him!"
>
> "My son," the father said, "you are always with me, and everything I have is yours. But we had to celebrate and be glad, because this brother of yours was dead and is alive again; he was lost and is found."[2]

The father wants the religious son inside, but his son prefers it in the backyard.

In this short passage, Jesus reveals two ways religion can destroy our souls. First, it can destroy the way we look at God. The religious son looks to dad as a slaveholder rather than a good father: "All these years I've been slaving for you . . ." He sees his dad not as a close friend, but a mean boss. Ironically, he's been close to home geographically, but far, far away in his heart. His religious obedience has kept him distant from the overflowing graciousness of his loving father.

Externally he's been close, but inside he's been on his own little island.

His father, however, does not call him "slave," "worker," or "grunt," but rather "my son." His dad calls him not by his works, but by their relationship: "My son, you are always with me, and everything I have is yours." The father rejects his son's distorted perception of their relationship and calls him to intimacy. He looks upon his religious son with filial devotion and care.

The second way Jesus says religion can destroy our soul is by the way we look at others. The religious son does not call the prodigal "my brother," but rather "this son of yours." When I would get in trouble as a kid, I remember my mom would jokingly tell my dad, "You'll never believe what *this son of yours* did!" It was a way of distancing relationship. I was no longer "my boy," but rather "your son." Only, my mom was joking; the older brother here is clearly not.

The religious son is distancing himself from his brother.

He not only distances himself *from* his brother, he also elevates himself *over* his brother. He reminds dad which one's been upholding the family name. Which one's been taking care of the farmstead. Which one's been contributing to the community. He lifts up his great track record ("all these years I've been slaving for you") in comparison to his brother's illicit track record (he "squandered your property with prostitutes.")

The religious son lifts himself up . . . by pushing his brother down.

And yet, the father rejects this power play. He calls the outlaw "this brother of yours." He insists on reaffirming their family relationship. He refuses to identify the prodigal by his past behavior and instead reaffirms his present identity: "[he] was dead and is alive again; he was lost and is found."

Dad rejects the religious son's rejection of his brother.

The father is *for* both sons. But he refuses the religious son's exalting of himself over his outlaw brother. Tragically, the older son clings to his pride, refuses this reality, and remains sulking in the backyard.

The Pride Inside

Jesus paints us a picture of a religious person in hell. The story ends with the older brother outside in the darkness, refusing the invitation to the party, weeping and gnashing his teeth in the backyard. His location in the backyard outside the father's house runs parallel to Gehenna's location in Jerusalem's backyard outside the city (chapter 3). Inside the Father's house is the great feast, the party of the year, the redemption celebration with the least likely guests of honor. Outside the Father's house is the destructive isolation, the sense of entitlement for one's good behavior, the clinging to the old world and rejection of the new world God has made.

Inside are the lights and laughter that mark the communion of grace. Outside are the darkness and tears that mark the vanquished self-reliance of sin.

Inside is the presence of the Father.

Outside is the presence of the self.

Jesus' picture here runs strikingly parallel with the rich man from the Lazarus parable, Jesus' most famous teaching on hell (chapter 6). There, the rich man gives himself to his greed; here, the religious son gives himself to his pride. Both refuse to give up the idols that have come to identify them. Both are called "son." Both refuse God's posture of embrace in preference for their self-chosen identity. There, the rich man still treats Lazarus like a slave; here the religious son still treats his brother like an outlaw. Both refuse the great redemption God has accomplished.

Riches and religion can keep you outside the kingdom.

What keeps the religious son outside the party is not the father's refusal to let him in. He is kept outside by his own refusal to repent of his sin and self-righteousness, to let go of the pride inside his heart, to loosen his kung fu grip on the idol of himself. While the father beckons him into the party, "pleads with him" to come inside, the son prefers the backyard. He is kept outside the party by his religion.

He is a slave to the sin he refuses to let go of.

A captive to his own self-righteousness.

He is bound by his religion.

THE THING ITSELF

So what does this mean for the world religions? I would propose the following: God's reconciliation of the world *is itself* a judgment on our religion. Let me explain. In Jesus' parable, the father's reconciliation of the outlaw son *is itself* what judges the pride and self-righteousness of the religious son. The father is not "out to get" the religious son, in a mean-spirited or vindictive sense. But the father *is* out to reconcile— the reconciliation of the outlaw son and the rejection of the religious son are not two separate plotlines, not two disconnected movements. They are integrally intertwined, two sides of the same coin.

The father's reconciliation *is itself* a judgment on the older son.

The religious brother is judged *by the thing itself.*

Reconciliation is a judgment.

God is on a mission, as we have seen throughout this book, to reconcile the world. That is, to reconcile heaven and earth: what we might call the *vertical* dimension of God and humanity, transcendence and immanence, all of creation. God is on a mission to reconcile east and west: the *horizontal* dimension of the human community, the nations of the world, the global social body. He is on a mission to reconcile good folks and bad folks: the *ethical* dimension of moralists and murderers, Pharisees and philanderers, the legalist and the lawless. God is on a mission to reconcile weak and strong: the *power* dimension of kings and slaves, the bullies and the battered, the president and the powerless.

We might call God's mission the Reconciliation Project.

God is *all about* reconciliation.

God's reconciliation *is itself*, I would suggest, a lens through which to understand his judgment on the world religions. We have seen this in Jesus' parable: God's desire to bring together good folks and bad folks (the *ethical* dimension) judges our pride and self-righteousness—symbolized by the older brother's rejection. Let's see what this might look like with a few other examples.

Heaven and Earth: Buddhism

God's reconciliation of heaven and earth *is itself* a judgment on the Buddhist concept of nirvana. As we have seen, God is on a mission to reconcile heaven and earth; Jesus will redeem creation from the destructive power of sin and flood the world with the glorious presence of his Spirit. God does not pull us out of this world or abandon it; he is out to redeem it.

Our world is destined for restoration.

Heaven and earth's reconciliation confronts, by its very nature, the Buddhist concept of nirvana as an otherworldly, or even anti-worldly, goal of redemption.[3] The Buddhist who distances herself from the physical, material world that God has made, in order to flee the cycle of suffering our world is bound up in, finds her escape confronted by God's coming reconciliation of heaven and earth.

God's new creation is a very different goal of redemption from that of nirvana. Gautama Buddha, for example, is quoted as saying of nirvana:

> There is that dimension where there is neither earth, nor water, nor fire, nor wind . . . neither this world, nor the next world, nor sun, nor moon. And there, I say, there is neither coming, nor going, nor stasis; neither passing away nor arising: without stance, without foundation, without support. This, just this, is the end of stress.[4]

Nirvana is depicted as a place *outside* creation: where there is no physical or material substance, no elements of the earth, no dancing or drinking, no emotion or movement, no sun or light.

The goal of salvation ("the end of stress") is to get there.

When set in contrast to God's redeemed world, nirvana starts to look a lot like the darkness outside the new creation. A lot like the aftermath of the "anti-creation." Nirvana starts to look an awful lot like hell.

While God opens his kingdom gates wide for the person in Buddhism, nirvana and its pursuit must be left at the door. The extinction of desire stands in stark contrast to the redemption of desire. The annihilation of personhood stands in stark contrast to the fulfillment of personhood. The extraction of oneself *from* God's creation stands in stark contrast to one's restored communion *within* God's creation.

God is *for* the Buddhist: they are image-bearers he beckons as daughters and sons to receive his mercy and enter the feast of his kingdom. But there are central aspects of Buddhism that must, by their very nature, be checked at the door. And it is not far-fetched to imagine some clinging to their religious ideals that have shaped their identity (similar to the rich man clinging to his riches against Lazarus, or the religious son clinging to his religion against the prodigal), preferring the pursuit of nirvana over receiving the reconciled creation of God.

This does not mean that God's grace is not big enough to encompass the Buddhist in the midst of a misdirected pursuit (the Christian must declare that God's grace has encompassed us as well in the midst of our misdirected pursuits). Or that there are not good reasons for a Buddhist's desire to escape the suffering of a corrupted world (we ourselves have all too often responded to suffering by settling for an otherworldly vision of salvation). Or that there are not good insights Buddhism has to offer the world (such as digging beneath the surface to see the destructive desires and affections that often drive our unhealthy behaviors).

But it is to say that in order to receive God's reconciliation of heaven and earth, there is something central to the heart of Buddhism that must be let go of. Jesus is not "out to get" Buddhists in a mean-spirited or vindictive sense, but Jesus is out to reconcile heaven and earth. And Jesus' reconciliation judges, by its very nature, all other-worldly visions of salvation and calls those who pursue them to turn and receive the kingdom.

Jesus' reconciliation of heaven and earth is itself a judgment on nirvana.

Weak and Strong: Hinduism

The way God reconciles weak and strong *is itself,* by its very nature, a judgment on the Hindu concept of karma. As we have seen, God identifies with the vulnerable, exploited, and outcast of our world. Jesus declares how we treat them is how we treat him. The King of all the earth is made weak on the cross, giving his life sacrificially for the weak as well as the strong, to gather them together in his kingdom.

God is with the weak. God is for the weak. God works through the weak to reconcile the world.

Karma, in contrast, starts with cause and effect. Our good actions will eventually give rise, like a boomerang come back to visit us, to future good experiences. Our evil deeds, on the other hand, will give rise to future suffering—even if in another life. Renowned Hindu scholar Pandurang Vaman Kane remarks on karma in the classic Dharmasastras texts:

> A good action has its reward and a bad action leads to retribution.
> If the bad actions do not yield their consequences in this life, the
> soul begins another existence and in the new environment under-
> goes suffering for its past deeds.[5]

Those with bad karma must undergo suffering for past wicked-ness in order to move closer toward salvation, or *moksha,* from the cycle of death and rebirth.

Social status is related to one's karma.[6] Upward social mobility is held out, like a carrot on a stick, as reward for merit in a future reincarnation, while downward social mobility is seen as punishment. Hindu texts frequently warn how wicked behavior can lead to rebirth as a weaker lower-caste person or even an animal.[7] One's ultimate goal is not simply to attain a higher social position, but rather to move closer to exiting the cycle of death and rebirth as a whole.

Jesus confronts the idea that the weak, poor, and outcast are farther from God and more distant from salvation than the strong. God is with the bruised, beat-up, and broken of our world in Jesus, declaring that how we treat them is how we treat him. God is downwardly mobile in Jesus, entering into our sin, suffering, and shame in order to gather humanity to himself. God approaches our world in and through the weak.

We do not climb to salvation by exiting the cycle of rebirth, suffering, and death. Salvation descends to us in the Son of God who is born, suffers, and dies—to reconcile weak and strong.

God's reconciliation confronts the caste system so prominent in Hindu societies (and similar systems throughout our world).[8] God's presence with the vulnerable challenges, by its very nature, any religious system that supports the segregation, marginalization, and oppression of people based on their wealth and class, that glories in the rich man while firmly pressing its boot on the neck of Lazarus, that uses the power of the violent gods to provide "spiritual" justification for this treason against God's compassion for his hurting children.

The gates of God's kingdom are wide open for the person in Hinduism, but in order to enter the party, something significant must be left at the door. God's party is a place where the outcast are given the best seats in the house, where the hungry are welcomed to the head of the dining table, where the last become first and the first become last. To receive God's new world, one must let go of caste status to encounter God in the face of the poor. One must give up karmic merit and receive the grace of God in the presence of the rejected, crucified, outcast Messiah.

God is *for* the Hindu: Jesus welcomes them into his city. The Great Physician extends his embrace with the healing the cross has made possible. But there are idols that must be left at the door. And it is not far-fetched to imagine some will be scandalized by the sick, the blind, and the poor who are dancing it up with Jesus at the center of the party, while they are offered a seat farther back.

This does not mean that Hindus have not frequently displayed extraordinary courage and compassion (that can put many of us who bear Jesus' name to shame). Or that other religious systems have not also been used oppressively (Christianity has at times been misused to justify slavery, genocide, and exploitation). Or that God's grace is not big enough to encompass the Hindu in the midst of what are often illusory and idolatrous assumptions (the Christian must declare that God's grace has encompassed us as well when we've made things ultimate other than God.

But it is to say that if we are to receive God's reconciliation of weak and strong, then things like karmic merit, caste status, and the bloodthirsty gods upholding the system must be left at the door of the kingdom. God has banished these gods and the system they justify in order to protect the beauty of the new world he will accomplish in Jesus.

Jesus' reconciliation of weak and strong is itself a judgment on karma and the caste system.

East and West: Islam

The way God reconciles east and west *is itself*, by its very nature, a scandal to Islam. As we have seen, God is on a mission to reconcile the nations: to heal the human social body from the destructive power of sin. That God's reconciliation occurs in and through Jesus is a scandal to Islam. Jesus is more than a prophet; he is the atoning Lamb through whom the nations are brought back to God. He is the sovereign King God has exalted with "all authority in heaven and on earth" in order to restore the world.[9]

Jesus is the Savior who reconciles the nations.

Jesus' reconciliation is so powerful, in part, because he is himself the Word of God through whom the world was made. For Islam, however, this eternal Word is reserved for the Quran. This gives rise to a major question dividing Islam and Christianity: Do we encounter

God most fully in the person of Jesus or the book of the Quran? In the words of Islamic scholar Daniel W. Brown, the question is:

> Whether the character of God is most clearly revealed in [Jesus'] perfect life culminating in redemptive death or in [the Quran's] perfect book giving rise to a perfect life. . . . Is the eternal Word ultimately revealed in flesh or in sounds and letters, on a cross or in a perfect law, in suffering or in success?[10]

As Brown's quote highlights, the scandal for Islam is more than simply *who* reconciles the world (Jesus), but also *how* he reconciles the world: through his redemptive death on the cross.

Celebrated Islamic scholar Kenneth Cragg suggests that the primary distinction between Islam and Christianity lies in this notion of suffering versus success.[11] While Muhammad enters Mecca successful in victory with sword in hand, Jesus enters Jerusalem on a donkey going willingly to his rejection, suffering, and death on the cross. Unlike Muhammad,

> [Jesus makes] no triumphal entry into a capitulating Mecca . . . Muhammad's more "effective" destiny is further seen as indicating his "finality" as "the seal of the prophets."[12]

While Jesus is respected in Islam, it is with nowhere near the prominence awarded Muhammad—and this is at least in part due to the nature of Muhammad's victory.

Suffering versus success. Many forms of Islam deny for this reason that Jesus actually died on the cross, arguing that God raptured him to heaven because a true prophet could not die such a shameful death.

For the gospel, in contrast, Jesus' suffering and death is not a problem to be avoided, but rather the center through which God redeems the world. East and west will ultimately be united not *under* sharia law but *through* the sacrificial power of Jesus' love. At the center of God's kingdom is not a prophet with a sword, but a Lamb once slain.[13] Jesus establishes his kingdom not through the love of power, but through the power of love: his self-giving enemy love that lays his life down for his enemies as we destroy him on the cross.

Jesus is *for* Muslims: they are beloved by God and invited into his kingdom. But at the center of the kingdom is Jesus, the King who invites them in. Islam rightly declares the world's need to submit to God's reign, but is challenged by the fact that Jesus is the one through whom God exercises this reign. Islam is right to exalt the holiness of God, but is challenged by the fact that this holy God is most profoundly revealed in the face of Jesus. God opens the gates of his kingdom wide for the person in Islam, but because Jesus is the King at the center of the city, lesser views of Jesus must be left at the door.

This does not mean that Christians are better than Muslims (whose integrity, honor, and devotion often put those of us who bear Jesus' name to shame). Or that God's grace is not big enough to encompass the Muslim in the midst of a reduced perception of Jesus (the Christian must declare that God's grace has encompassed us as well in our reduced perceptions of Jesus). Or that our seats at the feast are booked while theirs are denied (Jesus calls us to *expect* surprise on that day when he gathers the vast multitudes in from the nations to feast in his kingdom).

But it is to say that in order to receive Jesus' reconciled world, there is something central to the heart of Islamic belief that must be left behind: its view of Jesus.

THE DEATH OF IDEOLOGY

God's reconciliation *is itself* a judgment. It is not that God is "out to get" religious folks in a mean-spirited or vindictive way. But God is "out to get" his world in a positive way—and it is these good and glorious purposes of God for his world that give rise to his judgment upon the lesser things we settle for. Religion can be the very thing that binds us, keeps us, holds us captive, from receiving the better things God freely offers. And when this happens . . .

God's reconciliation is itself a judgment on the world religions.

Stopping there, however, is way too easy. Critiquing religion is in many quarters today simply preaching to the choir for cheap applause. There was perhaps a day when "religion" was considered the *good* side of the ethical spectrum and indifference to religion the *bad*. But the tables have turned.

Today, religion is often condemned as the new evil. It is seen to promote violence, irrationality, and sectarianism. Antireligion has become itself a new sort of religion. The growing popularity of authors from the "New Atheist" movement, like Richard Dawkins, Sam Harris, and the late Christopher Hitchens, speaks to a growing proselytizing atheism in the West that preaches the supposedly good news of a world without God.

New Atheism is merely antireligion's most extreme form, and it rides a deeper undercurrent of apathy in the West that increasingly considers religion irrelevant at best, and dangerous at worst.[14] It is all too easy today for the world's elite to mock the "naivete" of common religious folk. Ignoring or despising religion has become itself a marker of the "good": a benchmark of moral respectability and social righteousness in many quarters.

Jesus will judge this religion too.

Modern Religion

Where I live, being considered "good" has little to nothing to do with institutional religion. The social benchmarks for moral applause have more to do with whether one eats organic, rides his or her bike to work, and supports a humanitarian initiative in Africa. Things like these—even if *good* things that contribute to the flourishing of our world, in a manner similar to many traditional religious works—comprise our contemporary bars of righteousness by which one's social capital is improved.

In corporate culture, these bars may have more to do with how much money we've made or the size of our portfolio. In political culture, how much power we've attained or the heights up the ladder we've climbed. In popular culture, how much sex we've had or the number of Twitter followers who are interested in what we have to say. The cultural decline of institutional religion has simply meant the relocation, not the destruction, of social norms through which we pursue personal justification and social acceptance for our existence.

As Bob Dylan prophetically observed, "You're gonna have to serve somebody,"[15] and in the modern global culture of our world, the traditional gods of sex, money, and power still reign. They may have been stripped of the various gods and goddesses they were tradition-ally associated with (I don't know many today who would say they worship Aphrodite, Mammon, or Baal), but the idols are perhaps all the more seductive given their illusion of neutrality.

Sex, money, and power are still the popular idols of our day. They still have their prophets: Freud (sex), Marx (money), and Nietzsche (power) being the classic representatives. And our culture is flooded with the ghastly remnants of those who have handed over their person-hood in sacrificial devotion to their reign. The decline of institutional religion has not entailed the banishment of the gods.

Consumerism is perhaps the number-one religion in America today. Our shopping malls have become the new shrines, the public places of devotion where our culture gathers in search of salvation.[16] We identify ourselves through the fashions we wear, the music we listen to, the cars we drive. Our primary priesthood is a mixture of corporations, advertisers, and political machinations that mediate transcendence for us through the global market. Community has been replaced by affinity as we congregate with those who share our age range, cultural tastes, and socioeconomic bracket.

Religious devotion is not dead in the West; it has merely migrated toward a new center.

Ideology as Idolatry

This highlights a deeper problem: the word *religion* itself is a noto-riously complex animal to pin down. In the study of world religions, top scholars agree the very *concept* of religion is a category of thought unique to the modern West that is difficult, if not impossible, to define.[17] We all have a strong sense that we just *know* what religion is.

But attempting to articulate it is another matter.

Imagine, for example, the following ideologies shuffling into a police lineup for identification: capitalism, Buddhism, communism, Islam, nationalism, Christianity, environmentalism, Confucianism, agnosticism. At first glance, most of us probably *think* we know which are religions and which are not. But what criteria do we use to make this distinction?

It is more difficult than we might expect.

We can say religion is based on transcendent values that cannot be proven scientifically, while secular ideologies are based on concrete realities of our natural world. But capitalism orders and structures reality around transcendent values (such as the providential "invisible hand" of the free market) while Christianity claims to be based on the concrete historical events of the life, death, and resurrection of Jesus.

We can say religion is driven by utopian, otherworldly visions while secular ideologies work out of the givenness of what is. But communism is driven by a projected utopian vision of the future ideal society while Confucianism accepts reality as given with an emphasis on practical virtues for everyday life.

We can say religion is grounded in devotion to a leader who takes on a stature of mythical proportions. But fascism was driven by popular devotion to leaders like Hitler, Franco, and Mussolini, who took on a significance of mythical proportions in the social body's search for national salvation, while Buddhism, despite its name, revolves less around Buddha as a centralized leader than it does around the pursuit of enlightenment with assistance through a variety of guides.

We can say religion is more prone to violent sectarianism while secular ideology is more prone to peaceful tolerance. But the greatest violence of the twentieth century was perpetuated by atheist regimes and it is often proposed, correctly in my estimation, that a significant reason for this violence was the lack of any transcendent restraint upon the human pursuit of power.[18]

Each of these ideologies ultimately faces the problem of idolatry. Each exalts something over God and seeks to order our world around it: capitalism exalts "the market," communism exalts "the state," and nationalism exalts "blood and soil" (ethnic identity and land). While the market, the state, and blood and soil are all good things in their proper places, when exalted as ideological idols, as organizing centers for the world that seek freedom from any transcendent restraint by the reign of God, they have the power to unleash massive destruction in our world.

For God's kingdom to come, these idols must go.

Christ Our Brother

The category of religion is *way* too small. It is not only imams and gurus who find themselves confronted by the coming of the kingdom; it is presidents and CEOs as well. In fact, the term *religion* is probably more of a distraction from our most prominent contemporary allegiances. I would suggest *ideology* hits closer to the mark.

In the urban centers of the twenty-first century, the kingdom of God's primary form of confrontation probably has less to do with what we call "the world religions" and more to do with the political, economic, and social machinations we have created that seek to reign independently from God over his world. And their reinforcing ideologies.

But there is good news: the hope of the world is the death of ideology in the life of Christ. Jesus is not simply one more ideology competing for control of the world. Not one more power-hungry king with a bloodthirsty bent for global domination. Not just another imperialism. No. As Lesslie Newbigin observes, Jesus is the antithesis of our world's imperialisms:

> The Christian gospel has sometimes been made the tool of an imperialism, and of that we have to repent. But at its heart it is the denial of all imperialisms, for at its center there is the cross where all imperialisms are humbled and we are invited to find the

center of human unity in the One who was made nothing so that all might be one. The very heart of the biblical vision for the unity of humankind is that its center is not an imperial power but the slain Lamb.[19]

To use imagery from the prodigal son story, Jesus is a different kind of older brother. Jesus *left* the Father's house to come after us. Unlike the religious brother in his parable, Jesus left his Father's house to pursue us, the younger brothers lost in the distant land, wandering in rebellion, alienated from the family of God. He left the comfort and prestige of his Father's presence to be rejected and crucified, isolated and alone, in the darkness of Jerusalem's backyard outside the city gates. And he did it to bring us home.

Jesus is a good older brother. Though righteous, he does not begrudge us coming home. He gives his life to bring us back inside to the party. He invites us with arms open wide, welcomes us to lay down our idols and ideologies and receive the reconciling embrace of God, calls us to prepare for the coming of the kingdom that will turn this world into a celebration without end.

God's reconciling love *is* the ultimate judgment. God's love in Christ will reconcile the world. Our world will be judged by the love of God in Christ.

CHAPTER 11 KEY IDEA

HOW DOES GOD JUDGE THE WORLD RELIGIONS?

God's reconciliation is itself a judgment on the religions and ideologies of the world, inasmuch as they stand opposed to God's reconciliation for the world.

INTERLUDE

LOVE HAS A NAME

LOVE IS GOD?

Ian, a friend exploring Christianity, had decided to reject it. He explained: "I have come to believe not that God is love, but that Love is god." When asked what he meant, he continued: "When I'm hiking in the mountains or holding a newborn baby, I have these moments of epiphany where I feel the universe is motivated by love and sustained in love. I want to live into this reality more fully." Love was something like an animating force behind the universe, which Ian had come to believe we should make central for our lives.

I asked which parts of Christianity turned him off. Ian explained: "It seems limiting and restricting. If I believe in God, even if I believe God is love, I'm immediately saying my God is right and judging others. I want to respect Buddhists, Muslims, and atheists—not judge them. I want to be kind to my neighbors." Ian couldn't shake the sense that, if he believed in God, he was being judgmental.

Making love ultimate seemed like the best way to go.

I share this story because I believe Ian is not alone. He is simply articulating what is, in my experience, perhaps the most prominent ideology of the twenty-first century: love is god. We can't shake the sense that belief in God, or even more so Jesus, is inherently judgmental against the myriad other ways of life people prefer to pursue today. Doesn't Jesus' exclusivity promote divisiveness, arrogance, and closed-mindedness in a rapidly globalizing world? Don't we most desperately need openness, tolerance, and love? Shouldn't we replace the gospel's proclamation of God's love in Christ with our cultural proclamation that love itself, for its own sake, is the ultimate center around which our world should be ordered?

While I empathize with Ian's desire to love others and avoid being judgmental, I don't think "Love is god" gets him there. Let me share a few reasons why.

Love Is Personal

First of all, love is personal. Rocks don't love. Cars don't love. Inanimate objects don't love. People love. Love is not an abstract concept floating around in the universe somewhere; it is grounded in personhood. People love people. And people love things. But things don't love us back. I can love a car, a painting, or a hot fudge sundae. But I'll be sorely disappointed if I'm looking to my hot fudge sundae to return my affections.

When Ian talks about hiking or holding a baby and having an epiphany that the world is immersed in love, he is talking about a sense of *being* loved. Ian is not saying that he loves the universe; he is saying *the universe loves him*. But he is referring to the universe as a thing, not a person . . .

And this is like expecting your hot fudge sundae to love you back.

We associate love with affection, intention, and sacrificially putting the needs of another before your own. These are things that people do. Love that is just floating around in the universe somewhere as an abstract concept is like a fountain without a spring: it is missing its source. If the Love of the Universe that Ian wants to order his life around is to be more than a mere figment of his imagination, it is my conviction that there must be Someone on the other end.

Love must be personal.

The gospel proclaims that Love has a Name: Jesus. It also says that the universe is motivated by love, is sustained in love, and will be redeemed in love . . . but it is a love that arises from the personal existence of our Creator. Grounded in personhood. To cut God off as the source is like damming the spring and still expecting to have a fountain.

The Illusion of Neutrality

Second, while trying to not *be* judgmental, Ian's claim that "Love is god" is still judgmental. A Muslim would not agree with his claim. An atheist would not agree with his claim. I do not agree with his claim. Ian is making a judgment, a determination, a claim on the nature of our world. Ian's claim, by its very nature, implies that the Muslim, the atheist, and I are wrong.

Ian can be nice about this. He can treat us with kindness and respect. But he either believes we are wrong, or he doesn't truly believe what he claims.

In one sense, this is fine: we believe he is wrong too. The problem is not that Ian believes in something. The problem is Ian's impression that he alone is truly neutral. Ian has tricked himself into believing he is the objective one: that the Muslim, the atheist, and the rest of us are all biased and prejudiced with our religious notions, while he has somehow managed to climb the sacred mountain and look out over the world with unbiased, objective neutrality, unmired by the prejudices of tradition.

This is an illusion.

As Lesslie Newbigin poignantly observes, *There is no neutral standpoint, only that point from which I stand.*[1] And Ian's claim that Love is god is that point from which he stands, the center through which he filters, interprets, and (implicitly) judges the rest of the world.

The problem is the facade of humility, the illusion of neutrality. There is an underlying condescension beneath the humble facade: Ian has made a power play and is trying to pretend he hasn't. Ian has exalted himself over the rest of us, while sitting in the same boat with us. We are all making claims, implicitly or explicitly. But true dialogue begins when we at least acknowledge it.

Ian reaches for neutrality by saying, "Love is god." An agnostic may similarly reach for neutrality by saying, "Truth is unknowable," but then find herself in the awkward position of telling Muslims, atheists, and myself, "You should not be making truth claims." If we ask why, the response is, "Because truth is unknowable." Ironically, she has made a truth claim, a judgment on the nature of reality ("truth is unknowable"), one that marginalizes the Muslim, the atheist, myself . . . and also, ironically, my friend who believes that Love is god.

The point is not that we should not have beliefs; we all have beliefs. The point is this: there is no neutrality. We should hold our beliefs, but we can at least acknowledge that we are all in the same boat. The playing field is level. This is the starting point for real dialogue.

To say "love is god" or "truth is unknowable" is to make a claim on the nature of reality. It is to exalt a belief through which the world is to be received, interpreted, and ordered, a basis by which other beliefs are to be rejected when they clash. In other words, it is a center through which the world is to be judged.

The irony is that while many believe they are breaking with biased "religious traditions" in favor of independent autonomy to hold such a perspective, they are in actuality simply conforming to the predominant ideological fashion of our day, assimilating to the most popular "religious tradition" of modern Western culture. While assimilation to the majority is not inherently wrong, if you don't acknowledge it, you can be oblivious to the power you hold to marginalize and exclude others (like myself) who disagree with you.

A Love to Change the World

My question to Ian was this: Is love as an abstract concept enough? We might feel the love of the universe when holding a newborn baby, but what about when that baby grows up and is trafficked into the sex industry as a teenager where she is repeatedly raped and brutally exploited for the profit of others? Will it be enough to tell her, "There is a kind of love out there in the universe, I think, somewhere that, if you know when to look for it, can creep in at the good moments"?

We might feel the love when hiking in the beauty of the forested hills, but what happens when those hills become home to a million buried bones of those slaughtered in a genocide like Rwanda's? Or those forests are clear-cut, the land strip-mined, and the indigenous people removed to facilitate the profits of an international mineral corporation?

For a world torn apart by injustice, does "love is god" hold any redemptive power as good news? Outside the sheltered suburbs of the West, does it offer any real solace for the raped and ravaged of the world? Is it even coherent if it offers no transcendent power to rectify a world gone terribly wrong?

Can "love is god" deal with the skeletons in our ground?

Our world is desperately in need of love that is more than a *comfort*; we need love that is also a *confrontation*. If God is love, as the gospel proclaims God is, then we are in deep trouble, because we live in defiance of that love every day.

We only need pick up the morning paper, turn on the evening news, or take an honest look in the mirror, and the evidence is staring us in the face. We are inventors of destruction. We tear down what God wants to build up. We destroy that which God desires to prosper. We do violence to God's goodness, his *shalom*, his flourishing in the world. We create ways to live in opposition to God's holy love.

The gospel boldly proclaims, "God is love" and is unabashed in openly declaring what this means: the world will be judged by the love of God in Christ. God's holy love challenges: it confronts the world empires and calls us all into public obedience. God's holy love hits dirt and pavement: it is not an abstract philosophy chained within a spiritual prison, but an embodied kingdom that breathes life and redemption into the physical reality of our world.

And we are in luck, because God freely offers the mercy we all need: to forgive us of our sin, free us from ourselves, and fill us with himself—with his gracious Spirit—to make us fit for the love that permeates his coming kingdom.

God's love can redeem our skeletons.

12.

BODY AND BRIDE

What about the church? If God's judgment is a surprise, are our churches then irrelevant? If the King's arrival turns our expectations on their head, is there any point to being found among his friends when he shows up? If Jesus weeds out from his people, and gathers into his people, is the church then unnecessary and meaningless? By no means! It is precisely the church that Jesus weeds *out of* and gathers *into*.

God's surprise does not marginalize Jesus' bride; it magnifies her.

This is important. It's popular today to "like Jesus, but hate the church"—it would be a tragedy if what's been said in the last few chapters was used to throw fuel on that fire. To say we like Jesus but treat his church with disdain is like telling me, "Joshua, I think you're great, but your wife's a slut!"

You may find yourself waking up on the concrete with a black eye . . . because I love my wife. Jesus takes his bride seriously—if we claim to love him, we should too.

The problem arises when the church is defined as "the sum total of all those going to heaven." This is not the way the New Testament talks about the church. Rather, she is looked to as the body and bride of Jesus. An advance guard of the kingdom that's coming.

Let's look at why this is so revolutionary.

COLONY OF THE KINGDOM

The church is a colony of the kingdom, loyal to the rule of her King. What's a colony? Back in the day, if an empire wanted to establish itself in a foreign land, they would plant a colony: a group of people loyal to the mother country. The United States began as colonies of England: bastions of British rule on the North American continent. In Bible times, the Roman Empire started colonies because they wanted to spread their civilization across the land.

The colony was an outpost of the empire.

Similarly, the church is an outpost of God's kingdom: a different kind of colony for a different kind of empire.[1] God establishes his churches like little colonies scattered throughout a world of idolatry and injustice, as a foretaste of the glory that's coming. Jesus plants his people in the soil of a foreign land, as a signpost of his reconciliation for the world. The Spirit indwells her as bride, to make her ready for the King of the earth.

The church is an advance guard for the coming of God.

Citizens of heaven in the war zone of earth.

A colony in a foreign land.

What is she an ambassador of? *Reconciliation.* We've seen throughout this book that reconciliation is a major theme central to the heart of God. Let's explore how churches as colonies are ambassadors of God's coming reconciliation for the world.

The Church as Reconciliation

Jesus reconciles good folks and bad folks in his church. We are the modern-day tax collectors, prostitutes, and "sinners," worshipping alongside the once-uptight older brothers and model citizens who've been saved from their religion and civic pride. We've traded in our dirty rags for his clothes of righteousness, preparing together for the great Wedding Feast to come. We are the Evite "yes" list to God's wild wedding party. We're overjoyed to be more than simply spectators at the wedding; we're preparing to be the bride.

Jesus reconciles east and west in his church. We are gathered into an international body, with more than 2 billion Christians around the world. As I write this, I am in Vietnam, worshipping with Vietnamese brothers and sisters in Christ. You could not get much farther *east* from where Jesus told the Roman centurion about the upcoming gathering of the nations than where I am today. When I leave next week, I will return to Portland, Oregon, on the west coast of North America. You could not get much farther *west* from where Jesus was standing when he spoke those words than my hometown.

The gospel has gone global.

In the twenty centuries since Jesus walked the dust of the Middle East, the Atlantic Ocean has been sailed, the Ural and Himalayan mountains crossed, and the Sahara desert overcome—the world has "shrunk" and the good news of God's coming kingdom has spread throughout nearly the entire earth. Jesus is gathering the nations out of our empires and into his kingdom.

Jesus reconciles weak and strong in his church. We are gathered into a kingdom where all is given and nothing is earned. We are gathered not through imperial power, economic influence, or social strategy, but rather through the sacrificial love and atoning power of the King's blood shed in weakness for us. The poor, sick, blind, and lame worship alongside the presidents, generals, and CEOs. We are called by our King to give our time, our money, our imagination—our lives—to care for each other and serve a world Jesus loves generously.

And perhaps most important, the foundation of it all, Jesus reconciles heaven and earth: God and humanity, transcendence and immanence, loving Creator with beloved creation. Jesus marks his church by baptism: where we die to ourselves in his death and are raised through the power of his resurrection into the body of his people. Jesus marks us by Eucharist: where we feed on his body that makes us a body and receive his blood that washes and sustains and flows through our collective veins—bringing life to his holy, beloved community.

Together, we anticipate the glory of his new creation.

Jesus gives us his voice: we receive the words of God in Scripture and, more importantly, encounter him as the living Word *through* Scripture—as God's Spirit forms us in the midst of his sacred story for the world. Jesus marks us by worship: we abandon our freedom *from* God and find our freedom *for* God, giving all that we have in loving devotion to the One who has redeemed us from ourselves.

As the church participates in the life of Jesus, we are formed as a signpost of his reconciliation: an embodied witness *in* the world, an outpost of his victory *over* the world, a colony of his kingdom that's coming *for* the world.

The Significance of Surprise

Of course, we do not always participate in the life of Jesus. This is where the significance of surprise arises. When Jesus shows up, things get shaken. And Jesus shows up today—so things get shaken today. This is of major significance for life in the colony: we should expect shock and awe not only when God's kingdom arrives in fullness, but here and now.

For example, here's a common type of story I've seen play out dozens of times: Jack and Jill grew up together in church. Jack was an honor student and valedictorian, respected by all his peers, and a leader in his church's youth group. He went on to become a youth pastor. Meanwhile, Jill was a party animal, hung out with the "sex, drugs, and rock 'n' roll" crowd, and worried about pregnancy and STDs while jumping in and out of abusive relationships.

Church folks looked up to Jack as a role model and, rightly so, worried about the direction Jill's life was heading. If you had asked them which was bound for the Father's house and which would wind up in the backyard, the answer would have seemed obvious . . . but like the story of the prodigal son, would have been wrong.

Fast-forward ten years. Jill hit rock bottom, fell radically in love with the Savior, and left her former life behind to follow him. She suddenly found herself with Jesus' people, being formed in his image and growing tremendously over the years to come. Meanwhile, Jack realized he had been playing the religious game to please the community he grew up in. He left his family, left the church, and hit the clubs with an openly advertised life of short-term pleasures and one-night stands.

Jack was freed from religion and Jill from rebellion.

Jack was free from God and Jill for God.

And the outcome was a surprise.

We should anticipate surprise in the life of the kingdom. We should be wary of premature conclusions as to who will wind up in the Father's house and who will prefer the backyard. Because when Jesus shows up, appearances get shaken. Even today, Jack and Jill's story is not fully written. There is still room for humility on the one hand and hope on the other.

Paul and Judas

I have been shocked over the years as numerous friends I looked up to as pillars of the faith have turned their backs on Jesus and his people. Significant mentors in my own life have revealed downstream that their walk with God was a sham. Simultaneously, I am shocked at how many of my strongest friends in the faith are some of the least likely people I would have expected ten years ago. Some were apathetic toward God or even vocally anti-God, pursuing other agendas, yet have become some of the leaders I most respect today.

Today's gangsters may be tomorrow's preachers.

God's kingdom breaks in and shakes things up here and now. I'm sure the disciples were shocked when Judas came out of the closet as an enemy of Jesus. They had spent all that time together: eating meals, working miracles, sitting around the campfire, processing at the end of the day. Judas was part of the Jesus-tribe, a central part of the community.

The betrayal must have come as quite a surprise.

And I'm sure the early church was shocked when they heard Paul was boldly proclaiming the gospel! He was their arch-persecutor: hunting down and killing Christians, a vocal opponent of the Jesus movement, orchestrating the murder of their friends. Now he was a church planter writing the bulk of the New Testament and bound for martyrdom.

The turnaround must have come as quite a surprise.

With Judas in mind, we should remember that those we sit next to in the pew have not arrived, but are on a common journey toward a destination we have yet to reach. With Paul in mind, we should remember that our pagan neighbors, even if they are vociferously anti-God, are potential celebrants in the coming kingdom.

We should cling to Jesus and hold the rest loosely.

We should run toward Jesus, our destination.

And prepare for surprises along the way.

———

Jesus indwells the church with his presence, but Jesus is above the church as King of all the earth. The presence of his kingdom calls the church into existence, but his kingdom transcends the church. The church is the body of Christ, but Christ is the head of his body, exalted as Lord of the world. In the words of Lesslie Newbigin:

> It is not sufficient for the church to point to itself and say, "Here is the Body of the Messiah." It must point beyond itself to Him who is sole Judge and Saviour, both of the church and of the world. And yet the church is not merely the witness to Christ; it is also the Body of Christ. It is not merely the reporter of divine acts of redemption; it is also itself the bearer of God's redeeming grace, itself part of the story of redemption which is the burden of its message.[2]

The church is the steward of the gospel, but Jesus is the owner of the gospel. The church bears witness to God's coming salvation of the world from sin, but is simultaneously confronted by the very salvation it proclaims. We are but frail mud pots carrying the treasure of Christ's presence inside our breaking bodies.

LOVE TREES

"How then can I know if I'm saved?" the question is often asked. "Is there any security in salvation? If God's judgment is a surprise, can we have any confidence in Jesus' coming kingdom?" From an important angle, the answer, of course, is yes. But there is a major problem with the question, "How can I know if I'm saved?"

The problem is that the word *know* can mean two different things.

Riding the Bike

Imagine, for example, asking a scientist and a five-year-old, "Do you *know* how to ride a bike?"[3] The scientist might respond, "Of course!" and go on to explain gyroscopic forces, the location of the steer axis, and caster effects. And yet, when you ask, "Have you ever *ridden* a bike?" he might scoff and say, "Well, no, but I can tell you *all about* it!"

The five-year-old, on the other hand, might simply say, "Of course!" and then hop on her bike and go spinning around the block. She may be oblivious to how the mechanics of the bike work, yet have a more intimate knowledge of bike riding than the scientist. While the scientist has a *descriptive* knowledge of bike riding, the five-year-old has an *experiential* knowledge.

When many Christians ask, "How can I *know* if I'm saved?" the problem is that we often have the knowledge of the scientist, not the five-year-old, in mind. We look to a descriptive knowledge of Jesus, rather than an experiential knowledge, to tell ourselves we are "in." We can rattle off Greek words, point to a prayer we prayed, and sign off on complicated doctrinal statements. But do we *know* Jesus, in the five-year-old sense? Have we "ridden the bike," *experiencing* Jesus and the power of his love? Are we able to rejoice in more than simply *describing* him from a distance?

I am convinced Jesus will tell many theologians he never knew them, while many five-year-olds go riding their bikes into the kingdom.

Jesus invites his followers into a confident humility. Our

confidence is in who God is: God is a God who loves us, whose posture toward us is embrace, who wants to be reconciled to us. Our humility is in who we are: prone to wander, to deny him, to clutch our idols with greedy hands and run to a distant land. Our confidence is found not in a doctrine of eternal security, but in Jesus himself. To again quote Lesslie Newbigin:

> It seems to me clear from the whole New Testament that the Christian life has room both for a godly confidence and for a godly fear. The contrast between these is not a contradiction. If I know that God in his limitless grace and kindness has chosen and called me to be a bearer of his grace for others, my trust in him will not exclude the awareness that I could betray his trust in me, and that very awareness will drive me closer to him.[4]

Followers of Jesus are marked by a confident humility.
Our confidence is in who God is.
Our humility is in who we are.

The Sign Is Love

So how do we know if we're experiencing the real thing? That Jesus will claim to know us when his kingdom comes? Jesus gives us a good hint: he says a tree is known by its fruit, and the fruit of his Spirit is love.[5]

Imagine I tell you I have a cherry tree, but when spring comes it is bursting with apples. You would probably be thinking, *Apples don't come from cherry trees.*

Exactly.

In the same way, if we say God has planted us as oaks of righteousness in his lovely garden, but when tough times come we are bursting with greed, pride, and selfishness, folks will probably say, "I didn't think that grew on Jesus' trees."

Exactly. Our tree is known by its fruit.

Jesus says the fruit that marks his trees is love.[6] If our branches are connected to his vine, his Spirit will bring Jesus-fruit bursting off our branches. His holy love will come flowing through our veins. John puts it this way:

> God is love. Whoever lives in love lives in God, and God in them. This is how love is made complete among us *so that we will have confidence on the day of judgment.* . . . Everyone who loves has been born of God and knows God. Whoever does not love does not know God, because God is love.[7]

God is love. Union with God means God's love flows through you. If your roots are in Jesus, your fruit will be love.

Fruit takes time to grow; it doesn't appear overnight. We don't have to beat ourselves up for not being perfect Jesus-followers the day after we've started walking in his dust. It took the disciples a long time too. But the longer we're planted in God's garden, the deeper our roots grow in his goodness, and the more generosity, joy, and selflessness begin to spring forth from our branches.

If we realize there's no fruit on our branches, the solution isn't to grunt, muster up our willpower, and "try really hard to bear more fruit." The solution is to reconnect our branches to the life-giving tree, to turn our gaze back toward Jesus. Jesus is the Tree of Life, who longs to connect us to himself, to send his love flowing through us as branches, in order to bear much fruit in his hurting world.

The solution is to look to Jesus, in faith.

Faith: Becoming the Bride

Faith is not a work that gives us mastery over Jesus. Faith is that work in which we are mastered by Jesus. There is nothing we can use to lay claim upon God except his claim upon us. God accepts us in Christ; our obstacle is found in our rejection of God's acceptance in Christ.

Faith levels the playing field, because it is no longer our righteousness as upstanding citizens that makes us worthy of the kingdom, and it is no longer our lawlessness as criminals that makes us unworthy. It is Jesus' grace that makes both worthy—if we are willing to receive it.

This is why faith makes a city where murderers who have spilled blood, like Jeffrey Dahmer, can join with martyrs whose blood has been spilled, like Martin Luther King Jr., and both belt out the same wedding tune: the chorus of the Lamb who stands at the center of a city established by the mercy of his blood.

This is why the sign of faith is repentance. Repentance is not adding Jesus *to oneself,* but rather the conversion of oneself *to Jesus.* The gospel calls us, in light of Jesus' coming kingdom, to "repent and believe" that Jesus is Lord.[8] Our hope is built solely on Jesus—our solid rock, foundation, and reward—or it is not built at all.

God offers eternal life *freely* in Jesus. Yet this life is *eternal* precisely because it entails being grafted into the very life of God: becoming "partakers of the divine nature,"[9] bound in the Spirit to the Son into the life of the Father, living in the love of God that God wants to flow through us into his world. Entering eternal life entails the death of the mortal self, the forsaking of independence, the abdication of autonomy, in order to be bound in union with the very life of God.

The good news is that Jesus *wants* union with us: he wants to marry us. The Groom proposes on the cross to the world. The King offers amnesty. The Great Physician desires to heal. The Groom does not take the Barbie doll princess as his bride, but the battered and bruised whore—he is looking not for our trophies, but for our scars. The Vine says, "Join your branches to my life." And his life can begin to flow through us now, preparing us for the coming kingdom.

THE LOGIC OF COMMUNION

"Is it necessary to witness?" is also often asked. "If God's judgment is a surprise, does it make any difference to share our faith? If Jesus already knows the sheep who are his, what point is there in telling them?"

When we ask the question "Is witness necessary?" it usually depends on what we mean by the word *necessary*.

The Necessity of Witness

First off, some people imply that the salvation of the world is riding on our shoulders. In the Introduction, I shared of the visiting missionary who told us the world was "going to hell in a handbasket," and we needed to head overseas to intervene in their impending doom. It was *necessary* that we get them to "pray to receive Jesus," so that they might not be found on God's bad side at the great final judgment.

Witness is not necessary in this sense. As we've seen in the previous chapters, evangelism is not motivated by a guilt trip; it's motivated by good news. I could sit around watching football and eating Doritos all day and I'm not convinced it would impact the headcount in the kingdom. In fact, God might call that *Sabbath*.

But sharing our faith is *desirable*: Jesus is Life—in a world that is dying, how could we not share him? Jesus is Light—for captives groaning in darkness, how could we not proclaim him? Jesus is Love—for a society sinking in self-centeredness, how could we not shout him from the rooftops? "How beautiful are the feet of those who bring good news!"[10] To look on our decaying world and not want Jesus to be known is like looking on a dying friend and refusing to offer the medicine in your hands.

Jesus is the medicine our world needs.

And there's plenty to go around.

This reveals a second sense, however, in which sharing our faith *is* necessary: if we don't want to share the medicine, it probably reveals we haven't tasted it ourselves. If I am truly united with God, how could I not want to see his light, life, and love pour through me into the darkness, death, and destruction of our world? Jesus tells his followers, "As the Father sent me, so I send you."[11] If God's heartbeat of reconciling mission isn't pulsing through your veins, then you're probably not united with God.

Jesus' passion propels his people to participate in his pursuit of the world.

Witness will *necessarily* flow from one whose life is united with God.

The Church as Witness

We tend to emphasize witness as something *individuals* do, but in the New Testament the church *herself* is the primary witness to God's coming kingdom. Our collective life as the people of God *is* a witness to the watching world: how we treat each other in community, our neighbors in mission, and, above all, God in worship. This is, first and foremost, the way in which we demonstrate the kingdom of God to the world.

The church's primary calling is not to "fix" the world, but to *be* the church. Living together under the reign of God. An alternative community in the midst of the empire.

A refuge from the war zone.

A colony of the kingdom.

On earth as in heaven.

This is why God tells us to exercise judgment with each other. While we are not to judge those outside the community of faith, we are to lovingly confront unrepentant sin inside. For example, in Paul's day, Corinth was a hotbed of sexual immorality. As bad as things were outside the church, however, it was pretty bad inside too. One kid was even sleeping with his mom (there's a slang phrase for that I can't print in this book), and applauded for it.

That was just the tip of the iceberg. So Paul advises the church:

> What business is it of mine to judge those outside the church? . . .
> God will judge those outside. . . . Are you not to judge those inside?[12]

Paul says we're not to go play "morality police" in the city—that's God's territory, and he's got it covered. But we are to exercise judgment with one another.

So if my pagan neighbor invites me to a strip club, I can simply say, "No thanks," and trust God to sort that out. But if a buddy from church invites me to a strip club, we need to sit down and have a talk. There is a legitimate difference in how Jesus wants us to deal with sin inside and outside the church.

We often get this backward, wielding judgment like a teacher's whistle: trying to get all the naughty children on the playground of the world to come into our classroom and learn how to behave. But properly wielded, judgment is more like a broom: used to sweep the bad stuff out more than to get the good stuff in. To clean house. To pull the skeletons out of *our* closets, get the dust out from under our dark corners, and push the junk along until it has reached the welcome mat at the front door.

Because God cares about the integrity of our witness.

In Jeremiah's story (chapter 7), for example, we should have used much *greater* judgment as churches in proactively investigating child abuse accusations and removing pedophiles from the priesthood. The fact that, so often, priests were simply moved from one parish to another to protect the reputation of the church is a travesty. We abandoned the call to exercise judgment with one another.

And the world God loves was hurt in the process.

The church's witness was hurt in the process.

Jeremiah was hurt in the process.

Jesus calls us to lovingly confront blatant, unrepentant sin in his body, motivated not to tear the church down, but to build the church up. We are a bride preparing for our wedding day, so we should care about unrepentant sin flinging mud across our wedding dress. We are a community preparing for the coming of the kingdom, so we should care about the destructive power of hell in our midst that wants to rip our little community apart. The Spirit invites us to help prepare the bride for her wedding and care for the purity of her witness before a watching world.

Visible and Invisible?

A final observation: many talk about a "visible" and "invisible" church to try to deal with the surprise of judgment. While under-standable, the problem is that we tend to assume the "invisible" church is the real one: the true followers of Jesus are those we can't see. And the "visible" church is the fake: the messy institutions with all their pimples and warts are the facade we should ignore or avoid.

But the New Testament moves in the opposite direction. It is the "visible" church, the messy, pimply, warty whore, that is looked to as the *true* church. Jesus has identified with the communities of faith, scattered in particular cities and places around the world, bearing witness for better or worse to his coming kingdom.

What is "invisible" are the wolves in sheep's clothing, the imposters who sometimes come out in the open but more often work behind the scenes in the dark.

When Jesus compares the kingdom to a field, where wheat and weeds grow up together, he assumes that *the field itself* is a good thing.[13] The visible community marked by God's name is good, true, and real. The church belongs to God. What Jesus says we are not to pull up, however, are the weeds: because our perception is faulty and limited, we are to let them grow up together and not focus our attention on trying to make final proclamations on which are which. Good crops might get torn up in the process.

Jesus tells us God is good and will sort it out when he arrives.

In the meantime, the field of God is visible and good.

Invisible are the wolves, the weeds, and the weasels.

And we can have hope: Jesus is coming to vindicate his visible church, to weed out the invisible imposters. God will pull back the curtain on our deception of appearances, deal with the brutality of our history, and liberate creation from its bondage under sin. Jesus is coming to redeem the world.

When will he do this?

A ROBBER AT 2 A.M.

Jesus says his judgment will be a surprise—not only in its outcome, but also in its timing. First Thessalonians 5:2 says he will come "like a thief in the night." The problem with midnight intruders is they don't make an appointment. A robber at 2 a.m. doesn't ask for an invitation—and doesn't ring the doorbell when he arrives.

Jesus is saying the timing of his return will catch some unawares. The point is to make ourselves ready, like a bride anxiously anticipating the return of her groom.

When Jesus breaks into the house of the world, the irony is that he breaks into a house that's his. The good homeowner is returning to kick out the vandals; the Creator is coming to reclaim his creation; the King is arriving to establish his kingdom.

And his timing is a surprise.

Let's return to the colony image: in ancient times, if things got tough in the colony, the emperor would eventually come to rescue them and re-establish their safety in the land. Similarly, when times get tough today, we can lift our eyes to Jesus, the "good emperor," who is coming to rescue his colonies and establish his kingdom in the earth.

In light of God's arrival, we are called to "repent, for the kingdom of heaven [is] near!"[14] To hear this call and reject it is to walk in dangerous territory. Those who resist God today may find when he shows up that it is too late—their decision has already been made.

Jesus invites us to get ready faithfully for his return, like a bride longing desperately for the wedding party to get started. He calls us to light our lamps in the midnight dark of the world and to "keep watch, because you do not know the day or the hour [of his coming]."[15] Jesus encourages us, when things seem bleakest, to look up in hope and:

As his bride, to put on our best wedding threads of holy justice.

As his body, to bear his presence in the world here and now.

As his colony, to get ready for the coming of his kingdom.

———

We have dealt with *personal* judgment, but what about *structural* judgment? When Jesus arrives, how will he uproot the empire and establish his kingdom? How will he displace the rebellious powers that are tearing apart our world in order to make way for the new creation?

It is to this question we now turn.

CHAPTER 12 KEY IDEA

**DOES JESUS' SURPRISE IN JUDGMENT
MEAN THE CHURCH IS IRRELEVANT?**

By no means! It is precisely the church that Jesus weeds *out of* and gathers *into*. Jesus' surprise in judgment magnifies, rather than marginalizes, the church as his body and bride.

Part 3

THE HOPE OF HOLY WAR

Rachel came after the Sunday service, requesting prayer. She began sobbing as she explained. She made friends in her dorm as a new freshman at a local university, but when they learned she was a Christian, it sparked an interrogation:

> "How can you believe in a God who commanded the genocidal slaughter of the Canaanites in the Old Testament?"

> "Don't you realize what a dangerous and violent force religion is in the world?"

> "Haven't there been enough holy wars fought by people who think their religion is right and everyone else is wrong?"

Rachel's parents asked her similar questions years earlier. They were atheists and were concerned when Rachel started following Jesus. Rachel was wise enough to know the point is not to have "all the right answers." She'd learned it's more important to love our family and friends well and listen to their concerns, rather than trying to be the know-it-all with a perfect comeback for every challenge.

But she was also compassionate enough to want to be a good witness for Jesus, to rightly *address* the concerns of loved ones who had serious questions such as these. So what is going on with holy war in the Old Testament—and the New? Why does God get violent sometimes? God's violence is, for many people, the greatest skeleton in his closet.

13.

WEAK VS. STRONG

MUSCLE-BOUND MACHINE-GUN HEROES

Let's start with Israel's conquest of Canaan. I've found that, for many people, the caricature looks something like this: Canaan is an idyllic, peaceful paradise, once home to the garden of Eden. But one day there is a problem: Israel needs land. Canaan's people are minding their own business, keeping to themselves in their tropical utopia. But Israel comes out of the dry and dusty wilderness, lusting after Canaan's land of milk and honey. Fruitful land and flourishing resources are there for the taking, with only one obstacle: a bunch of indigenous people in the way.

So strong and muscle-bound, Israel simply decides to take it. They enter with machine guns (or whatever the ancient equivalent was) and begin mowing down those who were there before them. They leave no survivors and then have the audacity to invoke God and country and call themselves heroes—justifying the massacre by saying their civilization is greater than the one that came before them.

Muscle-bound machine-gun heroes using God to justify their greed and murder: Is this what's happening in the story?

While this is an obvious caricature, I've found it highlights three features many people associate with *holy war*.[1] First, those doing the fighting are "muscle-bound": they are strong, like Rambo. The strong have been using the gods to justify their wars since the beginning of time. Greek and Roman. Chinese and Mongol. Incan and Aztec. Everyone's gods are in the corner of the fight ring, backing them up.

And the angry gods coach their champions with a simple message, "Conquer your neighbors and take their stuff." All around the world, nations have used the gods to justify conquering their neighbors, plundering their resources, and assimilating their people, places, and things into an expanding civilization.

The bellicose gods are old as time.

But the general rule of thumb is this: you don't pick a fight unless you think you can win . . . even if your gods don't show up. When Alexander the Great, Genghis Khan, and Napoleon Bonaparte took on the known worlds of their day, they had the military might, manpower, and muscle to back them up. You can call on the deities to bless you, but you better think you've already got a pretty good shot. You better be training and have the goods to win.

A prime feature of mainstream holy war: the conquerors use God, or the gods, to justify picking the fights they already think they can win.

Second, the fighters have "machine guns": advanced weapons. Today we think of things like stealth planes, guided missiles, and atomic bombs. In ancient times, these would be things like swords, horses, and chariots. And they usually came with strategy, tactical advantage, and trained, experienced leaders.

You can be outnumbered as long as you've got the firepower. When Spanish conquistadors cut down New World natives in search of gold and glory, when Islamic raiders conquered and constructed the biggest empire of the medieval era, when British merchants shackled millions of Africans on slave ships, they were all outnumbered, but they had the weapons, strategy, and tactical advantage to win.

A second major feature of mainstream holy war: the conquerors use God, or the gods, to justify picking the fights they have the weapons to win.

Third, the winners call themselves "heroes": justified by the greatness of their civilization. Since the dawn of time, nations have been saying things like, "Just wait until you experience all our civilization has to offer you. Coca-Cola. Computers. Compact cars. It's in your best interest that we conquer you, because of how great we are. Trust us: this is for your own good."

This is the realm of ideology. Propaganda. War rhetoric.

The Roman Empire justified their many wars by the Pax Romana—the peace they would bring in the wake of the fighting under the greatness of their civilization. European colonists often saw themselves as having a "civilizing mission": justified to conquer because they were bringing the greatness of European civilization to the peoples of the world. This is what Rudyard Kipling famously called "the White Man's Burden": the "duty" of the white man to bring his civilization to bear on the "unenlightened" peoples of the world.[2]

A third major feature of mainstream holy war is the conquerors' strong belief that they are justified in fighting because of the greatness of their civilization.

Reading the Old Testament, however, I began to discover an alternative picture. It was not a slight variation on mainstream holy war, with a few lines drawn in subtly different directions or a few colors painted in slightly off-color shades. It was as if someone had taken the mainstream picture of holy war, painted across the historical canvas of our world, and turned it upside down. As if God was turning the unholy wars of our world on their heads and confronting them with a radically different picture.

God was confronting holy war. It is to this upside-down picture that we now turn.

SLAVES VS. EMPIRE

Israel vs. Canaan. A good first question to ask is this: *Who* is doing the fighting? And Israel is not who you'd expect. They are a nation of slaves going up against an empire. They've been getting their butts kicked on the outskirts of Egypt for four hundred years (yes, that's a *long* time!)

and are now going up against the mightiest imperial powerhouses of the day, who've been building their dominance for centuries. Israel's been wandering in the wilderness for forty years, eating strange food and wearing the same old clothes, and are now confronting the most advanced, heavily armored, and well-equipped armies of the day. They are one nation—a tiny nation—standing in the shadow of Canaan: an assimilator of nations, a devourer of peoples.

Israel should get routed.

Let's see how Israel turns mainstream holy war on its head.

Machine Guns: "Some Trust in Chariots . . ."

First, Israel does not have "machine guns": they are outrageously outgunned and outmanned. It's not like there was a stockpile of AK-47s waiting for them in the wilderness after they left Egypt. Israel has whatever they've been able to muddle together wandering through the desert for the last forty years. Canaan, in contrast, has weapons—the most advanced weaponry of the day. Their chariots can quickly take out Israel's foot soldiers. Their horses can easily knock down Israel's ground-fighters. Canaan's swords and spears can do their long-range damage well before Israel's sticks and stones come close.

Israel is a lone kindergartener taking on the high school senior class with a Wiffle bat.

Canaan also has defenses: heavily fortified military outposts like Jericho, with high walls, protective rivers, and top-of-the-line ramparts . . . Israel has a small wooden box they built in the desert that carries God's protective presence with them.

Canaan's generals have practiced strategy on the surrounding nations . . . Israel's commanders have learned to ward off snakes and animals in the wilderness.

Canaan has high-tech steel armor to protect their bodies from any incoming blows . . . Israel has the same ratty clothes they've been wandering around in for the last four decades.

Israel is storming Fort Knox with a water pistol.

Canaan is a land of giants, kings of the regional hill. They have strong, well-fed bodies that have been feasting off "the land of milk and honey" for generations. Israel, in contrast, has been enduring wilderness survival, living on prison food of bread and water: a strange heavenly wafer called manna (meaning "what is it?") and rivers from rocks.[3]

Canaan has wealth and affluence, with all the physical, emotional, and psychological confidence those things can bring. Israel is a comparative nation of runts with nothing but the name of their God.

Israel marches in like ants under elephants' feet.

This is something antithetical to mainstream holy war. You expect the grade-school bully to take on the weakling with lunch money; you don't expect him to take on the high school wrestling team. You expect a pirate to capture the vessel lost at sea; you don't expect him to declare open war on the Spanish Armada. You expect a Third World dictator to abuse scattered dissenters; you don't expect him to hop in his personal jet and take on the US Air Force.

To do so would be psychotic.

Unless something fundamentally different is happening.

Israel is not the bully, pirate, or dictator invoking the gods to justify her conquest of the weak. Israel is the opposite: the weakling who's been getting her lunch money taken every day by the playground bullies. She is the little nation whose vessel's been under constant attack by pirates while lost at sea. She is the dissenter among the nations getting railed on by the dictators.

Israel *is* the weak.

Canaan is not just a little bit stronger, not just overwhelmingly stronger—they are in a different league altogether. Their firepower puts them in a whole other category. Israel should get routed. Her only hope is that God goes with her:

"Some trust in chariots and some in horses, but we trust in the name of the LORD our God."[4]

Israel learned to sing this song in the valley of the shadow of the empires, with Egypt on one side and Canaan on the other: outrageously outgunned and outmanned.

Israel is the dramatic, laughable underdog. If the analogy is the NFL, this is not a lower-ranked team going up against a higher-ranked team and hoping for an upset. This is your local grade school team going up against the national Super Bowl champions who are sporting the rings to prove it.

Israel is a nation of fearful, intimidated slaves facing off with the mightiest imperial powerhouses of the ancient world, the extreme antithesis of *who* fights mainstream holy wars. They don't have a shot unless God is the one fighting for them.

Muscle-Bound: "God Will Fight for Us"

Second, Israel is not "muscle-bound": her strength and battle strategies are ridiculous. If God doesn't show up, they are not really strategies at all. Take Jericho, for example: the first fight in the promised land and a prototype of what's to come. Jericho is heavily defended, surrounded by high walls, protected by a river, and armed to the teeth. Jericho is the heavily fortified military city that is the gateway into Canaan.

So what brilliant military strategy is Israel going to use to take down Jericho? Joshua waits for instructions and is finally told to . . . wait for it . . . march around its walls for seven days and blow trumpets.

Seriously? Can you imagine the Allied Forces of World War II storming the beaches of Normandy with—not guns—but musical instruments? Or the Mongols marching up to the Great Wall of China and making—not war—but music? Or Canadians and Mexicans taking guitars and drums and marching along the US border as an act of war?

This is not a battle strategy; it's a recipe for disaster.

Unless God is the one leading the charge.

God continually gives Israel ridiculous battle strategies. Jericho is not the exception but the norm. Apparently it's part of the point:

so they will know God is the one, not them, who is really doing the fighting. Take Gideon's classic battle, for example. The Midianites, another biblical people group, have been brutally oppressing the Israelites for a while. So God raises up Gideon, like Moses before him, to liberate his weak and vulnerable people from their strong and powerful oppressors.

Gideon is, like Israel, not who you'd expect. He is the least in his family; his family is the weakest in his tribe; and his tribe is the last in Israel.[5] He is the last, the least, and the weakest within Israel, as Israel was the last, the least, and the weakest among the nations. God usually chooses the last kids picked on the playground when it's time for a revolution.

Gideon starts off severely outnumbered. Midian's militias are huge; in combination with their allies, their numbers "could no more be counted than the sand on the seashore."[6] Gideon's ragtag crew, however, *can* be counted. He is able to rally a battalion of 32,000 troops to take on the enemy's "sand on the seashore" militias.

God then gives Gideon the battle plan . . . wait for it . . . "You have too many men." Start sending folks home so that Israel may not boast, "My own strength has saved me."[7]

What? Seriously? Since when has too many troops been a bad thing?

God sends nearly all 32,000 troops home, leaving Gideon with only 300 men (less than 1 percent of the original crew) to go up against the incoming tidal wave of armies. Can you imagine Abraham Lincoln sending 99 percent of the Union's soldiers back north, then taking on the South with the remaining 1 percent just to make a point? Or William Wallace telling the Scottish battalions to leave the frontlines and just go home because he'd rather take on the English by himself?

This is not a battle strategy; it's a death wish.

Unless God is doing the heavy lifting.

Israel's battle strategies look ridiculous because they are designed to. They highlight that God is the one really doing the fighting. There is a famous psalm that says, "Be still, and know that I am God."[8]

People often quote this verse today, thinking it means something like, "Life is busy, so slow down, put aside your care and worries, sit in silence, and rest in God." The funny thing is, this is actually a *holy war* verse. It comes from God's deliverance of Israel from Egypt's armies at the Red Sea. When Pharaoh's chariots and swords are bearing down to destroy the ragtag slaves and it appears all hope is lost, Moses tells Israel:

> Do not be afraid. Stand firm and you will see the deliverance the LORD will bring you today. The Egyptians you see today you will never see again. The LORD will fight for you; you need only to be still.[9]

Be still. God will fight for you. Sit back and know that I am God. This became Israel's theme song, her battle cry, her national anthem in her encounters with Egypt and Canaan.[10] As one Old Testament scholar puts it:

> Every other nation in antiquity claimed that their gods participated in war and were responsible for giving their warriors victory. But only Israel came to understand this claim to mean that it was unnecessary to fight.[11]

Israel is not taking on the empire for God; God is taking on the empire for Israel.

"Be still and know that I am God" is not a private whisper made in the quiet of our closets for personal devotion so much as it is a public proclamation of God arising to defend the enslaved and exploited of our world from the mighty and powerful forces that oppress them. Our picture should not be the monk in the monastery in solemn reflection so much as the disabled kid on the playground being attacked by fifteen older, stronger bullies, when he suddenly hears the voice of his father stepping onto the scene and saying, "Sit back, son, be still, and watch me take care of these guys for you."

Mainstream holy war's motto is "We will fight for God!" But Israel turns this motto on its head, shouting instead, "God will fight for us!"

If God doesn't, they don't have a chance.

Heroes: "Not Because of Your Greatness"

Finally, Israel is not a nation of "heroes." As we have seen, nations tend to justify their wars by the greatness of their civilization. But Israel, in contrast, moves once again in the opposite direction. Her history books constantly remind her: "It is *not* because of your greatness." In one central holy war passage, God calls them a "stiff-necked people," reminding them that he will give them victory "not because of your righteousness or your integrity" but rather "on account of the wickedness of these nations."[12] God gives Israel victory in spite of herself, not because of herself.

"Victors write the history books," the classic saying goes, meaning the winners always tend to depict themselves in mainstream history books as strong, heroic, courageous, brave, and noble. But Israel, in contrast, constantly depicts herself as weak, fearful, idolatrous, unbelieving, dishonest, and disobedient. The Old Testament reads as if Israel hired a reporter to meticulously track all of her mistakes, weaknesses, and shortcomings. Her history books are written almost as an "anti-ideology": a glorying in the fact that things worked out in spite of how screwed up she was.

Israel finds it important that God's victory over the world's oppressive powers is not rooted in her greatness. Israel intentionally depicts herself as an anti-hero. This is something dramatically different from mainstream holy war.

Israel also had a numbers problem. In the ancient world, bigger was better. The more people you had, the stronger and greater you were. But God reminds Israel in another central holy war passage that he "did not set his affection on you and choose you because you were more numerous than other peoples, for you were the fewest of all peoples."[13] In a world where there was strength in numbers Israel did not just come in second or third . . . she came dead last.

She was the "fewest of all peoples."

Why was Israel's population so small? In part, she had a late start. Abraham was not called as the nation's founding father until the other nations had already been having kids for many generations—Israel arrived late to the starting line of the international population race after the other runners had already gone a few laps around the track.[14]

And then there was the genocide. When Moses was born, Egypt tried to murder all Israel's boys and destroy the nation—this did not help their numbers.[15] God found Israel in Egypt, to use a vivid image from Ezekiel, like a newborn baby abandoned in an open field, kicking and screaming in her blood.[16] Not a very flattering picture.

When we zoom out to the mighty empires of the ancient world, it is almost as if God is intentionally choosing the smallest, weakest, most vulnerable, helpless, and powerless nation he can, to demonstrate to the mightiest, wickedest, bloodiest, nastiest powerhouse empires of the day that there is a message he wants to send loud and clear to the ancient world. His message? "*This is who I am!* I am the rightful ruler of the earth, and I stand up for the weak, exploited, and oppressed!"

The kings of the hill may reign for a day, or even for centuries, but God will eventually arise for judgment on the empires of our world.

DAVID AND GOLIATH

So if you want to fight a *real* holy war, here's what you do:

1. Throw away your armor.
2. Burn your tactical training books.
3. Find the cheapest, most ineffective weapons you can.
4. Visit a drug rehab center to find military leaders with "issues."
5. Hire a reporter to meticulously track all your flaws and failures.
6. Boast to your enemies about how backward your civilization is.
7. Go find the biggest, baddest superpower who will surely kick your tail.

8. Pick a fight.

9. Walk onto the middle of the battlefield.

10. Pray that God shows up.

Everything we have looked at so far can be summed up in the classic story of David and Goliath. This tale of a boy shepherd and a Philistine giant is more than just a cute children's story: it is Israel's paradigm for holy war. It is the classic drama of the underdog facing a mighty oppressor and overcoming impossible odds—the storyline that has made millions for virtually every Disney movie ever made.

And it is the climax of Israel's experience in Canaan.

David is completing the conquest of Canaan. The battle takes place at the Valley of Elah, a significant location. While Israel's troops are encamped on one side of the valley, on the other side sits the remaining portion of the promised land yet to be entered.[17] Israel's encounters with Canaan are recounted in the previous books of Joshua, Judges, and 1 and 2 Samuel . . . now, here in David's epic battle, comes the climax of the conquest. What began at Jericho ends here. David goes after Goliath to complete what Joshua began.

This is not just another battle: this is the taking down of the final stronghold, the beginning of the end, the completion of the victory.

David and Goliath's encounter draws into itself all of the holy war themes we've looked at thus far: summarizing the major movements, epitomizing the driving ethos, and encapsulating the thrust of the story as a whole.

It is not just *a* holy war story; it is *the* holy war story.

Let's look at the warriors: David is the "weakling" going up against a giant, a fitting image for Israel going up against Canaan's empire. And Goliath is "muscle-bound" looking down upon the boy with a slingshot, like Canaan looking down upon Israel, ready to destroy. Goliath has the best weapons the ancient Middle East can buy. One swing of his massive sword can slice David's body in half; one thrust of his long spear can skewer David like a shish kebab. David's sling and stone, in contrast, are child's play: a laughable toy against an armored giant—like Israel's sticks and stones versus Canaan's horses and chariots.

Goliath's body is a fortress well defended as Jericho, covered in top-of-the-line armor. David's body, in contrast, is an exposed and open field. He approaches, like Israel, in shepherd's clothes—about to be led to slaughter. Goliath is a giant: his grandfathers have been feeding off "the land of milk and honey" for generations; he is nine feet tall and king of the regional hill. Like Canaan, his years have been spent preparing for war. David, in contrast, is the smallest and weakest in his family. He's spent his years herding sheep in the fields, like nomadic Israel wandering in the desert. He can't even fit into the armor he's offered; it's too heavy for his tiny frame.

Goliath's strategy makes perfect sense: go after your weaker opponent and chop off his head. David's strategy, like Israel's, makes no sense: throw pebbles at Mount Everest and hope it falls down. Goliath's trash talk embodies the belief that the strong can use their gods to justify their conquest of the weak:

> "Am I a dog, that you come at me with sticks?" And the Philistine cursed David by his gods. "Come here," he said, "and I'll give your flesh to the birds of the air and the beasts of the field!"[18]

Goliath sees himself as a "hero": he boasts in his strength, curses by his gods, and sets out to conquer the weak.

David, in contrast, boasts in God's strength rather than his own. He confronts Goliath's power with a God who arises to defend the weak and gives them victory against the tyranny of the strong:

> You come against me with sword and spear and javelin, but I come against you in the name of the LORD Almighty. . . . All those gathered here will know that it is not by sword or spear that the LORD saves; for the battle is the LORD's, and he will give all of you into our hands.[19]

David trusts God to fight for him in his weakness.

David's victory is more than just a runt killing a giant: it is a climactic image of all that has come before. Goliath is a picture of ancient empire: loud, arrogant, and strong; wanting to rule the world on their own while conquering the neighbors and taking their stuff; and using their gods to justify the whole ordeal. David is a picture of Israel, the last, least, and weakest, who are powerless to protect themselves but find God arising on their behalf.

God is taking back the ground that sin has tried to steal to establish his kingdom in the land. David, the shepherd with a slingshot, steps out in faith and takes down the armored warrior with a single throw. As we shall see in the coming chapters, David is also a foreshadowing of Jesus, who will take down the Goliath of modern empire in order to establish God's coming kingdom.

CHAPTER 13 KEY IDEA

IS OLD TESTAMENT HOLY WAR ONE MORE EXAMPLE OF THE STRONG USING THE GODS TO JUSTIFY THEIR CONQUEST OF THE WEAK?

No, it is God arising on behalf of the weak against the tyranny of the strong when it has raged for far too long.

INTERLUDE

GOD CRITIQUES HOLY WAR

Can Israel's history be used to support terrorism today? Don't terrorists believe themselves to be the weak, fighting on God's behalf against the tyranny of the strong? Even if Old Testament holy war is not the strong using God to justify their conquest of the weak, can't it still be used by terrorists to justify their war against the strong? This is an important question.

Fortunately, the answer is no.

As we have seen, a central feature of Old Testament holy war is that *God* is the one doing the fighting. The warriors are laughable. The strategies are ridiculous. They do not have the ideologies of greatness on their side. It is not *the weak fighting on behalf of God*, but *God fighting on behalf of the weak*.

When we hear the words *holy war* today, we think of terrorists strapping bombs to their chests and walking into crowded marketplaces, or flying planes into buildings while chanting, "We will fight for God!" But terrorist extremists don't need divine intervention; they are deceived into believing they *are* divine intervention.

In contrast, God is a warrior who is big enough to fight his own battles without billions of dollars from international oil money; who calls his people to stand defenseless on the open battlefield rather than crouch in the hidden darkness of caves; who uses a visibly vulnerable, identifiable people rather than a scattered network of cowards taking potshots at civilians from the shadows.

True holy war is not when we strap bombs to our chest and say, "We will fight for God!" but its contradiction: when God steps in for the vulnerable and defenseless and says, "I will fight for you!"

Israel's story does not vindicate the ways we tend to wage war in our world—it contradicts them (including terrorists).

As we have also seen, Israel's story critiques those who consider themselves "heroes," invoking the greatness of their civilization to justify their conquest. When many people hear the words *holy war* today, they think of Spanish conquistadores invoking God while cutting down indigenous peoples in the New World, English slave traders attending church while hauling millions of Africans across the ocean in slave ships, and French colonial administrators praying the Lord's Prayer while ruthlessly exploiting colonies in the Far East.

But if European colonization is the analogy, then holy war looks a lot more like a beleaguered motley crew of Native American, African, and Asian survivors shocked to find God rising up against the Western imperial powers marshaled against them.

And Israel's story critiques the strong using their pet ideologies as modern "gods" to justify their conquest of the weak. When many hear the words *holy war*, they envision Hitler's hordes invoking God while marching across Europe in pursuit of lebensraum. But if World War II is the analogy, then Old Testament holy war looks a lot more like God rising up in the concentration camps for those getting annihilated and taking down the Third Reich.

God critiques holy war, in its mainstream sense, as unholy. Israel's story reveals that a war is truly holy—transcendent, other, set apart—when God is the one doing the fighting. As we shall see, this is not only a part of the Old Testament; it is the hope of the New Testament.

14.

EVICTED FROM EDEN

DRASTIC MARCHING ORDERS

"Why does God have to be so brutal?" we may ask. And indeed, Moses and Joshua give some pretty drastic marching orders as they enter Canaan: "Utterly destroy them." "Show no mercy." "Do not leave alive anything that breathes."[1] At first glance, this can look like Israel is being commanded to slaughter civilians—to utterly annihilate all men, women, and children. God looks like an ancient military commander who's lost his marbles in war, suddenly unleashing rapid machine-gun fire on a conquered village of unarmed civilians.

Is God like William Calley, the US army officer who ordered the infamous My Lai massacre during the Vietnam War? Is God commanding the slaughter of defenseless noncombatants? This is an important question. Critics today load verses like these as ammunition in a rapid-fire assault on God, referring to Israel's holy wars as "bloodthirsty massacres," carried out with "xenophobic relish," one more example of "ethnic cleansing" in the bloody history of our world.[2]

Is God a genocidal maniac? Is this Israel's legacy in the Old Testament? Are Jesus' grandparents carrying out the vicious slaughter of unarmed civilians at his Father's command? Fortunately, if we take a closer look at the text we can quickly see that something substantially different is happening.

Military Cities

Three observations can help us make sense of Israel's drastic marching orders. First, the cities Israel takes out are military strongholds, not civilian population centers. Say the word *city* today, and most of us think of urban centers flooded with civilians. I live in the heart of Portland, a modern metropolitan city; when I walk outside my front door, I see houses, restaurants, businesses, hospitals, and schools. It is thus not surprising that when I come across Israel taking out a "city" like Jericho, the first image that comes to mind is a civilian population center.

But in the ancient Middle East, things were different. The Old Testament word for "city" (`ir`) would have, to Israel's ears, conjured up images of a fortified military garrison. Cities were frequently military outposts that defended the roads leading up to where the people were. Think "the Great Wall of China" as a military defense against invasion. This is where the soldiers were, not where the people lived. Women, children, and other civilians were in the towns and villages of the surrounding countryside, looking to the "cities" for military protection.

Jericho, for example, was only six acres with capacity for around twelve hundred soldiers. Richard Hess, an Old Testament scholar, has persuasively argued that Jericho and Ai, the two cities given the most attention in the book of Joshua, probably only held 100–150 soldiers each.[3] Jericho was the first line of defense, a fort guarding the travel routes up to Jerusalem, Bethel and Ophrah. Civilian populations lived in villages and towns up in the hills. Archaeology confirms that cities like Jericho were military outposts, not civilian centers:

> All the archaeological evidence indicates that no civilian populations existed at Jericho, Ai, and other cities mentioned in Joshua . . . Jericho was a small settlement of probably one hundred or fewer soldiers. This is why all of Israel could circle it seven times and then do battle against it on the same day.[4]

So when Israel "utterly destroys" a city like Jericho or Ai, we should picture a military fort being taken over—not a civilian massacre.[5] God is pulling down the Great Wall of China, not demolishing Beijing. Israel is taking out the Pentagon, not New York City.

Similarly, Israel conquers a lot of kings. When we hear the word *king* today, a "president" or top-dog political leader comes to mind, not a military leader. But in the ancient Middle East, kings were often local leaders who functioned a lot more as generals. They were military leaders who frequently led their soldiers into battle. The word for "king" (*melek*) "was commonly used in Canaan during this time for a military leader who was responsible to a higher ruler off-site."[6] In other words, the picture is one of Joshua's armies attacking military strongholds, knocking out generals, and putting their soldiers to flight; not invading cities, assassinating presidents, and slaughtering civilians.

Israel is taking on Napoleon and his militias, not Paris and her masses.

At Jericho, scholars believe Rahab the prostitute ran the fortress's hostel-tavern with her family.[7] These were common in military outposts: the hostel hosted visiting foreigners (like Israel's spies) so the military could keep a close eye on them. And it was not uncommon for the tavern to be run by a prostitute: some servicemen wanted more than just beer. It's telling that Rahab and her family are the only noncombatants specifically depicted as living in any of the cities destroyed in Joshua, and they are spared.

In a few places the phrase "all men and women, young and old" shows up, but in English this phrase is misleading. Hebrew scholars note this was a stock phrase used to imply totality, and to Hebrew ears the use of this phrase does not require that women and children were *actually present* in the militarized outposts, only that the forts were totally depopulated in the aftermath of victory.[8]

When a foreign army approached, civilians hanging around would have left the military to do the fighting and fled to the towns and villages in the hills. So it's unlikely there would have been many, or any, noncombatants in these cities.[9]

Another tricky issue involves numbers: the Hebrew word commonly translated as "thousand" (*'elep*), in a military context, often simply means "unit" or "squad." So some of the numbers might not be as high as English translations suggest. For example, when 12,000 are defeated at Ai in Joshua 8:25, Old Testament scholars note the more likely translation is actually 12 squads of combatants: "In this case, each squad may have included about 10 warriors, so that the total sum was between 100 and 150."[10] Ancient documents were not so concerned with statistical accuracy as we are today; they rather sought to give an overarching sense of the events that took place within the reporting conventions of the day.

So in summary, when the story says no survivors were left in a city, it is simply stating the obvious: the fort has been taken over, and all its defenders have either fled or been killed. Today, the majority of the world's population lives in cities. So it's not surprising that we think of cities as civilian population centers. But in the ancient Middle East, things were different. A city having no survivors is not a picture of a civilian massacre, but the taking over of a military stronghold. Civilians were not targeted; combatants were.

Ancient Trash Talk

The second observation that can help us is this: the Old Testament makes clear it is using ancient trash talk, exaggerated war rhetoric. This way of speaking was common throughout the ancient Middle East; when you beat an enemy in battle and the adrenaline was rushing, you bragged. But no one expected to take you seriously.

It was something like sports trash talk today. When a basketball team beats their opponents, you expect to hear them say things in the locker room like, "We wasted them! Wiped the floor with them! They had nothing on us, couldn't get a thing past us—we annihilated them!" If you'd just dropped in on this postgame locker room talk, you would think the score was 120–0. But when you ask your friend on the team what the actual score was, and he replies, "120–105," you realize it was *still* a decisive victory, but not anywhere *near* as drastic as the rhetoric alone would lead you to believe.

The basketball team is not telling lies in the locker room. They simply expect you to understand this is trash talk: an exaggerated way of speaking.

Similarly, in the ancient Middle East, this was the way people talked about war. This exaggerated war rhetoric was universally common. Here are a few examples:

Egypt claimed in a great battle of the fifteenth century B.C. that they "annihilated totally" the great opposing army of Mittani "within the hour," exterminating them fully to make them "like those not existent." In actuality, however, the great army of Mittani continued to fight on and cause Egypt trouble for more than a century to come.

The Hittites claimed in a great battle of the thirteenth century B.C. to have "emptied the mountains of humanity" and made its people extinct, when in actuality, they simply won sovereignty over the Mt. Asharpaya and Tarikarimu mountains. The people of the mountains lived on; this was simply military rhetoric for saying they had successfully subdued the area.

The Moabites beat Israel in battle in the eighth century B.C. and made the outrageous genocidal claim that as a nation, "Israel has utterly perished for always." In actuality, however, Israel lived on as a sovereign nation for a long time to come; this was simply a declaration of victory in battle.[11]

More examples could be added. But two things are clear when we read this ancient trash talk in context: first, that it is referring to *military* victories, *not* civilian massacres; and second, that the rhetoric greatly exaggerates the extent of the victory.

The Old Testament itself makes clear it is using hyperbole. Such drastic language is very rare; it only shows up a few times, and every time it does, we only have to go a little farther in the story to find the same enemies (that were supposedly wiped out) are still very much alive, still very powerful, and still causing problems.

For example, a central holy war passage is Joshua 9–12 (one of the few places this language shows up). In context, thirty-one kings from northern and southern Canaan rally their military forces to take out Israel. It is worth noting the battles are depicted as defensive for Israel; the ragtag group of slaves is facing genocidal extinction, going up against opponents "as numerous as sands on the seashore."[12]

Israel steps up to defend herself in battle. Joshua's armies are, as always, severely outgunned and outmanned. They should get routed. But once again, God fights for Israel and defends her against the hostile aggression of the stronger, more powerful nations that surround her. God provides a miraculous victory (this passage includes the famous story where the sun and moon stand still and God rains down hailstones on the enemy armies). Israel celebrates her victories with exaggerated war rhetoric, saying that Joshua defeated *all* the kings of Canaan, destroyed *all* the Canaanites, and captured *all* the land of Canaan.

But this is *clearly* not the case. Just keep reading: you won't have to go very far before discovering there are still plenty more kings, plenty more armies, and plenty more Canaanites who are still very clearly powerful and very much around for generations to come.[13] We are still in the book of Joshua: most of Israel's encounters with Canaan come in the following books of Judges and 1 and 2 Samuel. David's battle with Goliath is still many generations away. When we zoom out from the specific verse to the surrounding story, it is clear the basketball team is simply bragging in the locker room.

Israel is using ancient trash talk.

In the words of Christopher J. H. Wright, one of the most respected Old Testament scholars of our day,

> We must also recognize that the language of warfare had a conventional rhetoric that liked to make absolute and universal claims about total victory and completely wiping out the enemy. Such

rhetoric often exceeded reality on the ground. . . . This is not to accuse the biblical writers of falsehood, but to recognize the literary conventions of writing about warfare.[14]

While Israel's adrenaline is rushing, they say they "utterly destroyed" Canaan's army; they "showed no mercy" and "did not spare anyone that breathed."[15] But even *within* the Joshua passage, this is not accurate: some of Canaan's soldiers realize the battle is over and flee the battlefield to survive.[16] And Joshua's armies are clearly *not* fighting against civilians in the towns and villages; they are fighting against *soldiers* in their *fortified military outposts* and on the *battlefield*.

The story makes clear: these are military victories, not civilian massacres.

After the Joshua passage, every time this exaggerated war rhetoric shows up (and again, the times are very few), the same thing happens. All we have to do is go a little further in the story and we see that the same enemies are still running amok.[17] All we have to do is zoom out from the specific verse to the surrounding context in the broader story.

So, we are expected to read this language, not literally, but as exaggerated war rhetoric. As Paul Copan summarizes in his study:

> A closer look at the biblical text reveals a lot more nuance—and a lot less bloodshed. In short, the conquest of Canaan was far less widespread and harsh than many people assume. Like his ancient Near Eastern contemporaries, Joshua used the language of conventional warfare rhetoric . . . the language that everyone in his day would have understood. . . . The language is typically exaggerated and full of bravado, depicting total devastation. The knowing ancient Near Eastern reader recognized this as hyperbole; the accounts weren't understood to be literally true. . . . Joshua was just saying he had fairly well trounced the enemy.[18]

Israel is, like all her neighbors, just trash-talking.

"Driving out" vs. "Killing off"

The third observation that can help us is this: the Canaanites are "driven out," not "killed off." The phrase "drive out" is the primary language used for the Canaanites, showing up more than fifty times in the Old Testament. In contrast, the drastic marching orders are rare and show up in only a few places.

Being "driven out" is the language of eviction, not murder. And like a rowdy dancer bounced from a club, if you're driven out, the good news is you're still alive.

God is like a gardener chasing out the hooligans who've been trashing his vineyard. Like a landlord evicting the unruly tenants who've been destroying his home. Or an angry prophet with a whip, driving the mighty merchants out of his temple. (All these are *driving out* images that show up in the Bible.)[19] God drives the unruly, powerful tenants out of his garden home and gifts it to the last and the least, the homeless slaves, who've had the boot of empire on their necks for far too long.

If Canaan's getting the boot, God is the foot. Notice in the following passages how God, not Israel, is the primary one doing the evicting:

> The LORD will drive out all these nations before you, and you will dispossess nations larger and stronger than you. (Deuteronomy 11:23)

> Little by little I will drive them out before you, until you have increased enough to take possession of the land. (Exodus 23:30)

> The LORD has driven out before you great and powerful nations; to this day no one has been able to withstand you. (Joshua 23:9)

God is evicting "larger and stronger" nations that Israel could never take on by herself. He is doing this "little by little" over many generations: this is not an overnight ejection, but a gradual eviction. When Israel does enter the picture, they are simply finishing off a battle God has already won, jumping in on a victory God has already brought to the point of completion.

In context, the "drive out" passages inspire courage for the fearful, not bloodlust for the greedy. For example, Joshua tells his army: "Though the Canaanites have iron chariots and though they are strong, you can drive them out."[20] Joshua is calling for bravery among his outgunned, outmanned, underdog slaves, reminding them that God is the one leading the charge, and he will fight for them.

"Drive out" is the language of eviction, not murder—it is the language of exile. The first place the phrase shows up is significant: it is when Adam and Eve are "driven out" of the garden of Eden by God. Something very similar is happening here: now the Canaanites are being "driven out" of the garden of Canaan by God, like Adam and Eve so long ago. And for parallel reasons.

Adam and Eve were driven out because they unleashed the destructive power of sin into God's good garden. As we shall now see in the next section, something very similar is happening with Canaan.

BABYLON'S INVASION

Who was Canaan? I used to picture Canaan as a tropical utopia where native peoples lived in peace and harmony and fed each other grapes while strumming guitars and telling everyone how beautiful they were. This was home to the original garden of Eden, right? They were just minding their own business; why did God have to crash the party? Pharaoh and Egypt were the ones being mean to Israel; why didn't God simply give *their* land to his redeemed slaves?

Even if Israel is not brutal, like the caricature, we still have to ask: Why does God throw down on Canaan?

A couple of options come to mind. Maybe Canaan was simply in the wrong place at the wrong time. Maybe God woke up on the wrong side of the bed one day and decided if he couldn't be happy, nobody could. So he walked into town looking for a brawl, and Canaan was the first civilization he came across. Or maybe this is just who God is: an angry warlord on a perpetual warpath searching high and low for people to stomp on and destroy.

Fortunately, Israel's story gives us a radically different picture.

The Patience of God

In a haunting Old Testament passage, God comes to Abraham hundreds of years before the eventual holy war will take place. Abraham is living in Canaan: the ground beneath his feet is where his great-grandkids will be fighting one day. God promises to sustain Abraham's children through their coming slavery in Egypt, and he foreshadows why Canaan will eventually be judged:

> As the sun was setting, Abram fell into a deep sleep, and a thick and dreadful darkness came over him. Then the LORD said to him, "Know for certain that your descendants will be strangers in a country not their own [Egypt], and they will be enslaved and mistreated four hundred years. But I will punish the nation they serve as slaves, and afterward they will come out with great possessions. . . . In the fourth generation your descendants will come back here [Canaan], *for the sin of the Amorites has not yet reached its full measure.*"[21]

God tells Abraham the reason his grandkids are going to get beat up in Egypt for four hundred years, the reason they can't call this place home just yet, is this: he is being patient with Canaan.

There are three things I want to point out here. First, God is *way* more patient than the caricature would lead us to believe. Four hundred years is a *long* time. We misunderstand holy war if we think God is just out looking to pick a fight. God is not running around trashing mighty empires every day. His rumble with Canaan comes at the end of a long-suffering patience, a lengthy historical process.

I have a hard time fathoming four hundred years. I live in the United States, a country just one generation past its two hundredth birthday; our entire history is only *half* the length of God's patience with Canaan. I used to live near a Boston cemetery with tombstones from the early 1800s; my family hasn't kept records of our family tree even *that* far back. If I were an Israelite in Egypt, I'd have no clue who my grandpa Abraham was. My own country's two-and-a-half-century history is hard for me to fathom. And God's patience with Canaan is way longer.

God is patient with Canaan for a *long* time.

The Violence of Canaan

The second thing I want to point out: Canaan is *way* more violent than the caricature would lead us to believe. God tells Abraham "the sin of the Amorites" has not yet reached its full extent. Who are the Amorites? And what are they doing in Canaan?

Today we are not so familiar with the Amorites. But Abraham was. The Amorites were the founders of Babylon, perhaps the greatest empire of the ancient world. They were known for conquering their neighbors and taking their stuff. For aggressively waging war and violently dominating the surrounding nations. For their violent gods in the corner of the boxing ring, backing them up.

Abraham was from Babylon: the Amorites ruled his hometown. Abraham grew up in Ur of Chaldea, in the heart of Babylon. When God calls Abraham, he calls him out of Babylon and into Canaan. But as Abraham journeys westward toward Canaan, there is a problem: the Amorites are close behind. Babylon is expanding. God being patient with "the sin of the Amorites" in Canaan is an Old Testament way of saying he is being patient with their violent empire-building.

Four hundred years later: Canaan is not an idyllic paradise. It is a violent empire.

Babylon has invaded Eden. This picture becomes clearer when we zoom out to the broader story. When Adam and Eve are exiled from Eden, they move eastward. And their children keep moving eastward, farther and farther east of Eden, until they eventually settle to build Babylon. Consider the following passages (emphasis added):

> So the LORD God banished [Adam] from the Garden of Eden. . . . He placed on *the east side* of the Garden of Eden cherubim and a flaming sword flashing back and forth to guard the way to the tree of life. (Genesis 3:23–24)

> Cain said to the LORD, "My punishment is more than I can bear. Today you are driving me from the land." . . . So Cain went out from the LORD's presence and lived in the land of Nod, *east of Eden.* (Genesis 4:13–14, 16)

> As people *moved eastward*, they found a plain in Shinar [Babylon] and settled there. . . . Then they said, "Come, let us build ourselves a city, with a tower that reaches to the heavens." (Genesis 11:2, 4)

Babylon is depicted as *east* of Eden.

When God calls Abraham, he calls him *westward*: out of Babylon and back toward Eden. Here's a modern analogy to help give us a sense of the map. Imagine God planted a special garden in California and entrusted the care of this flourishing place to some gardener friends. But rather than care for the California garden, his friends started trashing the place. So God sent them east.

They worked their way through Arizona and New Mexico, eking out a living in the Southwestern deserts, until eventually one day they arrived in Texas. Here they began to settle and build a large, thriving Texan empire. Like Babylon, this Texan empire is east of the original garden.

Now let's say God paid a visit to the Texas project and called a man named Ol' Abe out of it, saying, "Come back west with me to California! You and your family will be my special gardeners and care for my California garden again. And together, we'll show Texas how it's really done." So Abe and his family set out to help God care for his California garden.

Only there's a problem. Texas is greedy. They want to colonize the California garden and establish outposts of the Texan empire there. When Abe gets to California, he finds the Texans are already there and more are coming. God tells Abe:

> I'm going to be patient with the Texans for a few hundred years, and let their empire have its way. Over time, they're going to thrash my garden pretty bad, but when it gets so bad I can't stand it anymore, I'm going to uproot Texas out of my garden and give it to your homeless, beat-up, and wandering grandchildren.
>
> Unfortunately, your children are going to get treated pretty rough in the meantime—they'll go to another empire, like Texas, down south called Mexico. They'll be enslaved there and treated bad: there's some hard times a-comin'. But when the time is right, I'll deal with Texas and Mexico. I'll put an end to their suffering and give your kids a home in California where we can finally care for my garden together.

This is the sense of the story. The Amorites are thrashing God's garden. Babylon has invaded Eden.

And God tells Abraham he's going to be patient for four hundred years. But when God's patience runs out, Babylon is going to get uprooted out of his garden. The Amorites will have to deal with their Creator. In a telling piece of imagery, the Amorites are said to have made the garden so sick that *the land itself* eventually "vomited out its inhabitants."[22] And God gives his garden over to the last and the least—a nation of homeless slaves who could never afford the garden on their own.

Canaan is not an idyllic utopia; it is a violent empire. The Amorites are not minding their own business; they have been thrashing God's garden for way too long. But their injustice does not have the last word.

"How Long, O Lord . . . ?"

The third thing I want to point out is this: God's patience involves the suffering of his people. God tells Abraham his kids are going to be in Egypt for four hundred years—*four hundred years!* And they're going to suffer there: "they'll be enslaved and mistreated."

I think I could endure just about anything . . . except the suffering of my children. If I were Abraham, I would be furious: "I've given everything to follow you! Why won't you protect my family? Why won't you care for my children? Why can't we live in our new home now?" And God's response: "I am being patient with Canaan." God's patience means Israel's suffering.

Abraham's family flips our question on its head. Israel's question is not, "God, if you are good, why would you ever intervene with the empires of our world?" It is instead, "God, if you are good, why do you wait so long?" And Abraham's answer to his suffering children: "God is more patient than we are."

Four hundred years can feel like an eternity. Especially if you're under an Egyptian whip: the same whip that your father was under . . . and grandfather. All because God is being patient with Canaan.

And Israel's cry in the midst of it is, "How long, O LORD . . . ?" This cry for God to intervene in the injustice of our world is threaded throughout the biblical story:

> How long, O LORD, must I call for help,
>   but you do not listen?
> Or cry out to you, "Violence!"
>   but you do not save? (Habakkuk 1:2)

> O Lord, how long will you look on?
>   Rescue my life from their ravages,
>   my precious life from these lions. (Psalm 35:17)

> How long, Sovereign Lord, holy and true, until you judge the
> inhabitants of the earth and avenge our blood? (Revelation 6:10)

God is not simply waiting for the flowers to bloom; he is enduring the suffering of his children.

We live in a world where the weak get beat up and the poor get exploited. The faithful suffer while the wicked prosper. In this world—our world—God's people participate in the pain of his patience with his rebellious world. The cry of protest for followers of Jesus is not, "God, if you are good, why would you ever intervene?" It is, rather, "God, because you are good, why do you wait so long?"

It can be easy today to think God has abandoned his world. We open the daily paper and are confronted with violence and scandal. We turn on the evening news and soak in the tragedy and corruption. We hear the ongoing "crack of Pharaoh's whip," like Israel of old. Companies pursue profits over people. Governments believe they can rule the earth without God. Injustice runs rampant and believes it has no one to answer to.

It can be easy to think God has left the building. But what if he is simply being patient? What if God is more patient than we are?

Many people have asked me, "If God is so good, how can he see all of the horrible things we do to each other and not intervene?" This is a difficult question, one we should feel the heartache of before we give a glib answer. But I have come to believe the answer has something to do with this: God is more patient than we are.

God was outrageously patient with the empires of old, and he is outrageously patient with us today. But his patience will not last forever.

And our demand highlights something: we are *crying out* for God to pick the fight, and wondering why he waits so long. This heart-wrenching cry arising from our blood-drenched, war-torn world has something central, I believe, to do with holy war.

When God's patience finally runs out, he arises to wage war on the empires of our world. God arises on behalf of the weak, whose resounding cries have ached his ears for ages. God is not an angry warlord on a perpetual warpath, smashing mighty empires every day. He is incredibly patient . . . but his patience will not last forever.

What does this mean for us today? It is to this question that we now turn.

CHAPTER 14 KEY IDEA

WHY IS GOD SO HARSH WITH CANAAN?

God is way less harsh, and way more patient, than
the caricature would lead us to believe. Canaan's
brutal empire is being evicted from Eden.

INTERLUDE

RAISING THE BAR

Israel raised the bar on warfare practice for the empires of the ancient world. Unlike her neighbors, Israel's soldiers were not paid for their military service and not allowed to take plunder in Canaan. This limited greed as an incentive for brutality and primary motivator for war. Strict rules were set on how defeated enemy populations and foreigners in the land were to be treated. Once in the land, Israel was not allowed to raise a standing army or expand beyond her borders. This defensive orientation set her apart from the imperial aggression and territorial expansion of her neighbors.[1]

Israel's neighbors could be much more brutal. Babylon and Assyria were known for massacring civilians, demolishing population centers, and developing grotesque public displays of mutilated enemy bodies to demonstrate their sheer power. On a spectrum of acceptable warfare practice, the surrounding empires looked much more like the caricature than Abraham's family did.

But what about modern wars? When people complain about holy war in the Old Testament, there is often an underlying assumption that they were brutish, backward, and brutal, while we are civilized, progressive, and humane. Is this really true? Are we less bloody today? Israel may not look like the caricature, but do we?

Modern warfare is deadlier than anything Israel could have dreamed of. We have perhaps been more like the caricature at times than we would like to admit. Israel may not have demolished urban population centers and massacred the civilians inside, but we have. Consider these statistics, taken from US foreign policy expert Walter Russell Mead's acclaimed historical work, on civilian deaths and urban destruction in a thirty-year span of wars:

WORLD WAR II: "More German *civilians* died in the three-night-long Anglo-American firebombing of Dresden than American *soldiers* died in [all of] World War I. . . . At the time the Dresden raids constituted the largest slaughter of civilians by military forces in one place at one time since the campaigns of Genghis Khan."[2]

WORLD WAR II: "In the last five months of World War II, American bombings killed more than 900,000 Japanese civilians, not counting the casualties from the atomic strikes against Hiroshima and Nagasaki. This is more than twice the total number of combat deaths (441,513) the United States has suffered in all its foreign wars combined."[3]

KOREAN WAR: "Out of a prewar population of 9.49 million, an estimated 1 million (North) Korean civilians are believed to have died as a result of the actions of American forces during the 1950–53 conflict there. . . . Almost 34,000 American soldiers were killed during [the Korean War], meaning that US forces killed approximately 30 North Korean *civilians* for every American *soldier* who died."[4]

VIETNAM WAR: "Some 365,000 Vietnamese civilians are believed to have died as a result of the war during the period of American involvement. . . . [This would mean] a ratio of 8 Vietnamese civilian deaths for every American killed in the war."[5]

This comparison is not of soldier-to-soldier deaths, but of soldier-to-*civilian* deaths. The language of "utterly destroy them," "show no mercy," and "do not leave alive anything that breathes" could be used of our wars here not as exaggerated trash talk—as in Israel's case—but as description of fact.

And the scope of urban destruction is unprecedented. These cities were not military outposts—as in Israel's case—but civilian population centers with women, children, and the elderly inside. Within thirty years, we killed *drastically* more civilians in our wars across enemy lines than the soldiers we lost. The civilian casualties and urban destruction we've inflicted make Israel's battles look like child's play.

The point is not whether or not we can make contemporary justifications for our modern warfare tactics. The point is simply that we tend to hold the ancients to a much higher standard than we hold ourselves. We tend to look back and pick the civilizational specks out of their eye while conveniently ignoring the planks in our own. And Israel's practice ends up being much more humane, and way less bloody, than the tragic scope of modern warfare.

The Angry Gods

"Yes, but we fight for practical reasons," some might say. "They fought for religious ones." This is misleading, however, on two fronts. First, Israel's wars were way less "religious" than we tend to think. Gerhard von Rad, one of the most renowned and influential scholars on Old Testament holy war, observes that Israel was not "fighting for God" in a contemporary sense:

> We would be greatly misunderstanding these wars if we sought to comprehend them as religious wars in the sense that has become current for us . . . Israel did not arise to protect faith in Yahweh, but Yahweh came on the scene to defend Israel.[6]

Israel was not fighting to impose her ideology on the surrounding empires. God was arising to protect a weak and vulnerable people from the political and socioeconomic powerhouses that sought to either exploit or destroy them. Nothing could be more "practical" than that.

Second, modern warfare is way more "religious" than we like to admit. The gods are still around; they just go by different names.

The twentieth century was the most violent the world has ever seen. Its opposing powers fought in the name of communism and capitalism, nationalism and free markets, "blood and soil" and the "will of the people," the sovereignty of the state and the autonomy of the individual.

Ancient civilizations used the gods to justify their violence; we use our ideologies. The angry gods are still in the corner of the boxing ring, backing us up; they have just taken on more discreet form.

And the regimes that sought to banish God most explicitly from their civilization, the communist regimes of the Cold War era, wound up being the most violent of the century. As Alister McGrath notes in his influential study on atheism:

> The twentieth century gave rise to one of the greatest and most distressing paradoxes of human history: that the greatest intolerance and violence of that century were practiced by those who believed that religion caused intolerance and violence.[7]

Freeing our societies *from* God would appear to make us not less violent, but more.[8] When we zoom out from communism to the broader modern world, David Bentley Hart offers a provocative thought in a similar direction, claiming:

> We live now in the wake of the most monstrously violent century in human history, during which the secular order (on both the political right and the political left), freed from the authority of religion, showed itself willing to kill on an unprecedented scale and with an ease of conscience worse than merely depraved. If ever an age deserved to be thought an age of darkness, it is surely ours.[9]

15.

THE GREAT CITY

WHITE HORSE RIDER

Jesus is coming to wage holy war on Babylon. Holy war is more than an Old Testament phenomenon; it is New Testament hope. Jesus is the resurrected King of the New Testament, who will return to "[destroy] all dominion, authority, and power" that stands opposed to God, and "[hand] over the kingdom to God the Father."[1] In Revelation, Jesus comes as the rider on a white horse, leading the armies of God to take down "the great city" of Babylon that rules over the peoples of the earth.[2] Jesus takes out the empire to bring in the kingdom.

This is holy war language.

So what is Babylon? If Jesus is going to wage holy war on "the great city," it would be helpful to know what that city is—especially if we are in it.

We need to guard against a popular danger here: it is all too easy to find "Babylon" in our own national enemies—to picture ourselves as the heroic good guys and those outside as the epic villains. For example, during the Cold War, some Americans looked to Russia as the "great beast." During the Vietnam War, many portrayed America as the angelic forces of good while the Vietnamese played the apocalyptic forces of evil. Today, some Americans identify the Islamic world as a reemerging "Babylon" of sorts.

It seems we are good at finding Babylon everywhere we are not.

But what if Babylon hits closer to home? What if "the great city" is not simply a place we in the West can point to from the outside, but a reality we live in from the inside? What if its walls and towers are not simply a coming event for the future, but a structure we have been constructing for centuries? What if they are still growing taller and taller—what if we are building Babylon today?

In this chapter, I want to explore three of Babylon's primary characteristics, asking if we might find ourselves within her walls. Let's start with economy.

BABYLON AS ECONOMY

Babylon is an economic powerhouse. She is described not so much as a political machine in Revelation as an international economy. There is no lone king barking orders across the earth, no "one-world government" ruling over the nations. Rather, Babylon is depicted as an international playground where the "kings" (political leaders) and "merchants" (economic leaders) come out to play.

Babylon is an economic brothel: she promotes vice in the world. Vices like lust: the kings are said to commit adultery with her. Vices like greed: the merchants are said to grow rich off her. Vices like gluttony: the nations are said to get drunk off her wine. Babylon is not a dictator restricting our freedom, but a vending machine giving us everything we could possibly want.

Babylon is in the import/export business: a global Walmart with ships going back and forth across the oceans in trade. Shoppers are satisfied with everything their hearts desire. Her merchants are called "the world's great men" (think Donald Trump, Rupert Murdoch, and the "1 percent" who own 39 percent of the world's wealth[3]). When Babylon goes down, her economic leaders weep and gnash their teeth over her expired shopping list:

The merchants of the earth will weep and mourn over her [Babylon] because no one buys their cargoes anymore—cargoes of gold, silver, precious stones and pearls; fine linen, purple, silk and scarlet cloth; every sort of citron wood, and articles of every kind made of ivory, costly wood, bronze, iron and marble; cargoes of cinnamon and spice, of incense, myrrh and frankincense, of wine and olive oil, of fine flour and wheat; cattle and sheep; horses and carriages; and bodies and souls of men.[4]

Babylon's shopping list offers everything from riches to restaurants; clothes to construction materials; perfume to pets; spices to slaves.

And Babylon is connected with injustice. Around the world, the blood of the oppressed cries out against her, into the ears of God. Does this bear any resemblance to our world today?

The Invisible Center

Our world has an economic center. Historically, the great powers of our world were *politically* centered: Pharaoh's palace drove Egypt. Caesar was centered in Rome. The Aztecs had Tenochtitlán, and the Ming had Beijing. Kings were sovereign over their kingdoms. You could point to a capitol. You could visit a visible center.

But things are different today. Our world is economically centered: there is no sovereign president, no central government, no judicial capital presiding over the international economy. The great powers of our world participate in an economic network that is bigger than them all. In the words of Immanuel Wallerstein:

Empires . . . were a constant feature of the world scene for 5,000 years. . . . In the late fifteenth and early sixteenth century, there came into existence what we may call a European world-economy. It was not an empire yet it was as spacious as a grand empire and shared some features with it. But it was different, and new. It was a kind of social system the world has not really known before and which is the

distinctive feature of the modern world-system. It is an economic but
not a political entity . . . a "world" system . . . because it is larger than
any juridically-defined political unit . . . a "world-*economy*" because
the basic linkage between the parts of the system is economic.[5]

We call the market free precisely to the extent it has freedom from
political constraints. We say an "invisible hand" drives it precisely
because it has no governing body. Our international economy has an
invisible center.

I remember a time this came to life for me. Living in Boston,
I went to hear a lecture at Harvard Square by Dr. Owens Wiwa, a
Nigerian leader, on a recent massacre of Ogoni people in Nigeria.
The Ogoni were an ethnic minority, an indigenous people group in
Nigeria. Wiwa gave the following backstory to the massacre.[6]

The Ogoni had massive oil reserves beneath their land, discovered decades earlier by Shell, a US-based oil company. Over the
years, more than $30 billion in oil revenue had been pulled out from
beneath the Ogonis' feet. Because the Ogoni were an ethnic minority,
with next to no political clout or voice in the country, they had seen
next to nothing of this money.

While the Ogoni didn't receive money, they did receive something else: the destruction of their land. Over the course of fifteen
years, there had been nearly three thousand separate oil spills in the
Niger Delta, averaging seven hundred barrels each and contaminating local water supplies. Gas flares would burn twenty-four hours a
day near some Ogoni villages, covering the area in thick soot and constant noise, causing air pollution, acid rain, and respiratory problems,
while further contaminating local water supplies.

The Ogoni sang a song about the gas flares: "The flames of Shell
are flames of hell; we bask below their light."

In contrast, Shell grew extremely wealthy: 14 percent of Shell's
global oil production came from Nigeria at the time. And Nigerian
leaders made a killing: 80 percent of Nigeria's government revenue
came from oil during those same years.

The kings and merchants were doing well.

Fed up, the Ogoni protested. Three hundred thousand Ogoni showed up at the first protest, wanting greater voice and participation in political decisions affecting their land. The Nigerian military was sent in to deal with the situation. The military had recently appointed Ernest Shonekan, Shell's former Nigeria director, as interim president of the country. Political, economic, and military force was stacked in an intimidating bloc against the Ogoni.

As community tensions increased, brutal attacks on Ogoni villages led to more than seven hundred people being killed, with twenty-five thousand left homeless. It was a massacre. To make sure the Ogoni got the point, nine of their key tribal leaders were arrested and publicly executed.

It's a Small World

I had heard stories like this before. But what got me came next. The Nigerian professor began to list major international investors in Shell's operations. I had a part-time job at the time as a mail carrier in the business district in downtown Boston. Every day, I entered some of Boston's largest high-rises, rode the elevator to the top, said good morning, and passed off the mail. As the Nigerian professor read through the list, I was shocked to realize that some of Shell's top investors were companies to whom I delivered mail every day.

In the weeks to come, it was an eerie feeling to enter the massive revolving door, step behind the concrete walls, take the rising elevator to the top of the lofty tower, walk through the expansive lobby to reception, and as I stood suspended above the Boston skyline . . . remember the Ogoni bodies lying dead halfway around the world.

Our world is radically interconnected. Sometimes in ways that are not so good.

My world became much smaller that day. What struck me was this: an indigenous people group in rural Nigeria was connected to a high-rise tower in Boston, was connected to a military dictatorship in a Third World country, was connected to a twenty-one-year-old

American delivering mail, was connected to African land halfway around the world, was connected to money in the bank and gas in the tank, was connected to a community massacre and execution of political leaders, was connected to me.

It's a small world after all.

Our world has become increasingly interconnected. And when injustice occurs in the world today, it often occurs in the space of those interconnections. This does not mean the global economy is inherently unjust. Oil gets drilled all the time without local people being killed. It is not the case that every time you fill your tank, someone in the world dies. Texas has massive wealth from massive oil fields without mass graveyards to accompany them.

International business does a lot of good and has raised the livelihood of many around the world. But *sometimes*, and perhaps more often than we like to admit, international economics and injustice are intertwined. How many Third World governments have exploited or displaced local communities to facilitate the interests of First World business? How many Middle Eastern regimes have been propped up by international oil dollars while brutalizing their people? How many skyscrapers have been built on the backs of the poor?

How many skeletons do *we* have in the ground?

The market may be free, but is it a freedom *from* God or *for* God? Is its invisible hand a benevolent leader or a violent dictator, particularly from the perspective of the poor? People have been killing each other since the beginning of time; that is nothing new. What is unique today is the international context in which this killing frequently occurs.

Jesus calls us, in the midst of Babylon, to create ethical businesses that care well not only for investors, but also for employees and the local communities where our products are made. Jesus calls us, in the midst of Babylon, to be conscientious consumers and to pay attention to where our products are coming from.

If it's cheaper than it should be, there's probably a story behind it—and it's probably not a good one.

Our Products Have Histories

Our imports have histories that, like Babylon's, are not always pretty. To cite just a few well-known examples: Diamonds mined in war zones, or "blood diamonds," are cheap and prominent on the international market and worn on wedding fingers throughout the West. But their international profit has fueled local warlords and violent insurgencies throughout West Africa and galvanized demand in these countries for child soldiers and child laborers.[7]

Chocolate produced by international companies such as Hershey's and Nestlé relies on cheap supplies from cocoa plantations where thousands of children are trafficked, enslaved, abused, and exploited under extremely inhospitable conditions in forced slave labor.[8]

Land conflicts have frequently erupted over property owned by international companies and contested by local peoples. For example, Dole's, Chiquita's, and Del Monte's banana plantations were at the heart of the infamous US-backed overthrow of Guatemala's democratically elected government and the deaths of more than two hundred thousand indigenous Mayans and other Guatemalans in the ensuing civil war.[9]

Yes, our imports have a tale to tell—and it's not always a fairy tale.

Babylon is also in the export business. Our exports, like Babylon's, have histories that are not always good. For example: soft drinks like Coke and Pepsi are often sold cheaper than water in much of the developing world, leading to epidemic diabetes, obesity, dental disease, and other health problems in impoverished communities.

Cheap meat is grown on American factory farms by overcrowding animals into inhumane living conditions, injecting them with antibiotics to keep them alive while they suffer, and exporting their cheap remains around the world for fast-food companies such as McDonald's and KFC to profit off the increasing obesity epidemic in our world.

Corn is infamously cheap in America, subsidized by the US government at the astronomical level of more than $10 billion a year. The resulting cheap corn has flooded Mexico's market for almost two decades, pushing Mexico's 15 million corn farmers into unemployment and severely reduced incomes, as the price of corn dropped in Mexico by more than 70 percent.[10]

If our exports could talk, we might not like what they have to say.

Babylon is also, as we saw earlier, an economic brothel promoting vice in the world and profiting handsomely. Our international economy behaves like Babylon in this way too. Advertising frequently plays off our basest motives, using sex (*She'll want to sleep with you if you wear this cologne!*), pride (*Everyone will want to* be *you if you drive this car!*), and greed (*The Joneses have this; do you?*) to produce dissatisfaction—a hole to be filled by consuming the latest product.

And if you don't have the money for these things, Babylon will give you a credit card. Banking services offered through major companies like Chase and Bank of America pull exorbitant interest and profits out of local communities (including already impoverished ones) and into major international trading centers, like New York, London, and Tokyo. The rich get richer and the poor get poorer.

And if you feel uneasy about this arrangement, simply turn on the television: Babylon will give you a new story to live in. Media not only reflects reality; it helps shape and create it. Hollywood movies, reality TV, and video games not only frequently glorify violence, promiscuity, and our basest motives; they provide new, self-justifying narratives through which we make sense of our world—and they're not always healthy ones.

Babylon is a prostitute: she'll dress up sexy and get you to sleep with her, then leave you with a hole in your heart (and your wallet) . . . and possibly a nasty disease.

The point is, our modern international economy looks a lot like Babylon. We do not need to look outside ourselves to find "the great city" in our newest national enemies; it would appear we ourselves live inside its towering walls. The West is not the hero of this story—we have historically been its prime architects, not its virtuous detractors. We have led the way in developing, and profiting greatly from, the international economy over the last few centuries.

We are part and parcel of the global construction project.
We bear the marks of the great city.
We are builders of Babylon.

BABYLON AS AUTONOMY

Babylon is defined not only by its economy, but also by its autonomy. Babylon wants to rule the earth without God: this is her driving political ethos. Babylon's roots are at the famous Tower of Babel. In Genesis 11, the nations declare war on God and storm the heavens, building the tower in an offensive assault on his kingdom. The Tower of Babel's soaring walls were built with "bricks" and "tar" (v. 3), and Israel knew from her experience enslaved in Egypt who was making the bricks.

Babylon calls herself an enlightened civilization: her children build the tower to "make a name for ourselves,"[11] rather than receive their name from God. But Abraham's grandchildren laugh that she is a "city of confusion" (the Hebrew word *babel* means "confusion," like our word *babble*). As her tower walls get higher and higher, Babylon seemingly gets farther and farther from God.

Babylon wasn't built in a day. She has a history: it takes time for her walls and towers to rise . . . and God is incredibly patient. When Babylon later invades Canaan, God is patient for hundreds of years before giving the land to his nation of homeless slaves. And later, when Babylon demolishes Jerusalem and takes her people captive, God again waits hundreds of years before sending the Messiah.

God shows extreme patience with Babylon's violent attempt to rule the earth on her own. Does the long, historical process of Babylon's development bear any resemblance to our world today?

Conquest and Colonization

Just like Babylon's ancient tower, our international construction project takes time. The modern global economy has been developing for centuries; it will likely keep developing for a long time to come. Where has it come from? Does it have an apocalyptic history? If "the great city" is currently under construction, who laid its modern foundations?

What are the invisible center's political roots?

Western civilization was not always poised to lead the way. As historian Paul Kennedy observes, in the year 1500 Europe was the least likely continent to arise to global dominance. The major world powers of the day were China's Ming dynasty, the Middle East's Ottoman and Persian empires, and the Incan and Aztec civilizations of the Western Hemisphere. Europe, in contrast, had remained a "hodgepodge of petty kingdoms and principalities," politically fragmented since the fall of the Roman Empire a thousand years earlier.[12]

What happened to change all that?

Conquest and colonization were key factors. From the fifteenth to the twentieth century, the European powers conquered and colonized the world. Across the earth, they carved out many of the borders we recognize on a world map today. For example, in 1500 Portugal gave birth to the colony of Brazil. Prior to 1500, the borders of the country we call "Brazil" today did not exist. These borders were not created to reflect the interests of local people on the ground. Portugal created the colony's borders to represent her overseas interests there.

Brazil, like most colonies, was a commercial success. By 1600, the sugar alone exported from Brazil *doubled all* of England's total exports to the world at the time.[13] Just sugar. But Portugal had a much bigger shopping list to pick up from Brazil than just sugar: she exported gold, jewels, spices, construction materials, and more. The list actually looks an awful lot like Babylon's shopping list from Revelation 18, quoted earlier.

Portugal grew extremely wealthy off Brazil.

European colonies like Brazil represented Western interests over those of local people. For example, if we zoom out from Brazil, the rest of Latin America was colonized by Spain. Between Christopher Columbus's arrival in 1492 and the year 1640, Spain extracted as much as 360 tons of gold and 34,000 tons of silver from the Americas. This was 85 percent of the world's total silver production at the time. With this massive influx of precious metals, Europe's production of metal coins multiplied approximately eight to ten times in one century. And once again, Spain had much more than gold and silver on its shopping list.[14]

Europe made bank off Latin America.

An Apocalyptic History

If we zoom out from Latin America to the rest of the Southern Hemisphere, the European powers similarly colonized most of Africa, the Middle East, India, and Southeast Asia. For example, during the infamous "Scramble for Africa," the European powers carved the African continent into borders and governments to represent Western interests in their respective spheres. Dr. Adu Boahen, a famous African historian, observes that "by 1900 practically the whole of . . . the entire African continent had been appropriated by European nations to meet their selfish economic, political, and social ends."[15]

For England, India became the "jewel in the British crown," funneling massive wealth and resources back home and helping the English expand their empire to become a place "where the sun never set." France played a particularly strong role in Southeast Asia, colonizing countries like Vietnam, Cambodia, and Laos—with tensions created and fueled that would blow up in that region for a long time to come.

Western civilization arose to world dominance, in part, through its imperial expansion around the globe. As world historian J. M. Blaut observes, Europe's rise to global dominance occurred "because of the immense wealth obtained by Europeans in America and later in Asia and Africa—not because Europeans were brighter or bolder or better than non-Europeans, or more modern, more advanced, more progressive, more rational."[16]

Western civilization has its fair share of apocalyptic images in this history: the eradication of indigenous peoples in the Americas, the enslavement of tens of millions of Africans, the exploitation of the masses in India and Southeast Asia. This is not to say the world was a utopia beforehand, or that the West is at the root of all our modern world's problems—sin and destruction have been around since Eden—but it is to say that the West has historically led the way in developing our modern global economy.

Babylon's great city is under construction, and we have laid its modern foundations. The invisible center's political roots are in Western civilization. We are the builders of Babylon. And if her history is a play, it has many apocalyptic scenes.

Storming the Heavens

Babylon's ancient tower stormed the heavens—declaring war on the kingdom of God. Ironically, the higher her tower walls climbed, the more distant she grew from God. Similarly, we have sought to rule the earth on our own. And the higher our global walls climb, the more distant God seems to appear. As Western civilization has expanded throughout the modern era, God has increasingly been pushed out of public life.

Charles Taylor opens his acclaimed work, *A Secular Age*, asking the provocative question, "What happened between 1500 and 2000?" to so dramatically change the cultural landscape of belief:

> Why was it virtually impossible not to believe in God in, say, 1500 in our Western society, while in 2000 many of us find this not only easy, but even inescapable? . . . The change I want to define and trace is one which takes us from a society in which it was virtually impossible not to believe in God, to one in which faith, even for the staunchest believer, is one human possibility among others . . . and in which moreover, unbelief has become for many the major default option.[17]

While Taylor's argument is multifaceted and profound, there is an illuminating central word he borrows from historians to describe this modern process: *disenchantment*. Our disenchanting of the world is our banishing of transcendence from public life, the pushing of

God out from earth and away into heaven. This is the modern world we have made. A world disenchanted with God.

A world enchanted with ourselves.

If we are to rule the earth on our own, God must go. If the empire is to reign unchallenged, the kingdom must be pushed away. If our civilization is to "make a name for ourselves," the one who names us must be silenced. Ironically, the more our skyscraping towers penetrate the heavens, the more distant God becomes.

This leads to our final observation.

BABYLON AS EXILE

Babylon is, finally, a place of exile: where the people of God await the coming of the kingdom. When Adam and Eve head east to build Babylon, there is hope in the exile that redemption is coming. When Abraham is called out of Babylon, he looks toward the coming of a "city with foundations, whose architect and builder is God."[18] When Babylon destroys Jerusalem and carries her children into exile, they sing from behind the empire's walls:

> By the rivers of Babylon we sat and wept
> > when we remembered Zion. . . .
> How can we sing the songs of the LORD
> > while in a foreign land? . . .
> May my tongue cling to the roof of my mouth [O Jerusalem]
> > if I do not remember you,
> if I do not consider Jerusalem
> > my highest joy.[19]

God's people live in Babylon, but it is not their home. They lift their eyes over Babylon's walls and look toward the coming city of God.

What does this mean for us today?

Every Nation, Tribe, and Tongue

Around the world, the church waits in exile for the coming of God's kingdom. Many have an outdated tendency today to think of Christianity as a "white man's religion." But that picture couldn't be farther from the truth. Jesus' church has gone global. The largest Christian populations in the world are found in Africa, Latin America, and increasingly, Asia.[20] There are more Christians at church on Sunday in China than in all of Europe today.[21]

Jesus' people are a global phenomenon.

With this global growth, the geographic centers of the church have also shifted. As John Mbiti, a Kenyan scholar, observes, "The centers of the church's universality [are] no longer in Geneva, Rome, Athens, Paris, London, New York, but Kinshasa, Buenos Aires, Addis Ababa, and Manila."[22]

Christianity's influence is increasingly coming from the Southern Hemisphere.

Jesus' church is not only global and southern, but also poor. Many in the West have an inaccurate perception of average Christians today as "elite aristocrats," living secluded lives in the suburbs of the West. But this picture couldn't be any less accurate. The majority of today's Christians are poor. They live in slums, work in factories, struggle to make ends meet—and are vibrant followers of Jesus. As Philip Jenkins observes, "If we want to visualize a 'typical' contemporary Christian, we should think of a woman living in a village in Nigeria or in a Brazilian favela."[23]

All around the world, Jesus' followers live in the midst of global Babylon, crying out to God from inside her walls. They want intimacy with God, not distance; communion with God, not independence; worship of God, not autonomy. They want God's kingdom to come on earth as in heaven.

They want God to come and end the exile.

Their hope is not only for themselves, but also for the world. They have found in Babylon not only "the blood of prophets and of the saints," but also the blood "of all who have been killed on the earth."[24] As they cry out, they may not call it "Babylon," they may not see the international construction that holds it all together, but they cry out nonetheless.

And God hears.

Piling Up Crimes

As we saw earlier in the Cain and Abel story, death does not silence the cries of the murdered; it amplifies them. God hears Abel's blood crying out from the ground, screaming into the ears of God. And as Cain's children fill and flood the earth with violence, the blood of the exploited, oppressed, and enslaved rises through history like a tidal wave in a crescendoing cacophony that climaxes on the great and terrible day of the Lord.

When the cries from our world are too much to bear, when God's patience with Babylon finally runs out, the great city will be judged.

God hears the blood.

Babylon is piling up crimes. Revelation says the great city will be judged when "her sins are piled up to heaven."[25] The bodies of the dead are stacked like money in her account. The body of Abel. The bodies of the Ogoni. The corpses of the murdered rising up from the earth. The cries of the poor are in the mortar, precariously holding together her walls. But God has not forgotten.

"God has remembered her crimes."[26]

While Babylon rages upon the earth, the prayers of the saints rise to God's throne. These prayers are pictured as incense in Revelation, rising before the presence of God.[27] God smells the prayers of his people, hears the cries erupting from his blood-soaked world. The cries are gathered to fill the bowls of wrath before God's throne waiting to be poured out in his final judgment upon Babylon.

Our cries fuel the wrath of God that will tear down Babylon.

Babylon's future is not glory but destruction. Yet, God does not destroy the great city because he delights in her destruction ("We would have healed Babylon, but she cannot be healed"[28]), but to pave the way for the coming of his kingdom. As Babylon continues to grow upon the earth, and the cries continue to rise against her, she moves ever closer to that day when God shall arise in holy war against the great city.

Closer to Home

Babylon hits closer to home than we realize. We live out a twenty-first-century version of it every day. Its walls and towers are not simply a coming event for the future, but a structure we have been constructing for centuries, growing taller and taller by the day. We are the architects of autonomy, the builders of Babylon, the constructors of confusion, the engineers of exile's empire.

God is patient, more patient than we are, but he will not be patient forever.

CHAPTER 15 KEY IDEA

WHAT IS "THE GREAT CITY" OF BABYLON?

Babylon is not simply a place we in the West can point to from the outside, but a reality we live in from the inside. We bear its characteristic marks of economy, autonomy, and exile. God's coming holy war on the great city is a source of confrontation, not vindication, for our civilization.

16.

AGENTS OF WRATH

WAR AND PEACE

Does holy war have any practical implications for us today? Can modern nations wage holy war? Should believing in Jesus' conflict with Babylon make us more violent or less? As someone who personally finds great hope in God's coming holy war, I believe—ironically—that reclaiming holy war is quite possibly one of the greatest resources for living peacefully in our violent world today. In this chapter, I want to explain why.

Nonviolent Resistance

Miroslav Volf is a Croatian theologian. Writing from the genocidal war zones of his homeland, he asks: When your brother has been gunned down by a local militia, where can you find the strength to forgive? When your mother has been gang-raped, where can you find the ability to not retaliate? When you hold in your arms the lifeless body of your slaughtered child, where can you find the conviction to not pick up an AK-47?

God's coming justice for our world is, Volf argues, the greatest resource that can empower us to live peacefully today. Because justice is in God's hands, we don't have to take it into our own. Volf argues that without this belief, ironically, it may be impossible to truly forgive today:

My thesis that the practice of nonviolence requires a belief in divine vengeance will be unpopular with many Christians, especially theologians in the West. To the person who is inclined to dismiss it, I suggest imagining that you are delivering a lecture in a war zone. . . . Among your listeners are people whose cities and villages have been first plundered, then burned and leveled to the ground, whose daughters and sisters have been raped, whose fathers and brothers have had their throats slit. The topic of the lecture: a Christian attitude toward violence. The thesis: we should not retaliate since God is perfect noncoercive love. Soon you would discover that it takes the quiet of a suburban home for the birth of the thesis that human nonviolence corresponds to God's refusal to judge. In a scorched land, soaked in the blood of the innocent, it will invariably die.[1]

Our world is crying out for God's justice. Hope in its coming can break our cycles of violence today. If God holds vengeance in his hands, then we do not have to take it into our own. Jesus proclaims God's kingdom will be victorious in the end. And it is with this confidence that Jesus calls us to confidently suffer well, as he did: to receive the blows and turn the other cheek, to love those who abuse us and forgive our enemies.

We can look toward God's arrival and find the power to love and forgive, knowing it will not be in vain because our world's Savior will ultimately establish his justice in the earth. When we are abused and exploited in an unjust world, we can pray for God's kingdom to come and express our raw, honest desire for vindication.

I love this about the psalmists: they frequently ask God to arise and vindicate them against their enemies. Some people complain, "Why are they so violent? Why can't they just be nice, forgive, and move on?" But those who complain this way have usually never been horrifically wounded. And the complaint misses a central miracle that is happening: in bringing their raw, honest desire for vindication before God, they are removing it from their own hands.

By entrusting vengeance to God's hands, they are taking it out of their own.

Just War or Pacifism?

A related question arises: Does holy war, properly understood, support just war or pacifism? Ironically, I believe it can be used to support both. The pacifist will point out that in the Old Testament, *God* is the one doing the fighting. Indeed, God being the primary warrior is precisely what makes it holy. It is not a *holy* war unless God himself picks the fight and does the heavy lifting.

By contrast, God's people are called to "be still": to step out in faith and look for God to show up. A war initiated by human hands is not holy, so we shouldn't presume to fight in the many unholy wars of our world. We should suffer well under the unjust powers of our world, as Jesus did, abstaining from their violence and waiting for God to come and set things right.

Just war, on the other hand, will point out that the Old Testament shows us *the kind of wars* God fights. God arises to defend the weak from the tyranny of the strong. He protects the vulnerable from those who would exploit them. God vindicates the poor from the hand of the oppressor. The murdered mothers and brothers Volf mentions needed this kind of protection. Part of the tragedy is that they did not receive it.

This is why God has given us authority to defend and protect the vulnerable under our care from outside aggression or exploitation. Like a parent protecting a child from an intruder, or a mother hen protecting her baby chicks by batting away the incoming wolves, government is justified in using violence to the extent that it protects the vulnerable under its care from hostile forces. A war is just to the extent that it is defensive, not offensive; protective, not aggressive.

God's violence is, in both the pacifist and just war traditions, oriented toward the protection of the shalom of society, particularly for the weak and vulnerable. The question is the extent to which we may participate with God in this protective action.

While I have great respect for the pacifist tradition (indeed, many of the authors I've drawn from in this holy war section are pacifist[2]), my own convictions land firmly in the just war tradition. A common critique of just war is that everyone, of course, thinks *their* wars are just. In the Croatian conflict to which Volf refers, both the Bosnians and Serbs believe their side is right. Calling any war *just* is simply a quick and easy tool to legitimate our side.

When properly understood, however, I believe it has the opposite effect.

Justice raises a bar with criteria by which the injustice of our wars can be measured. For example, Augustine is one of the most influential thinkers of the just war tradition. Yet Augustine uses justice not to legitimate the Roman Empire's many wars but to radically critique them. In *The City of God*, his monumental magnum opus, he spends a massive chunk of the book showing how Rome's wars were fought for vanity, pride, self-centered glory, and violent aggression against their neighbors in greedy pursuit of the empire's expansion.

Just war is a bar that, when properly understood, prophetically confronts and seeks to restrain the flood of unjust wars raging in our world. For example, justice might affirm Bosnians' and Serbs' need to defend their daughters and sons from hostile invasion, but confront their offensive retaliation and aggression against their neighbors.

Loving Our Enemies

How does this square with Jesus' command to love our enemies? A man once told me if he came home, walked into his bedroom, found an intruder about to rape his wife, and saw a gun on the nightstand, he would not shoot the intruder. Instead, he would fall to his knees and pray for the intruder . . . while his wife was raped.

I think this man is tragically confused. He thinks this is radical obedience to Jesus' command to love his enemies, while I think it is grievous disobedience and an offense against God.

When I am personally mistreated, insulted, and abused, I believe Jesus calls me as a disciple to "turn . . . the other cheek," to forgive "seventy times seven," and not retaliate.[3] But I also believe Jesus calls me to preserve the *shalom* of our household, entrusted under my authority and care, to protect my wife and daughter. If someone attacks my beloved bride or my little girl, I will beat them senseless to the best of my ability to protect my family. And I will do it *because of* God's authority, not in spite of it. God has given me authority, as a husband and father, to protect and defend the family he has entrusted to my care.

The Christian tradition has by and large distinguished between public authority and personal responsibility. For example, Moses tells the people of Israel not to murder (personal responsibility), but a few chapters later, Moses the governor leads the government in wiping out the rebels (public authority).[4] This is not a contradiction. It is simply the obvious: government is allowed to do things individuals cannot. We use the same logic in society today: a judge and a police officer are allowed to do things a private citizen cannot.

Similarly, Jesus suffers willingly *under* the Roman authorities in his crucifixion (submitting himself through the humility of his incarnation to atone for the sin of the world), but when he is exalted *over* our governmental authority upon his resurrection (exalted to the throne of God and given "all authority in heaven and on earth"[5]) the hope is for his coming to vindicate God's kingdom in the world. Jesus now carries the weight of government "on his shoulders"[6] and is coming to tear down Babylon.

This raises the question, *why* does God give government "the sword"? What is its purpose and when is its violence improperly used? Does holy war shed any light on this controversial topic?

PROTECTING *SHALOM*

God loves the world and wants it to flourish, to experience his *shalom*. And God cares for those whose flourishing is under threat—particularly the weak and vulnerable of society. This is where the logic of government arises: God establishes government to protect the *shalom* of society, to preserve its flourishing, particularly for the powerless whose well-being is most in danger.

God calls government to protect the flourishing under its care. Along these lines, Paul tells the church in Rome:

> Let everyone be subject to the governing authorities. . . . For the one in authority is God's servant for your good. But if you do wrong, be afraid, for rulers do not bear the sword for no reason. They are God's servants, agents of wrath to bring punishment on the wrongdoer.[7]

God's servants. Agents of wrath. Paul is talking about pagan authorities. What is going on here?

A few observations. First, Paul does not say everything the government does is good. He's not advocating for Hitler. Paul knows full well how evil leaders can get. He is writing to the church in Rome, who are being persecuted and killed by the government. The biblical story is loaded chock-full with government doing evil things: Babel building towers using slave labor, Pharaoh massacring Israelite babies, David murdering Uriah, Israel's kings worshipping idols, Nebuchadnezzar slaughtering cities, and Haman plotting the genocide of God's people. The Bible does not have a Pollyanna view of government.

Hitler is truly evil.

Another thing: Paul is talking about the *purpose* of government done right, not when it is abused. Paul says government's purpose, the reason it's given the sword, is "for our good"—for the well-being of society, the flourishing of God's *shalom* in the world. Whether the Roman authorities know it or not, God's purpose for them is to protect and preserve the thriving of his world.

Caesar, whether he knows it or not, is God's employee.

God's Servants

Finally, when government fulfills this purpose, Paul says they are acting as "God's servants." Even if they don't know God, even if they are anti-God, even if they are pagan, like the Roman emperors, God is working through them when they protect the *shalom* of society to preserve the vulnerable prospering of his world.

This came to life for me once when I joined a police officer on patrol for a ride along. Thirsty, we stopped at a convenience store to get a drink. As we walked in, the owner came out from behind the counter, ran up to the police officer, and gave him a bear hug. His wife came out from the back to greet the officer as well. They were an immigrant family from Southeast Asia, and I wondered, *Why are they so excited to see this police officer?*

I was confused so the husband explained, "We used to get robbed regularly, a couple times a week. After my wife had a gun waved in her face a few times, she was afraid for her safety and I was afraid for our lives. We called the police for a while, but nobody came. Then this officer took notice and began to visit regularly. As he showed up more frequently and made a few neighborhood arrests, the crime dropped off. Now we have not been robbed in a few months and are so happy."

This illustrates the reason God gives government the sword: the police officer's presence protected *shalom*, particularly for a vulnerable immigrant family. The threat of "the sword" scared off the criminals. It made them think twice. The family's vulnerable business and livelihood were safeguarded from hostile invasion. The officer defended their flourishing.

Preservative vs. Redemptive

Some argue that this buys into the myth of redemptive violence, misleading us to believe that government can redeem evil by inflicting vengeance on our enemies and thus bring an end to the cycle of violence. But nothing of the sort is being said: government cannot *redeem* sin; it can simply *preserve shalom*.

For example, if I protect my daughter from a would-be child molester, my protection does not redeem the lust of the child molester; it simply preserves the *shalom* of my daughter. If a police officer protects an immigrant family from a robber, his protection does not redeem the robber's greed; it simply preserves the prospering of the family's business and livelihood.

Government's authority is *preservative*, not *redemptive*. Its purpose is to protect *shalom*.

Paul says when government does this, they act as God's "agents of wrath." Hold on a minute—*wrath* . . . that is holy war language. God's wrath is central to the concept of holy war: when God's patience with the destructive powers runs out, God arises in wrath. Paul is saying that today, God wages war on sin *through* government.

God's wrath. Through government.

This leads to a shocking conclusion: If there is a modern analogy for holy war, it is not when one country wages war on another, and not when terrorists strap bombs to their chests and blow up buildings. Rather, it is when government punishes sin to protect *shalom* entrusted under its authority. In other words, when judges and police officers do their jobs properly, they can act as modern-day holy warriors, agents of God's wrath—soldiers cannot.[8]

There may be such a thing as a just war for a soldier, but not a holy one. If there is a legitimate contemporary application for holy war, it is this: government is given authority to inflict God's wrath on the destructive power of sin *within society* in order to protect the flourishing *shalom* of society—particularly for those who are the most helpless.

Violence Against Violence

Can we reconcile God's love with his violence? Some people fear God's violence makes him look like a bipolar schizophrenic. Miroslav Volf, the Croatian theologian mentioned at the beginning of this chapter, asks: How can we reconcile the crucified Messiah with the rider on a white horse? Volf's powerful answer is that God's is a different kind of violence from our everyday brand, a *violence against violence*, flowing from his holy love against the destructive power of sin.[9]

We can unpack this with a few helpful considerations. First, God is *holy love*. The Scriptures tell us that "God is holy" and "God is love"[10]—these are part of his eternal character, his essential attributes, who he is. If there were no sin, God would still be holy love. In contrast, we are never told that "God is violent" in this sense of an eternal attribute. If there were no sin, God would not be violent. Violence is not essential to his being.

Holy love is *internal* to the life of God; violence is not.

Sin, on the other hand, *is* violent. As we saw earlier in this book, it is inherently violent. It wants to tear God's good world apart. It *violates* the integrity of God's world. Because God is holy love, he wants the world to flourish, to experience his *shalom*, to overflow with his goodness flooding and spilling over. Sin, in contrast, is a destructive parasite, a cancerous foreign invader, that devours and destroys God's good world and doesn't care if it dies in the process.

Violence *is* essential to sin.

So, God exerts a *violence against violence*. God arises in holy love against sin's destructive power to contain it and to restrain its devouring impulse in order to protect the flourishing *shalom* of his world. God's violence is not an essential part of his eternal character, but rather a holy, loving response to sin's vicious assault.

This "violence against violence" illuminates God's purpose in both government authority now and the holy war to come. *Wrath* is the language used. Government protects the flourishing of society as "agents of wrath" by exerting an authoritative violence against the violent power of sin. And ultimately, when God's fractured *shalom* is so far gone as to be obliterated beyond recognition, God's wrath arises in holy war against the society itself.

IDENTITY IS SOCIAL

So when does God stop inflicting wrath *through* government, and start inflicting wrath *on* government? When does Jesus show up on a white horse, riding sword in hand, to throw down on empire? When does the fire fall from heaven and real holy war begin?

We Are Our People

It is tempting to simply answer: When government is beyond hope. When leaders like Hitler and Stalin and Genghis Khan reign. When the very authority God gave to *protect shalom* is turned as a weapon *against shalom*, destroying the very flourishing it was entrusted to protect. There may be some truth to this—the idea of Antichrist, the antagonistic leader who wants to rule the earth without God.

But this is too easy, a cop-out. When we think of our president, mayors, and everyday leaders, very few of us are actually in positions of government leadership or know what it is like to bear that weight. The reality is, there is much in the biblical story that suggests it has much more to do with the state of society as a whole.

For example, God says things in the Old Testament like, "If I can find just fifty righteous people in this city, I will spare it . . . Okay, fifty's not realistic; forty . . . Okay, if I can just find ten . . ."[11] God seems to be *looking* for righteousness, longing for it, hoping to find it. Willing to lower the bar as low as it can possibly go to spare the city. Looking at the state of the society as a whole.

Similarly, in Canaan, God waits for "the sins of the Amorites" to reach their full extent. Waits patiently. Four hundred years. While the cries rise up against Babylon into his aching ears, mounting like a tidal wave, being stored up patiently until the dam finally bursts and God's wrath pours out on the society like a flood. God looks upon the society as a whole.

This leads to an inescapable conclusion: identity is social.

We are our people.

Community and Personhood

This concept is not unique to the Hebrews; it shows up around the world. This came to life for me when I lived on the Navajo reservation. People would invariably introduce themselves to me by the family and place they were from: "Hi. I'm John Babbitt, from the Kin yaa'áanii clan on Black Mesa." For the Navajo, the people they were from—like the Kin yaa´áanii clan—shaped their identity. And the land they belonged to—like Black Mesa—gave them context.

People and place formed their personhood.

The community came first.

This was a striking contrast to what I was used to. Back home, my friends and I identified ourselves by things we did, like our jobs and hobbies: "Hi, I'm Joshua. I work at a software company, I enjoy playing guitar and going to Timbers games." Where I'm from, the individual is king. I'll gladly tell you what music I like to listen to, clothes I like to wear, and books I like to read. But if you want to know about my family or where I'm from, you better get to know me a bit first.

We start with the individual; then work our way out to the community.

My community revolves around me; not me around my community.

America is the exception, not the norm in this regard. Throughout history, people have generally been a lot more like the Navajo. If a traditional African or Chinese society were attacked, their gut reaction would not necessarily be, "How unfair to all the innocent!" but rather, "Are we as a society innocent?" The social nature of identity implies that not only individuals, but society as well, can be just or unjust, righteous or unrighteous, guilty or innocent. What does this mean for us today?

I am responsible for my people.

I am responsible to my people.

I am part of the society that falls under God's blessing or judgment. When we as a society are guilty, the weight of our gathered iniquity drags us all down. Similarly, when we as a society are good, the weight of our gathered goodness elevates us.[12]

We rise and fall together.

The Company of Prophets

I need to live righteously not only for my own sake, but for the sake of my community. If my community is unjust, I can still, of course, choose to live justly. This is to be in the company of the prophets: living faithfully in unfaithful times. But living justly does not mean God will spare us from suffering. We can walk upright and still get caught in the social torrent when judgment comes down. Jeremiah lived faithfully before God, but still suffered greatly when Babylon destroyed Jerusalem and carried her people into exile.

It is good to be in the company of the prophets. But the fate of the prophets is often persecution, suffering, and death. God's promise for the faithful is not to protect them from suffering, but to vindicate them through suffering on the other side of the grave. Our hope is to be like Jesus: not to avoid suffering, but to encounter God on the other side of our suffering through the power of his resurrection.

When we suffer injustice in our blood-soaked world, we should remember that God is being patient; but he will not be patient forever. Suffering under the unjust powers of our world should cause us to lift our eyes to the God who is coming.

To lift our eyes in hope.

CHAPTER 16 KEY IDEA

DOES HOLY WAR HAVE ANY PRACTICAL IMPLICATIONS FOR US TODAY?

When properly understood, God's coming holy war helps us live more peacefully, rather than more violently, in our sin-struck, ravaged, war-torn world today.

17.

THE RUBBLE OF BABYLON

THE LAKE OF FIRE

We are now in a position to deal with what is, for many people, the most troubling image in the New Testament: the lake of fire. The lake of fire can be a skeleton in God's closet all by itself: it brings together many people's worst fears about hell, judgment, and holy war. At first glance, it can seem to stand opposed to everything we've looked at in this book thus far, to depict a sadistic, closed-minded, and unforgiving God.

I still remember the first time I encountered this image. I was in college, walking home from class, when I happened to cross paths with a street preacher. He had just finished preaching to the passersby on campus, packed up his things, and begun heading home. As our paths crossed, I decided to strike up a conversation.

"How's it going?" I asked.

"If you were to die tonight, do you know where you'd go?" he quickly responded.

Man, this guy really doesn't have an off switch, I thought. I knew where this was headed, but decided to play it dumb. "What are my options?"

"Well, you've currently got a reservation at *the hotel lake of fire.*" He pointed at the people walking by. "All these folks do too." He opened a small booklet and pointed to a picture of a fiery pit, filled with people screaming out in pain, surrounded by words like "communists," "homosexuals," "liberals," and continued: "This is a place where God will burn you with unquenchable fire. You'll be writhing in agony forever, but it will be too late."

Don't invite this guy to our upcoming house party, I thought.

"But there's good news, my friend." He stopped and put on his salesman face. "God loves you and doesn't want you to go there." He opened to the last page of his booklet. "If you pray this prayer, and follow Jesus like I do, you can avoid this awful place."

God, I thought, *I don't want to follow Jesus like this guy does.* He didn't even have time to say hello, dismissed everyone around him with a sweep of his hand, and was convinced he was right and everyone else was wrong. Believing in the lake of fire seemed to make you mean and judgmental. His way of following Jesus seemed to make you very un-Christlike.

I felt sorry for him. My impression was that he was cold, isolated, and lonely. He seemed trapped in paranoid illusions that fueled his pride and need to feel special and above the world around him. He seemed to be trapped in a hell of his own making . . .

I thanked him for his time, shook his hand, and moved on. But as I walked away, I wondered what the lake of fire was really all about.

BURNING DOWN BABYLON

The street preacher saw the lake of fire as a place where God tortures people for eternity. But was he right? Is torture really the point of this image? The lake of fire has, perhaps more than any other image in the New Testament, contributed to the caricature of "the underground torture chamber" we opened this book with. But is God really like a master chef anxiously waiting for evening to come so he can roast people over his barbecue spit forever? Fortunately, the answer is no.

Not only is the caricature wrong. The lake of fire is, more importantly, a powerful image that can inspire hope in our world today.

An Apocalyptic Symbol: "Sheep vs. Godzilla"

To help us reclaim a healthy understanding of the lake of fire, we must first understand that it is an *apocalyptic symbol*. It is found in Revelation, a book filled with apocalyptic symbols: God is on a throne. Jesus is a lamb. Beasts are roaring, trumpets blowing, and scrolls unfolding. Revelation is written in the apocalyptic genre—a type of literature that relies heavily on symbolic imagery.

There is a danger in interpreting these symbols too literally. For example:

> To say that God is on a throne does not mean he is literally a sedentary old man sitting on a big, gold chair in the sky contemplating his day.

> To say that Jesus is a lamb does not mean he is literally saying, "Baa!" and chewing grass while wandering around heaven on all fours.

> To say that a beast rises out of the ocean to terrorize the earth does not mean Godzilla has suddenly stepped out of the Atlantic to trample down our cities.

If we did interpret these images this way, John (the author of Revelation) would probably scratch his head and say, "How did you get *that*?" We'd be missing the point.

So how *do* we understand these images? A good first step is to turn to the Old Testament, from which Revelation draws much of its imagery, and ask: "Where does this image come from?" "What is it a symbol of?" "What is the metaphor for?" For example:

> God's throne is a prominent Old Testament symbol for his kingdom reign. God is a King who reigns over all of heaven and earth.

Lambs were central to the Old Testament history of sacrifice. Jesus is a Lamb whose death atones for the sin of the world.

Beasts are an Old Testament apocalyptic symbol for empire. The beast is an empire that rages against God in his world.

The Old Testament can help us understand these symbols as they were meant to be understood. God's sovereignty, Jesus' sacrifice, and our empires are much better interpretations than armchairs, sheep, and Godzilla.

So the street preacher I bumped into may be interpreting the "lake of fire" *too* literally, in a way the author did not intend. While he might defend his interpretation of this apocalyptic symbol by saying he is "just reading the Bible literally," he may in actuality be doing an injustice to Revelation's intention. He may be painting a picture equivalent to God being a sedentary old man in the sky, Jesus saying, "Baa!" and chewing on grass, or Godzilla arising out of the ocean to stomp on our cities.

He might be missing the point.

The Context: "The Smoke of Her Burning"

We'll get to the lake of fire's Old Testament backdrop in a second. But first, another great question to ask is: "What context does the symbol show up in?" And there is definitely a context. In Revelation 19, just before the lake of fire steps onstage for its first appearance, something dramatic has happened: God has just judged Babylon with fire.

God is burning down Babylon. This is the immediate context for the symbol: God is judging an empire, not torturing individuals. In the following passages, notice how God is judging Babylon, how the instrument of his judgment is fire, and how people are looking on (emphases mine):

> *Fallen! Fallen is Babylon the Great!* . . .
> *for her sins are piled up to heaven*

and God has remembered her crimes . . .
  She will be consumed by fire,
    for mighty is the Lord God who judges her. (Revelation 18:2, 5, 8)

When the kings of the earth who committed adultery with [Babylon] and shared her luxury see *the smoke of her burning,* they will weep and mourn over her. Terrified at her torment, they will stand far off and cry:

> *"Woe! Woe to you, great city,*
> *you mighty city of Babylon!*
> *In one hour your doom has come!" (Revelation 18:9–10)*

The merchants of the earth will weep and mourn over [Babylon] because no one buys their cargoes any more. . . . All who earn their living from the sea, will stand far off. When they see *the smoke of her burning,* they will exclaim, "Was there ever a city like this great city?" (Revelation 18:11, 17–18)

God is using fire here to judge an empire, not to torture individuals. This is structural judgment, not personal judgment. God is waging holy war on the great city; his heavenly fire is directed at its towers and walls.

God is burning down Babylon.

Babylon's judgment has implications, of course, for individuals whose lives are invested and hopes are set in all that she represents. The "kings" (political leaders) and "merchants" (economic leaders) are weeping and gnashing their teeth because of all they've lost in her destruction. But it is worth noting that they are not in physical anguish because God is torturing them; they are in emotional anguish over the things they've lost in the fire.

God is not roasting them over a spit. Like the rich man in the Lazarus parable, they are crying because their toys have been taken away.

Empire vs. Individual

Judging an empire and torturing an individual are two very different things. Consider, for example, when the Allied powers bombed Nazi Germany to bring an end to World War II. Most people today think this was the right thing to do. And this is a picture of an empire being judged by fire from above.

But let's say after the war ended, convicted Nazi soldiers were lifted high on stakes and piles of wood set aflame beneath their feet. Let's say they were slowly roasted in agony over the torment of the flames. What's more, let's say they were lifted just high enough to stay alive indefinitely. Most of us would think this a cruel and inhumane thing to do—a picture of torture.

There is all the difference in the world between bombing an empire and torturing an individual.

Fire is used very differently in these two examples. Bombing an empire is done to end a war; burning an individual is done for revenge. Bombing seeks peace, and in the interest of that peace takes up violence against hostile, aggressive, powerful forces; burning seeks violence, and in the interest of that violence inflicts vengeance on defeated, helpless, powerless forces. Bombing is a picture of fire falling from heaven; burning, of flames set from earth below.

Judging an empire has obvious implications for its citizens. If you're a Nazi soldier, it's bad news when Germany gets bombed. It's bad news when your side gets defeated in the war. It's bad news when all you're left with is the smoldering rubble of your once-glorious civilization. You will probably weep and wail, feeling an internal sense of anguish and torment at all you sought to build that has now been lost. But this is very different from your victorious enemy throwing you into a concentration camp and torturing you.

So how does the lake of fire fit into all this? When God has destroyed Babylon by fire, all that is left is a smoldering pile of rubble. A steaming pillar of stones. A sunken puddle of flame. The great city that once destroyed the world has been reduced to ashes. The lake of fire does not depict the torture of individuals, but rather God's judgment on empire. This is the meaning of the apocalyptic symbol: it is the smoldering rubble of Babylon.

As we shall now see, its Old Testament backdrop confirms this.

JUDGMENT ON EMPIRE

The lake of fire is a holy war image. Revelation draws extensively on holy war images from the Old Testament. Consider the following examples:

SEVEN TRUMPETS: Babylon is surrounded by seven trumpets (Revelation 8–9). This image draws from Joshua's famous battle of Jericho, where Israel surrounded the fortified city with trumpets and, after seven days of trumpet blasts, the mighty walls of the great city came tumbling down. Similarly here in Revelation, the seven trumpet blasts bring God's judgment on the great city of Babylon, opening the way into the promised land of the new creation.

SEVEN PLAGUES: Babylon is afflicted by seven plagues that start small but get greater and greater in a consecutive stream because her people refuse to repent (Revelation 15–16). This image draws from Israel's exodus, where God rains down plagues on Egypt in a consecutive stream that gets greater and greater because *her* people refuse to repent.

WHITE HORSE RIDER: Jesus appears as a rider on a white horse, leading the armies of God into the promised land (Revelation 19). This image draws from Joshua's leading the charge as the people of God enter Canaan. Only now, with Jesus, the promised land has expanded to encompass the whole earth.

Holy war images are used extensively in Revelation to depict God's coming judgment on Babylon. And the lake of fire is one of them.

Sodom and Gomorrah: "Like Smoke from a Furnace"

Let's look at three Old Testament backdrops that can help us reclaim a healthy understanding of the lake of fire. The first is Sodom and Gomorrah: the first cities destroyed by fire in Scripture. Sodom and Gomorrah are more than just cities; they are regional power-houses, rallying coalitions to wage war on their neighbors.[1] They have regional influence over their smaller, weaker sister cities—and their influence is not good. They are depicted as brutally unjust.

God explains why they were judged: "This was the sin of your sister Sodom: She and her daughters [smaller, regional cities under her influence] were arrogant, overfed and unconcerned; they did not help the poor and needy. They were haughty and did detestable things before me."[2]

The cries against Sodom grow so loud that God finally comes down to see "if what they have done is as bad as the outcry that has reached me."[3] This image of the "outcry" reaching God is the same language used later when Israel cries out under Egypt as Pharaoh brutally oppresses her in slavery and murders her children, until God "hears the cry" and comes down to take out the oppressor.[4] God steps in, with Sodom as with Egypt, to see if things are as bad as he has heard.

When God enters Sodom, everyone gathers to gang-rape (and presumedly murder) his messengers. God finds a place so corrupt and violent he is unable to find even *ten* righteous people inside—they've all been destroyed by the empire.

So God burns down their city.

Sodom burns down God's patience, so God burns down their empire, waging holy war against it, because "the outcry to the LORD against its people is so great."[5] When Sodom's crimes are piled up to heaven, God arises against her. When her sins have reached their full measure, God throws down—in a prophetic foreshadowing of what he will do later to Egypt, and eventually, to Babylon.

The next day, Abraham goes out to examine the scene. Looking down upon the valley, he now sees, where Sodom and Gomorrah once were, "dense smoke rising from the land, like smoke from a furnace."[6] The great cities of Sodom and Gomorrah have been judged by fire, and all that is left is their smoldering remains.

This verse is alluded to in Revelation. When Babylon is destroyed, we are told "the smoke from her goes up for ever and ever."[7] God judges Babylon by fire, and all that is left, like Sodom and Gomorrah, is smoke rising up from the land. Two things are noteworthy about this backdrop. First, in the context of Sodom and Gomorrah, the "smoke from a furnace" image is not being used to describe an underground torture chamber. It is simply a picture of the destruction of empire. The context of the backdrop makes this obvious.

Second, when Revelation says the smoke from Babylon "goes up forever and ever," it is simply speaking to the finality of Babylon's destruction. After Sodom and Gomorrah were destroyed, when the smoke faded and the rubble was cleared away, they could eventually be rebuilt. But Babylon will never be rebuilt, because God has won his victory over her forever. So the smoke going up *forever* is simply an image that says: "When Babylon goes down, she ain't gettin' back up."

The prophets also use Sodom and Gomorrah's destruction by fire as a picture of hope for God's coming victory over Babylon. Jeremiah declares:

> *As God overthrew Sodom and Gomorrah*
> *along with their neighboring towns . . .*
> *so no one will live [in Babylon];*
> *no man will dwell in it. . . .*
> *Babylon's thick wall will be leveled*
> *and her high gates set on fire;*
> *the peoples [building Babylon] exhaust themselves for nothing,*
> *the nations' labor is only fuel for the flames.*[8]

The lake of fire draws upon Sodom and Gomorrah's destruction as a backdrop for God's coming judgment on Babylon. In its Old Testament context, this backdrop does not depict individuals being tortured, but rather an empire being judged.

Topheth: "Prepared as a Fire Pit"

A second backdrop for the lake of fire can be found in Topheth. Topheth was located in Gehenna, that cruel valley just outside Jerusalem's walls that we looked at in chapter 3, Jesus' primary image for hell. Topheth means literally, "the roasting place," because this was where Israel roasted her children, burning them as human sacrifices to false gods. Topheth was the epicenter of Gehenna, and God cried out against his people about it:

> They have built the high places of Topheth in the Valley of Ben Hinnom [Gehenna] to burn their sons and daughters in the fire— something I did not command, nor did it enter my mind.[9]

Topheth was the altar where Israel murdered God's children. It was the creaky bed in the cheap hotel where she cheated on God. Topheth was a symbol for how far gone Israel was: cheating on her faithful husband and murdering his kids.

Topheth held the skeletons buried in Jerusalem's backyard.

So God promised that when he returned, he would redeem Jerusalem and kick the rebellion out to Topheth. Isaiah described Topheth as a "fire pit" God was preparing for the rebellion:

> *Topheth has long been prepared;*
> *it has been made ready for the king.*
> *Its fire pit has been made deep and wide,*
> *with an abundance of fire and wood;*
> *the breath of the Lord,*
> *like a stream of burning sulfur,*
> *sets it ablaze.*[10]

Isaiah is creatively turning the image of Topheth on its head. Topheth "has long been prepared" by the powerful as a "roasting place" for the vulnerable. But when God returns, he will make the empire lie down in the very bed it has made.

This passage of Isaiah is soaked in holy war imagery. When God arises as victorious King, he "will cause men to hear his majestic voice and will make them see his arm coming down with raging anger and consuming fire, with cloudburst, thunderstorm and hail."[11] God will shatter the empire that has carried his people into exile, and will "[fight] them in battle with the blows of his arm."[12] When God is finished, he will kick the empire outside his holy city and lay it in Topheth as a bed of rest.

The lake of fire draws upon this Topheth imagery. In Revelation, God destroys Babylon with consuming fire and her smoldering rubble is located, like Topheth, outside Jerusalem. The New Jerusalem has a posture of welcoming embrace, with gates flung open wide, but the ravaging flame of sin's destructive power is contained outside the city. God redeems Jerusalem and kicks the power of Babylon outside his holy city.

The lake of fire draws upon Topheth's "fire pit" imagery outside Jerusalem as a backdrop for God's coming judgment on Babylon. In its Old Testament context, this backdrop, like Sodom and Gomorrah, does not depict individuals being tortured, but again, an empire being judged.

Daniel: "The Slain Beast in the Blazing Fire"

A third backdrop for the lake of fire can be found in Daniel. Daniel has an apocalyptic vision, much like Revelation, while living in Babylon in exile. In it, he sees four beasts representing four empires he is told will rise to power in the ancient world: commonly interpreted as Babylon, Medo-Persia, Greece, and Rome. The fourth beast, or the Roman Empire, is said to be particularly brutal: "[it] will devour the whole earth, trampling it down and crushing it."[13]

The meaning of these beasts is clear: they are empires.

Daniel is terrified by the bestial power of these empires that come to rage over God's world. But there is hope.

When the time has come, God will arise to wage holy war on these bestial powers and replace them with his good kingdom: "His dominion is an everlasting dominion that will not pass away, and his kingdom is one that will never be destroyed."[14] As God arises in victory, Daniel sees that "the beast was slain and its body destroyed and thrown into the blazing fire."[15]

The meaning of the blazing fire is clear: it is an apocalyptic symbol for imperial destruction.

The blazing fire into which the beast is thrown is a grave for empire, not a torture chamber for individuals. It is a bed for the beast to lie in. Daniel joins the Old Testament hope that, when the time is right, God will arise to end the exile; to wage holy war on the oppressive powers that oppose him and establish his kingdom on earth as in heaven.

Daniel tells us that when the empires go down, they're not getting back up: their bed is in the fire.

This Daniel imagery is picked up in Revelation, where the apocalyptic beasts of empire gather the nations against God. Although they appear unstoppable, God eventually arises to wage holy war on them: "fire came down from heaven and devoured them."[16] The imperial beast is slain and its body thrown into the ensuing lake of fire: Babylon's smoldering rubble.

The lake of fire draws upon Daniel's backdrop of God's coming holy war on the apocalyptic beasts. In its Old Testament context, this is yet one more example that does not depict *individual torture*, but rather *imperial judgment*.

THE HOPE OF THE WORLD

Like a chorus in unison, these three holy war passages all sing the same tune: God will judge empire. This is the hope of the world. The lake of fire is about the end of empire, not the torture of individuals. If God's kingdom is to come, our empire must go. If God is to rule on earth as in heaven, then our attempt to rule the earth without him must be put away. God stands against Babylon because God stands for his world.

It is for this reason that the lake of fire is an image of hope. Its significance is that Babylon shall never rise again. The exile will be over; the great city and all that she represents will be replaced by Jesus' kingdom. Sin's destructive power will no longer be allowed to terrorize the earth. And when Babylon falls, she ain't gettin' back up. This is the hope of the world.

Judgment vs. Torture

A final reflection on the lake of fire: God does not torture people; we do. We put a lot of creativity into our brutality. We've developed some pretty horrific methods of torture. The rack. Mutilation of body parts. Electroshock to the genitals, waterboarding, and breaking of bones.

Around the time Revelation was written, the Roman emperor Nero even impaled Christians by thrusting stakes through their rectums, covered them in wax, lifted them high in his backyard, and lit fires at the base—slowly roasting them alive to light his garden at night.[17]

God does not slowly roast people on stakes; we do.

In college, I developed a dark fascination with the horrific things we do to each other. I dove into our world's most brutal civil wars with every documentary I could find. I spent hours reading Amnesty International accounts of torture. My dorm room was littered with books on genocide. I figured if these things were happening in our world, I didn't want to turn a blind eye; I wanted to face them head-on.

Over time, the weight became a lot to bear. I had trouble sleeping. I would lie awake in bed at night. I could hear screams erupting from around our apocalyptic world, crying out in agony to a vaulted sky. I knew if these reports were true of what happened yesterday, then somewhere around the world the same things were happening today.

The screams flowing violently into the ears of God were keeping me up at night.

Big Eyes and Ears

God's ears are big. Every day he hears the screams of his sin-scarred, war-torn world. What would it be like to be God, to hear the daily avalanche of cries—sometimes whispered quietly, sometimes shrieked in agony—for help? God's ears are bigger than ours; he hears them all.

And I think his ears are aching.

I began to wonder: What would it be like to be God, exposed daily to the carnage that erupts around our world? What would it be like to know intimately the lives of those who are daily destroyed? The many stories I was exposed to were only a small snapshot into the daily wreckage. God sees it all.

And I think his eyes hurt.

Babylon must be reduced to rubble because these stories are embedded in her foundations. The blood of the innocent is mixed in the mortar that binds the bricks that build the walls that thrust her towers skyward, raging against the heavenly reign of God.

God is patient; more patient than we are. But his patience will not last forever. For a time, God will allow us to build the walls of our exilic empire higher and higher, feeding our craving for a world without him. But a time will come when our sins have reached their full measure, when the outcry has become too great in his ears, when God arises to end the exile and wage holy war on Babylon to bring his kingdom come.

The end of Babylon is the hope of the world. It marks not simply an end, but a beginning: the inauguration of God's kingdom come in fullness on earth as in heaven.

CHAPTER 17 KEY IDEA

WHAT IS THE LAKE OF FIRE?

The lake of fire is an apocalyptic symbol for the smoldering rubble of Babylon. It speaks to God's judgment on empire, not the torture of individuals. Its context in Revelation and backdrop in the Old Testament make this clear.

INTERLUDE

THE SPIRIT OF EMPIRE

SERPENT AND DRAGON

What about Satan? We have talked about hell and the lake of fire, but have not up to this point looked very closely at the Prince of Darkness. In part, this has been to avoid another common caricature: Satan is, in the popular imagination, a little red man with a long tail, pointy ears, and a pitchfork. Not to mention a goatee. He seems relatively harmless.

But in Revelation, he is a monstrous dragon. He wages war on the nations. He devours the world. And his home is in the lake of fire.

So this is perhaps a good place to give him his due.

A Political Figure

Satan is a political figure. We do not tend to think of him this way. "Politics is secular," we tell ourselves. "The spiritual has no place *there*." But the biblical story would beg to differ.

When Satan tempts Jesus, he offers him *the kingdoms of the world*: "All this I will give you, if you will bow down and worship me."[1] Satan assumes he has them to give. He assumes the world's kingdoms are his. And Jesus does not correct him, saying, "Sorry, buddy, those actually belong to God." What is going on here? How do the empires of the world belong to Satan?

The story, I would suggest, goes something like this. When Adam and Eve turn *from* God, they turn implicitly *toward* the serpent. When they believe his lie, they join his rebellion. Prior to this, Adam and Eve's authority was *under* God; they were called to co-reign together with him. But when they turn, they implicitly place themselves *under* the serpent's lie: tearing heaven and earth, severing the world from God, unleashing the Accuser's destructive power in God's good world.

They co-reign, whether they know it or not, with Satan.

And Satan's rule is political; it is an authority. Satan wants to rule the earth without God. So when we seek to rule the earth without God, using our authority for freedom *from* God, we join sides with the arch-traitor. This is similar to what we saw at the outset of this book: the destructive power of hell (and Satan, the chief Arsonist) works its way into God's good world through us.

Whether we know it or not, whether we like it or not, Satan's power is unleashed through us.

This is why Jesus proclaims, in response to Satan's temptation, that God alone is worthy of our worship. He refuses to worship Satan. Jesus chooses to reclaim the kingdoms of the world: not through an alliance with the enemy in pride *against* God, but rather, through the sacrificial love of the cross in devotion *toward* God.

The Dragon

So let's return to the dragon of Revelation. Some people are surprised that the dragon is identified with both Satan and the Roman Empire. Which is it? Is John trying to depict the devil, or Rome? A spiritual power or a political power? The answer should now be obvious: both. Revelation sees Satan as the spiritual power, the driving force, the animating ethos behind Rome's attempt to rule the earth without God.

Satan is the Spirit of Empire.

Interestingly in this regard, Revelation calls the dragon that "serpent of old,"[2] a reference to the slithering snake that deceived Adam and Eve in the garden of Eden. The sense is that when it was just

Adam and Eve in the garden, Satan was just a little snake, slithering around with sweet whispers. But now, as the human population has grown throughout history, Satan's power has grown with us. Satan has grown to monumental proportions over the years, feeding on our rebellion, living through our expanding empires.

He is now a monstrous dragon that does not whisper—he roars.

The Roman Empire is the vehicle Satan is driving, smashing into other nations and leaving a trail of car wrecks in the rearview mirror—with dead bodies piling up in the morgue. In the apocalyptic language of Daniel, the Roman Empire is a brutal beast come to "devour the whole earth, trampling it down and crushing it."[3] Satan's demonic power shows up in the bestial brutality of empire.

Adam and Eve's grandchildren are the ones building first the Tower of Babel . . . then Egypt . . . then Rome. When Pharaoh whips Israel in Egypt, she is being whipped by Adam's great-grandson. Egypt's empire is the political culmination of humanity's rebellion. Same with Caesar: he is Adam's offspring. The Roman Empire is, like Egypt, the structural outflow of our rebellion.

Its power is rooted in the serpent's lie.

In the words of Richard Bauckham, John's apocalypse confronts Caesar's kingdom because it "sees God's rule over the world apparently contradicted by the rule of the Roman Empire, which arrogates divine rule over the world to itself and to all appearances does so successfully. He faces the question: who then is really Lord of this world?"[4] Politics is, for the biblical authors, anything but "secular." It is the climactic arena in which Satan's attempt to rule the earth without God is played out through us.

A Dirge for Babylon

This challenges our tendency to divorce the physical and the spiritual in the West, to compartmentalize politics and religion, to keep the things of Caesar as far as possible from the things of God. Christians often reinforce this dichotomy today. For example, mission teams will go to Africa and pray rigorously against the local witch doctor, missing all the while that Satan's dark forces are showing up most powerfully in the dictator's regime. We will look for demons in Southeast Asia's temples, even though their raging power is being unleashed much more prominently in the country's presidential palaces. We will raise the alarm about atheism and the New Age movement in America, while the country bows down at the shopping mall to the gods of consumerism.

We are kings of missing the point, brilliant at missing the obvious right in front of our eyes. And at the root of it all is our divorce of the physical from the spiritual, our bifurcation of sacred and secular, our compartmentalization of politics and religion. But the Hebrew worldview is more holistic: it does not believe such a separation is truly possible.

The divorce does not exist.

Jesus shares this perspective. In a famous passage, Jesus tells his disciples, "I saw Satan fall like lightning from heaven."[5] At first glance, Satan falling out of the sky may look like we are back to abstract mythology again; but we are not. Jesus is quoting Isaiah, and if we go back to Isaiah, we find, surprisingly, that nowhere in the passage Jesus quotes is Satan mentioned—it is about the fall of Babylon.

So did Jesus miss it? Did he intend to talk about Satan and accidentally reference Babylon? Was he talking about a spiritual power or a political one? The answer is again: both. Just like Revelation, Jesus sees the spiritual and political intertwined. Jesus sees Satan as the spiritual power, the driving force, the animating ethos behind Babylon's attempt to rule the earth without God.

And in the passage Jesus is quoting, Babylon falls.

Jesus identifies the fall of Babylon with the demise of Satan.

Babylon will be reduced to rubble . . . and Satan's power will go down with it. Satan's home is in the lake of fire because his power is embodied in Babylon. The end of empire entails, by its very nature, his destruction. When the great city goes down, he goes down with it.

Satan's home is in the rubble of Babylon.

A fitting place to end our discussion of Satan, and Babylon, is the passage Jesus quotes from Isaiah. It is a passage of God coming to establish his kingdom with justice for the world. It is a passage of hope for the exiles who suffer under the empire's power. When God's victory comes, Isaiah prepares this ensuing dirge for Babylon:

> *You will take up this taunt against the king of Babylon:*
> *How the oppressor has come to an end!*
> > *How his fury has ended!*
> *The Lord has broken the rod of the wicked,*
> > *the scepter of the rulers,*
> *which in anger struck down peoples*
> > *with unceasing blows,*
> *and in fury subdued nations*
> > *with relentless aggression. . . .*
> *The realm of the dead below is all astir [O Babylon]*
> > *to meet you at your coming. . . .*
> *All your pomp has been brought down to the grave,*
> > *along with the noise of your harps;*
> *maggots are spread out beneath you*
> > *and worms cover you.*
> *How you have fallen from heaven,*
> > *O morning star, son of the dawn!*
> *You have been cast down to the earth,*
> > *you who once laid low the nations!*
> *You said in your heart,*
> > *"I will ascend to the heavens;*
> *I will raise my throne*
> > *above the stars of God;*
> *I will sit enthroned on the mount of assembly,*
> > *on the utmost heights of Mount Zaphon.*
> *I will ascend above the tops of the clouds;*
> > *I will make myself like the Most High."*
> *But you are brought down to the realm of the dead [Sheol],*
> > *to the depths of the pit.*[6]

18.

CITY OF GOD

RECONCILED WORLD

God's city will reconcile the world. At the end of Revelation, John sees the New Jerusalem, God's holy city, coming down out of heaven. The context is a wedding: the city has been "prepared as a bride beautifully dressed for her husband."[1] Jesus is the husband and his New Jerusalem wedding celebrates union: the union of heaven and earth, of east and west, of good folks and bad folks, of weak and strong—of all the major themes we have seen throughout this book.

God's city is a city of union.

The New Jerusalem is *huge*. There is room for everyone. The measurements of the city are given as 15,000 miles long by 15,000 miles wide and 15,000 miles high. That is no ordinary city—this is the size of a massive country!

While we should understand these dimensions symbolically[2] one can still not get away from the impression that this city is colossal! The base of the city is given as 1.9 million square miles—the weight of a city that large, landing on top of the earth, would tilt us off our axis. Dropping a rock that big would spin us out of orbit. So either God's city will set off a massive cataclysm that unintentionally destroys our world, or creation will be made new, transformed and filled with glory as a home for God's holy city.

The New Jerusalem is a perfect cube, patterned after the Holy of Holies in Jerusalem's temple where God's presence dwelled most intimately. Only now the Holy of Holies has expanded to become *the city itself.* The holiest place has become a city, the city has become a country, and the country has become the center of the world.

God's city will consummate creation.

At first glance, some might find this a scary prospect. Our cities often *exclude* creation: if we want to see trees, rivers, and mountains, we have to *leave* the city. But God's city is a garden city: it *consummates* creation. At its center is the tree of life, from which flows the river of life, lined with trees bearing God's life-giving blessing to the world.

Creation starts in a garden.

And climaxes in a city.

A garden city.

How is this garden city, this city of union, the hope of the world? As we wrap up this book, let's use the New Jerusalem imagery to summarize each of the major themes we've explored thus far.

Heaven and Earth

God's city reconciles heaven and earth. John sees the New Jerusalem coming "down out of heaven."[3] It is worth noting which direction the city is moving: it is *descending* out of heaven. We are not going "up" to heaven; heaven is coming "down" to earth. This reminds us of the major theme from chapter 1: God is not on a mission to get us out of earth and into heaven or hell. He is out to reconcile heaven and earth *from* the destructive power of sin, death, and hell. His goal is to reconcile the world.

God's city is a place where we live with God: "They will be his people, and God himself will be with them and be their God."[4] The New Jerusalem wedding celebrates the union of God and humanity, the interweaving of transcendence and immanence, the threading back together of heaven and earth.

Life with God.

It is this story that confronts our popular caricature of hell. When we say that God's goal is to get us out of earth and into heaven, it is not far downstream before hell begins to look like an underground torture chamber. If our eternal destiny is in heaven *above*, then its negative counterpart must be in hell *below*. If heaven's primary purpose is to *reward* the righteous, then hell's primary purpose must be to *torture* the wicked.

As we have seen, however, this picture is upside down. The gospel story provokes a paradigm shift. Heaven's primary counterpart is not hell; it is earth. God's goal is not to get us out of earth and into heaven; it is to reconcile heaven and earth from the destructive power of sin, death, and hell. Jesus is the Savior who reunites heaven and earth, in order to fill it with the glorious presence of God.

This is the biblical story: God's grand objective is to get heaven into earth—and get the hell out.

God's goodness gives rise, in this framework, to the doctrine of hell as something consistent with, rather than contradictory to, his good character. Hell's location shifts from *underground* to *outside the city*, as Jesus the good King establishes God's perfect kingdom inside the city with justice and righteousness for the earth. God's purpose becomes *protection* rather than *torture*: establishing a boundary of mercy that not only protects the new creation from the continued onslaught of sin, but also gives unrepentant rebels the autonomy they crave while limiting the extent of their self-imposed destruction. Rather than a "chamber" God locks from the outside against our repentant will, hell is seen to be a "coffin" we latch from the inside through our unrepentant will, fueled by our insatiable desire for freedom *from* God, others, and ourselves as given by God.

Hell's destructive power arises in this paradigm not from God, but from us.

Reconciliation is the centerpiece of this paradigm shift. God's goal is not to abandon the created order, but to redeem it. His redemption magnifies his glorious grace and mercy toward our world.

East and West

God's city also reconciles east and west. The masses come streaming from around the world to worship in a New Jerusalem whose gates are wide open in a posture of welcoming embrace: "The nations will walk by its light. . . . The glory and honor of the nations will be brought into it."[5] The citizens of God's kingdom are comprised of every nation, tribe, and tongue.[6] The tree of life is inside the city and "the leaves of the tree are for the healing of the nations."[7]

God's city heals humanity.

This reminds us of the major theme we saw earlier: God's mission is not to pluck a few folks from a few nations out of the human social body and into an acultural kingdom. It is to heal the human social body by reconciling the nations *to* himself and *through* himself to one another in his multicultural, international kingdom. God is out to heal the human social body from the destructive power of sin.

God's throwing a cosmic wedding bash, and he wants the world to come. His only requirement for entry is not our behavior, but simply receiving his mercy, being washed in the blood of the Lamb, and letting him freely clothe us in his righteousness.[8] God doesn't want the cosmic celebration spoiled, so he confronts the marriage-rejecters who don't take the invitation seriously and the wedding crashers who try to bring their sin in with them. God takes the wedding seriously because he loves the world that his wedding reconciles.

God's love in Christ *is* the judgment that is coming upon our world. It confronts our idolatries and ideologies inasmuch as they settle for lesser things and stand opposed to his reconciliation. Reconciliation is, once again, at the center of the paradigm shift.

Our world will be judged by the love of God in Christ.

God's love in Christ will reconcile the world.

This again gives rise to judgment as something consistent with, rather than contradictory to, God's good character. It is God's gracious response . . .

> *to all that refuses his mercy and destroys his world . . .*
>> *to all that sets itself against Christ's healing of the world . . .*
>>> *to all that stands unrepentantly opposed to his reconciliation . . .*

And this, too, magnifies his grace and mercy toward our world.

Weak and Strong

God's city reconciles weak and strong. In the New Jerusalem, our loving Father will embrace the weak and "wipe every tear from their eyes."[9] And the strong are not excluded; the Mighty King welcomes "the kings of the earth [who] bring their splendor into it."[10] In Jesus' holy city, "there will be no more death or mourning or crying or pain,"[11] for "the old order of things has passed away"; the new has come.[12]

God wages holy war on the old order to bring in the new.

God takes down the empire to bring in the kingdom.

This confronts our popular caricature of holy war: it is not the strong using God to justify their conquest of the weak. It is God arising on behalf of the weak when the tyranny of the strong has raged for far too long. When we look at God's holy war as one more example of the strong justifying their conquest, it is not far downstream before God can look like a tyrant from whom our world needs protection. God becomes simply one more source of powerful fuel thrown on the flames that are tearing our violent world apart. The strong and powerful can simply use God to justify whatever it is they want to do in the world.

But as we have seen, this picture is upside down. The gospel story demonstrates that God's holy war is a source of hope for the downtrodden, a world in which all too often the powerful use their strength to oppress the weak; the rich use their advantage to exploit the poor; and leaders use their influence to be served rather than to serve.

God's holy war does not legitimate the world's unjust structures; it confronts them. In a world where the structures arising from our histories of rebellion seem so intractable, bigger than our ability to heal, God's coming holy war is a source of hope. The knowledge of its coming should restrain our injustice, not justify it. When properly understood, it does not throw fuel on the fires that are tearing our world apart, but buckets of cold water.

Our world is desperately in need of God to come and set things right. The real question is not why God wages holy war. It is why he waits so long. God is more patient than we are: patient with our empires and the destruction entailed in their development. But the time will come when God will arise to reclaim his world from the powers of idolatry and injustice—political, personal, and spiritual—establishing his justice and righteousness in their place.

Reconciliation is, once again, the centerpiece of this paradigm shift. In this framework, the doctrine of holy war is consistent with, rather than contradictory to, God's good character. God's goal is not to exacerbate tensions between the strong and the weak; it is to heal them. God's redemption brings hope to the abused, the exploited, and the downtrodden and reveals his grace and mercy for what it really is: glorious.

God's city will reconcile the world.

And the center of the city is Jesus.

JESUS IS THE CITY

Jesus is the King of the reconciled world. We are told the city revolves around "the throne of God and of the Lamb."[13] Jesus is the atoning Lamb at the center of the city, who reconciles the world in sacrificial love and, from the throne, establishes the kingdom reign of God in power upon the earth. He is at the center of the new creation because it is through him that creation is made new.

The city revolves around Jesus because Jesus reconciles the world.

To enter the city is to be grafted into the life of Jesus himself. Admission is free, for the Lamb who was slain has atoned for our sin and opened its gates for all who will come. Yet, it costs us everything, for to enter is to be grafted into the very life of God, dying to ourselves that we might be united in him as one. God's city has a posture of embrace, but to receive that embrace is to be filled with his Spirit and drawn into his very reconciling presence as part of the city itself.

The Body of Christ

Jesus builds his city with people. The foundations of the city, we are told, are the twelve tribes of Israel and the gates of the city are the twelve apostles.[14] The people of God *are* the city, grafted into the life of the metropolis itself. This means when we are united with Jesus, we become the building blocks of his home for the world, receiving the nations to come worship God and dwell with him forever. God floods us with his glorious presence and makes us part of the city itself.

Jesus invites us not only to enter his city, but to *become* the city.

Jesus will not be content for us to simply observe as tourists; he calls us to participate as citizens. As Jesus fills us with his Spirit, he unites us to himself and turns us into "living stones"[15] united to himself, participating in his Father's bringing together what was once torn asunder: humanity. We ourselves are built into the home God is making, in which he dwells on earth as in heaven.

United to Jesus, we become part of the city "whose architect and builder is God."[16] A city whose foundation is secure, for the foundation is none other than Jesus himself. He is the "chief cornerstone," rejected by us but elected by God to become the foundation upon which the rest of God's city is built.

Jesus is in the city as its center, under the city as its foundation, around the city as its walls, and reigns over the city as its King. Jesus *is* the city that reconciles the world.

This is why it is a mistake to ask, "If I reject Jesus, will he kick me out of his city?" To reject Jesus is to reject *the city itself.*

For Jesus is the city.

The Resurrection of Christ

As we wrap up, tackling one final question will be illuminating. Throughout this book, we have said that God's purpose is to redeem creation, not abandon it. But a few passages do seem to indicate God is going to destroy this old world. Perhaps the most famous is when Peter says:

The present heavens and earth are reserved for fire. . . . The heavens will disappear with a roar; the elements will be destroyed by fire, and the earth and everything in it will be laid bare.[17]

Which is it? Does God redeem this world or destroy it? Does Jesus pull out the ol' toolbox and renovate his home? Or light a match and burn it down?

The answer, as has so often been the case throughout this book, is: both.

Jesus himself, from the earliest days of the church, has been looked to as the model. His death and resurrection are a signpost of what's to come for all creation. Similar to the way Jesus' body was crucified, so this old world will be put to death and laid in its cosmic grave. Through the atoning power of Jesus' death, creation's corruption will be purged to bring an end to its groaning under the bondage of our sin . . .

But this is not the end.

As Jesus was raised up out of the grave, so God will raise creation out from its cosmic grave, through the power of Jesus' resurrection, and into the life of his kingdom. God will baptize the world with fire, then raise it up from the roaring flames of judgment into the power of the new creation. Creation itself will be baptized by the Father, through the Son, in the Spirit—then God will be, in the words of Paul, "all in all."[18]

Will it be the same creation? Yes, in an important sense. Like Jesus' resurrection body, the new creation will still be the same creation, continuous with the old. When Jesus was raised, he didn't come back as a Brazilian woman, a Japanese sumo wrestler, or a twenty-first-century hipster. His friends recognized him; they talked with him, ate with him, felt the nail wounds, and put their fingers into his pierced side.[19]

Similarly, when God resurrects his world, we'll recognize it. It will be the same world, familiar, known. God doesn't dump creation in a cosmic wastebasket and start over. Like an old '57 Chevy, God's world is worth redeeming. He'll pull out the old toolbox and get to work on the renovation.

But in another sense, it won't be the same creation. It will be different from the old. When Jesus was raised from death, his body wasn't the same: he's walking through locked doors, appearing out of nowhere, and ascending into heaven.[20] Some friends don't recognize him at first—and when they eventually do, he has to tell them not to be afraid.[21] His body has been glorified, raised incorruptible, made new.[22]

Similarly, when God resurrects the world, it will be made new. Brighter. Stronger. Glorious. When God's glory floods the earth as the waters cover the sea, things will look different, feel different, be different. Creation will participate in the glory of God through Jesus in the power of the Spirit. It will be made new.

Jesus' resurrection is what makes the new creation possible.

Jesus' resurrection is what makes the holy city possible.

Jesus' resurrection is what reconciles the world.

The New Creation

Jesus has taken the fire and darkness of our old world into himself on the cross. He has borne the anticreative power of our sin. Carried the weight of its darkness. Extinguished its wildfire. Buried it in the grave and conquered it through the power of his resurrection.

Jesus now ushers in the reconciling life of the kingdom. In his presence is the new creation. He has borne the holy judgment of God and now embraces the world with the holy salvation of God.

Jesus welcomes us to receive his kingdom. The King wants to pardon. The Lamb desires to forgive. The Great Physician longs to heal. We cannot get him dirty; he can only make us clean. On the cross, his arms were opened wide to embrace his sin-sick world. And now, in resurrection power, he raises his voice strong and calls to the ends of the earth to be gathered to his kingdom, to receive his reconciling presence and prepare for the resurrection to come.

His city gates are wide-open. Though we are rebels, his voice calls to us, "Daughter," and "Son." To receive his embrace is to enter the new. To refuse his embrace is to remain in the old. Jesus has conquered the anti-creation.

Jesus is the new creation.

CHAPTER 18 KEY IDEA

WHAT IS THE GOAL OF HISTORY?

God's city—a city that will reconcile the world. God's city reconciles heaven and earth, east and west, good and bad, weak and strong—through the power of Jesus' resurrection, it establishes the new creation.

CONCLUSION

THESE BONES CAN LIVE

SKELETONS IN THE GROUND

Our questions are Israel's answers. This thread has been woven subtly throughout this book, but this is the first time it has been articulated explicitly, so it is worth saying again: our questions are Israel's answers. Let me explain.

We opened this book with the image of skeletons in the closet. Israel also had skeletons: only theirs weren't in a closet; they were in the ground. And they weren't metaphorical; they were real. Israel's skeletons in the ground also provoked questions. Big questions. About whether God was good and could really be trusted.

Ultimately, however, these were not just questions Israel asked of God. They were questions God asked of Israel. In Ezekiel's "Valley of Dry Bones," a central passage of the Old Testament, God asks his people about the skeletons in the ground.

Babylon's Bones

The date: circa 550 BC. God picks Ezekiel up by the scruff of the neck and carries him out to a valley of dry bones. The valley is a massacre memorial: bones flood the valley. There are more than can be counted. God makes Ezekiel walk back and forth through this valley of the shadow of death, side to side through this containment pit of destruction, until he has soaked in the entire gruesome scene.

The bones are dry. They have been baking in the midday sun, scorched by the brutal ball of fire bearing down upon the earth. Like Israel in Babylon, they are cooking in the humidity of exile's oven.

They are the bones of those butchered by Babylon. Babylon: the empire of exile that wants to rule the earth without God. Babylon: the apocalyptic beast that devours the nations with an insatiable thirst for its own glory. Babylon: the city of confusion that rages against God.

As Ezekiel surveys the pile of bones in dismay, God's voice thunders loud, raging, mighty in the prophet's ears: "Son of man, can these bones live?" (Ezekiel 37:3). God hears the blood of his murdered children crying up from the ground. He rages at the massacre memorial. God weeps over his slaughtered children.

"Son of man, can these bones live?"

God calls Ezekiel "son of man." He does not call him "prophet," "holy one," or "ambassador of the Most High." These titles would indicate you are someone important, significant, part of the solution rather than the problem. Instead, he calls him son of man, a son of Adam. Adam: beloved. Adam: rebel. Adam: you and me, the beloved rebels whose rebellion has produced the valleys of butchered, baking bones that mark our fallen world.

As God speaks to Ezekiel, a son of Adam, we can hear him speak to us. The prophet, before he is a prophet, is part of the problem. He is a son of man. And the question God asks Ezekiel is a question he also asks us. God's question to his sin-struck, war-torn world is, "Can these bones live?"

Ezekiel gives a safe answer: "Lord, you alone know." This is a polite answer. A respectful answer. One that acknowledges God's sovereign power, but doesn't impose expectations on what God could, would, or should do. It is a risk-free answer.

But it is the wrong answer.

It is not the answer God is looking for. It does not share God's rage over his slaughtered children. It does not wail with God over his murdered kids. It is not an answer that protests the butchery of Babylon, the inhumanity of humanity, and the cemetery that marks his tragic world.

God must answer his own question. If the prophet is not angry, then God must teach him. The child must learn the ways of his father; the student, the lessons of his master; the ambassador must be taught to represent the God whose presence he bears. Ezekiel's prophetic rage must be fueled from the raging fury of God's own broken heart.

The prophet must encounter the Father's mourning love.

Resurrection Is the Answer

And God's answer to his own question is this: resurrection. These bones *can* live. The exile will end. Babylon's unstoppable power will come to a close. The sheet of death that separates us from the face of God will be put away forever. Our cosmic distance will be done away with in a dramatic finale.

Death will be put to death. Exile will be sent into exile.

Resurrection will come.

These bones can live.

Resurrection. God does not give an abstract explanation of why it had to be this way. He does not develop a philosophy on how this is the best of all possible worlds. God does not look back.

God looks forward.

God is angry at the past. And his answer to his own anger is resurrection. New creation.

Resurrection is not a trite, pithy statement on a Hallmark card sent to sugarcoat a suffering world's terminal wound. Resurrection is the raising of life that sin has destroyed, out of death and into the glorious presence of God. Resurrection is the power of new creation breaking into the destruction of the old. It is the raising of the dead to stand before our world's Redeemer.

Resurrection is the opening of *our* dark closet doors, the bringing of *our* dead skeletons out of the graveyard, to be dealt with by a God who is gracious, glorious, and good.

Resurrection.

The scariest doctrine in the New Testament is not hell, it is not judgment, it is not holy war.

It is resurrection.

Resurrection means we will not be able to hide in our graves from the presence of the living God. Death cannot hold us, as much as we may want it to. We may wonder how resurrection can be the New Testament's scariest doctrine when it is simultaneously the greatest doctrine of Christian hope. Ironically, resurrection is so scary *because* it is so packed with hope.

It is hope because death cannot hold us. It is fear because death cannot hide us from the living God before whom we must stand.

It is hope because sin will be defeated. It is fear because sin must be defeated in us.

It is hope because the dragon, that serpent of old, will be cast outside God's reconciling city. It is fear because we have made ourselves his allies and must defect if we are to be made ready for the coming world.

Resurrection is the catalyst for the coming new creation. Because of this, resurrection is simultaneously the catalyst for God's judgment on the old creation.

Resurrection has implications.

RAZING BABYLON, RAISING THE DEAD, REDEEMING THE WORLD

God promises Ezekiel three things in light of resurrection: he will come to raze Babylon, raise the dead, and redeem the world.[1] These are the three main topics we have explored throughout this book. God promises to *raze Babylon* through holy war, *raise the dead* for judgment, and *redeem the world* from the destructive power of hell. Hell, judgment, and holy war are God's good answers to Israel's tough questions.

Resurrection gives rise to them all.

Let's look at each in turn.

Razing Babylon

God is coming to raze Babylon. This comes first. This is holy war: God arising on behalf of the weak against the tyranny of the strong. God waging war on our empires when their crimes have piled up to heaven. God taking down the apocalyptic beasts that rage violently in his world.

God hears the cries of his murdered children screaming up from the cracked and thorny ground. He hears the affliction of his groaning world longing for liberation from our rebellion. God's ears are tired, ringing, exhausted. He is patient—but he won't always be.

Holy war is God's *structural judgment*: his response to the political, economic, and social oppression of our world, along with the dark, spiritual realities that lie behind them.

God is coming to raze Babylon to the ground, until all that's left is debris.

Raising the Dead

Next, God is coming to raise the dead. This is judgment: God drawing us out of our graves, pulling back the curtain on our deception of appearances, and addressing the brutality of our history in his righteous judgment.

God's purpose in judgment is to ensure that sin's destructive power is not allowed to disrupt the flourishing of his new creation. God's mercy is freely offered in Jesus, but sin will not be allowed to enter the holy city. God judges the world through Jesus: he has been exalted and given authority to reconcile creation to God.

Jesus is a good judge. He's a better judge than you are, a better judge than I am. He knows what he's doing, and he knows us better than we know ourselves. His judgment is good news for a world racked by sin, destruction, and death.

This is God's *personal judgment*: addressing the wicked root that lies at the heart of sin's ruin in the world, and placing a tourniquet on the wound of all that refuses to be healed by his mercy.

Redeeming the World

God is coming to redeem the world. This is the final movement. God will redeem his world from the toxic power of sin, death, and hell. God will protect his kingdom from all that would seek to disrupt, deface, or destroy the flourishing *shalom* of his holy city. God will banish all that stands unrepentantly opposed to his reconciliation for the world.

It is here that the logic of hell arises. God's city has a posture of embrace toward the world, but sin will not be allowed inside. God redeems the world *from* sin, so we must face the reality of which we prefer: God or sin. Freedom *from* God or freedom *for* God.

Freedom from God will be cast outside the city, because it is opposed by its very nature to the glorious goodness of what is happening inside the city. The destructive power of sin will find its home in the rubble of Babylon.

Hell is distance from God, and its closet is latched from the inside.

FLIPPING THE SCRIPT

Throughout this book, we have sought to flip the script on popular understandings of these topics. Now, in one final coup des grace, we flip the script on the script itself. We have explored these topics in reverse order. We started with hell, then moved to judgment, and finally landed on holy war. This was done to develop a particular *logical* flow. But *chronologically*, as Israel's answers, these topics move in the opposite direction. First comes holy war (God's razing of Babylon), then judgment (God's raising of the dead), and finally hell (God's redemption of the world).

God takes down the empire, pulls back the curtain, and establishes his kingdom.

Reversing the order of this book, the flow of God's finale for the world is:

razing Babylon
raising the dead
redeeming the world

God answers Israel's tough questions about the skeletons in the ground with powerful promises:

> Israel asks, "Will you end the exile and put a stop to the imperial powers that rage in arrogance against your world?" *God's answer is holy war.*

> Israel asks, "Will you address the brutality of history, the deception of appearances, and the bondage of creation?" *God's answer is judgment.*

> Israel asks, "Will you redeem the world and protect your kingdom from the continued onslaught of evil?" *God's answer is hell.*

God's answers are good news for the skeletons in the ground.

While this is good news for Israel, it is precisely these answers that give rise to our tough questions. Our grappling with topics like holy war, judgment, and hell are our attempt to come to grips with God's powerful answers to Israel's hard questions. Our skeletons in the closet arise from God's passionate responses to Israel's skeletons in the ground.

Our questions are hell, judgment, and holy war.
Holy war, judgment, and hell are Israel's answers.
Our questions are Israel's answers.

When we pull these topics out from the caricatures and place them back within the story where they belong—Israel's story for the world, the Old Testament framework where they were always intended to be—they begin to make sense again. Not only do they make sense, they begin to be seen as good news, part and parcel of the broader story of God's gloriously good purposes for his world. They arise because of resurrection. To proclaim, "These bones can live!" is to imply, by its very nature, that Babylon will be destroyed, the dead will be raised, and the world will be redeemed.

Resurrection is the melody at the center of God's symphony for the world, a symphony in which holy war, judgment, and hell are seen to be minor movements within resurrection's broader major sweep.

Resurrection proclaims that the skeletons in the ground are not forgotten; God remembers. Their blood does not cry out in vain; God hears. They are not abandoned; they are God's.

God's skeletons.

IN CLOSING . . .

God is good. Gloriously good. Better-than-we-could-ask-or-imagine-good. God is good *in his very bones*: not just in what he does, but in who he is; not only in his actions, but in his character. God's goodness is the hope of the world. It is God's goodness that gives rise to resurrection: as hope for our sin-struck, war-torn world. It is his goodness that gives rise to reconciliation: as hope for the fragmentation we have inflicted upon his world. And it is his goodness that gives rise to restoration: as hope amid the destruction we have unleashed in his glorious world.

Resurrection. Reconciliation. Restoration. These are proclamations of coming glory, hope for a world torn apart by the destructive, divisive, aggressive power of sin. Holy war, judgment, and hell arise within this broader major symphony as minor movements that contribute to the beauty of the whole. They are more than episodes we can learn to live with; they are plotlines we (literally) cannot live without.

They are not embarrassing artifacts of the Christian faith that need to be defended; they are offensive proclamations in light of Christ's resurrection against the idolatry, injustice, and presumption of the world. They declare loudly, boldly, and clearly that God is good.

And that he is coming for his world.

APPENDIX

LOOSE ENDS

Let's tie up a few loose ends by addressing some common questions that often arise when talking about these topics:

NOT OF THIS WORLD

QUESTION: Jesus tells Pilate his kingdom is "not of this world."[1] Many think this implies we leave this world when we die to go to Jesus' kingdom in heaven. But a centerpiece of this book has been that Jesus' kingdom *does* actually lay claim to this world. How do you make sense then of Jesus' statement to Pilate?

RESPONSE: Great question. When Jesus says his kingdom is "not of this world," the word "of" can mean different things. Jesus is not saying his kingdom is "not *for* this world" (this would contradict the entire thrust of Scripture), but rather that the origin of its power is "not *from* this world" and the way its power is exercised is "not *in the way of* this world."

So Jesus is speaking to the *origin* of his kingdom's authority—it comes from a different place than the empires of this world (like Caesar's Rome) that seek to rule the earth apart from God. While Rome's power arises up from the earth in rebellion against God's heavenly kingdom, Jesus' power comes down from God's heavenly kingdom and lays claim upon the earth. While Pilate understands his authority to come from Caesar, Jesus understands his authority to come from God.

Of course, Jesus challenges Pilate even deeper here, a challenge that cuts to the very roots of the Roman Empire's self-understanding, saying, "You would have no power over me if it were not given to you from above."[2] Whether Pilate knows it or not, his authority has ultimately been given to him from above. Jesus thus frames Pilate's authority as *beneath* God's kingdom reign, a kingdom that lays claim upon Pilate and the empire he represents.

So Jesus actually issues a prophetic challenge in this passage to Rome's supposed autonomous rule over the earth, ironically and climactically at the very moment the empire is crucifying him as the Son of God, the rightful King of the earth.

Jesus is also speaking to the *character* of his kingdom's authority. As Jesus tells his disciples elsewhere, "You know that the rulers of the Gentiles lord it over them, and their high officials exercise authority over them. Not so with you. Instead, whoever wants to become great among you must be your servant."[3] Jesus says Rome's leadership is frequently characterized by the love of power, but his disciples are to lead through the power of love. Authority in Jesus' kingdom is not exercised in the same manner as it tends to be in the kingdoms of this world, driven by the love of power.

So Jesus is saying both the *origin* of his kingdom, and the *character* of his kingdom, are of a wholly different nature from Rome's empire. Jesus' authority comes from a different place, and is exercised in a different style—his kingdom is "not of this world." But the *destination* of Jesus' kingdom lays claim to the same earth that Rome's does—it is "for this world." To say otherwise would contradict the entire thrust of Scripture.

As Jesus speaks these words to Pilate, it looks like Rome will win this "contest of kingdoms"—while Jesus is crucified, the kingdom marked by the love of power appears to be triumphing over the kingdom marked by the power of love. But this is, ironically, precisely the event through which Jesus is about to atone for sin and redeem the world—establishing God's kingdom upon the earth through the eventual displacement of our empires under the power of his redemptive love.

POWER OR PLACE

QUESTION: In some parts of the book you talk about hell as a "power," but in others as a "place." Which is it: a *power* or a *place*?

RESPONSE: Both. As is often the case with Scripture, this is a *both/ and*, not an *either/or*. The destructive "power" of hell makes its way into the world from the "place" of hell. For example, in the James passage we looked at earlier, this dynamic can be seen clearly:

> Consider what a great forest is set on fire by a small spark. The tongue also is a fire, a world of evil among the parts of the body. It corrupts the whole body, sets the whole course of one's life on fire, and is itself set on fire by hell [Gehenna].[4]

James sees hell as a *place* whose destructive *power*, like a wildfire, makes its way into the world through us. Power and place go together.

To use an analogy: let's say the United States invades Iraq (I know, use your imagination). And let's say you live in Iraq. And let's say as the bombs fall around you, they destroy a local hospital, a school, and a few homes. And someone asks you, "Is the United States a *power*, or a *place*?"

The obvious answer would be: both. You are experiencing the *power* of the United States invading your country, dropping bombs, destroying buildings. But it is a power that comes from a *place*; its origins are not in Iraq, but on the North American continent, across an ocean, far away. This is what makes it an *invasion*: a power is infiltrating your country from an outside place.

Similarly, in Scripture, the power of hell is seen as an invasion into God's good world. Sin wants to root itself within the garden, Gehenna creeps inside Jerusalem's walls, the adulterous affair lusts after the marriage bed, the rebellion stakes its claim in the capital, Babylon wants to tear down the temple, Satan wants the kingdoms of the world for himself, the wildfire wants to take down creation.

Earth is contested territory.

We often speak today of "heaven breaking into earth," and I love this language: God's heavenly kingdom invades, interrupts, crashes into earth even now. So we pray as Jesus taught, "Your kingdom come, your will be done, on earth as it is in heaven." I've found, however, that we don't often make the flip side of this observation: hell breaks into earth too. This is, in many ways, simply a reflection on the obvious other side of this popular coin.

But the gospel hope is that hell does not have the last word. The invasion will be kicked out. God's city will be established. Jesus' kingdom will reign on earth. Creation will be redeemed. The wildfire will be removed: the *power* will be pushed back into the *place* that it came from and contained from ever invading again.

Personally, I tend to emphasize hell as a "power" when speaking of it in the present tense, tearing apart our world today; and as a "place" when speaking of it in the future, when it is kicked out and contained by the victory of God. You see this, for example, in chapter 2 where I emphasize hell as a "power" while addressing the contemporary state of our world versus chapter 3 where I emphasize hell as a "place" while focusing on the future hope of the gospel.

This is because I believe we experience hell today more as a destructive *power* tearing our world apart, but our hope is that it will eventually and ultimately be contained in its *place*. We are living in Iraq getting bombed, but our hope is that one day the bombs will be kicked out of our country and kept back in North America.

PROTECTION OR PUNISHMENT

QUESTION: You've said God's primary purpose in hell is "protection" (containing hell's destructive power to protect the new creation), but it is also described as "punishment" in places like 2 Peter 2:9; 2 Thessalonians 1:8; and Jude 1:7. Which is it, protection or punishment?

RESPONSE: Once again, this is not an *either/or* but a *both/and.* God's containment *is* the punishment. We use this logic all the time in society. Take prison, for example: we want society to flourish, and we recognize rape and murder are a threat to society's flourishing. So we lock up rapists and murderers in order to protect society. And when a judge sentences someone to prison for rape or murder, we call that sentence a "punishment."

Their containment *is* the punishment.

Now, if the judge says, "You're sentenced to being waterboarded and electroshocked daily for the next fifty years," we would probably have a different response. This is torture of a vindictive sort, not punishment of a protective sort. We are accustomed to seeing containment as punishment, and (rightly) disturbed by the idea of torture as punishment.

I chose to avoid using the punishment terminology in the first section of this book because, pastorally, I know that as soon as I say the word *punishment* these days in a conversation on hell, everybody's mind immediately goes to torture. And I don't think that's what Scripture has in mind.

But once we clear the ground from our modern distortions and reclaim the Hebrew narrative worldview that Jesus and the New Testament are operating in, the word *punishment* fits naturally into the paradigm we've been exploring. And I think it's actually quite similar to the common-sense logic we use for dealing with crime in our society today.

Now, there are of course some glaring differences between our justice system and God's. For example, our justice system is frequently limited by our insufficient knowledge (innocent people go to prison); our justice system is afflicted by, and unable to account for, the radical racial inequities of our society (our prisons are filled with black and Hispanic minorities[5]); and unlike our justice system, God freely offers mercy in Jesus, a salvation that can transform us from the inside out, to all who will receive it (our justice system cannot deal redemptively with the "wicked root" in our hearts). God's justice is, thankfully, able to deal with and not be afflicted by all these radical limitations of our justice system.

But the justice system analogy is helpful to clarify an important point: the paradigm we've outlined in this book does not say that hell is not punishment; simply that it is not torture. The containment *is* the punishment. The paradigm we've outlined simply highlights the Hebrew narrative worldview in which containment-as-punishment makes sense.

WRATH

QUESTION: Some people speak of hell as a place where God "continually pours out his wrath" on unrepentant sinners. What do you think of this?

RESPONSE: It all depends on what we mean by the word "wrath." Like *punishment*, when most folks hear the word *wrath* today in a conversation on hell, I think their minds go immediately to God punching people in the face for eternity or something of the sort—the image of eternal sadistic torture. I don't think this is the correct picture at all.

Wrath as God's violence or force is best understood, in my estimation, in relation to the *events* of holy war and judgment, rather than the *state* of hell that follows on their heels. For example, in holy war God's wrath is unleashed on Babylon. Revelation's imagery here is the "bowls of God's wrath" being poured out on the great city as God burns down the empire with fire. When God's wrath is spent, completed, finished, we're left with the aftermath *state* of the smoldering rubble of Babylon, the post-apocalyptic landscape of the "lake of fire" that follows on the heels of the empire's destruction.

Wrath here is seen in the holy war *event* of Babylon's destruction, not in the *state* of hell that follows. God is not "continually throwing down on Babylon"—this would be an awkward image: the city continually rising up so God could throw back down on it again. God's violence on the empire has a start-time and end-time on the divine stop-watch. Wrath as God's violence is appropriate to holy war, not to hell.

Similarly, God's wrath as *force* is seen in the event of judgment: God raises humanity from death to set his world right and *casts out* those who stand opposed to his good kingdom. This "casting out" imagery, continually used by Jesus in his parables, is a picture of wrath: the landlord arriving to kick out his unruly tenants, the king booting the wedding crashers, the master removing his unfaithful servant. Judgment is the wrath-event of "casting out," hell is simply the aftermath state of having been cast out.

God is not "continually casting out" impenitent rebels—like a bouncer at a club repeatedly tossing an unruly dancer who keeps sneaking back in. Wrath here is seen in the *event* of judgment, not in the state that follows.

So wrath as *violence* is holy war language; wrath as *force* is judgment language. What about hell?

If we want to use the language of wrath for hell, I would suggest it works so long as we more carefully frame the word (given its awkward modern linguistic associations) as something like: "God continually protects the flourishing of his kingdom by actively containing the destructive power of our unrepentant sin." So wrath here is something more like *handing over*, or *containment* or *restraint*.

This is more congruent with the biblical storyline and also resonates with the depiction of God's wrath in Romans 1, where God's handing unrepentant sinners over to their desire for autonomy from him is described *itself* as a revelation of the wrath of God. Paul does not say here that *if* we want freedom from God, *then* he will pour out his wrath on us. He says, rather, that our life apart from God *is itself* the revelation of God's wrath: our being handed over to the sin we so desire. While the context of Romans 1 is world history, this dynamic of being handed over to what we want is similar to what we've explored in this book in the context of the coming of the kingdom.

So in summary, God's wrath as *violence* is holy war language; as *force* is judgment language; as *handing over* is hell language. God's

wrath being "poured out" is holy war language; "casting out" is judgment language; "containing" is hell language.

THE UNDYING WORM

QUESTION: Jesus describes hell as a place where "the worms that eat
them do not die, and the fire is not quenched." Is this not a picture
of hell as torture?

RESPONSE: Jesus is quoting Isaiah 66:24 here. As we have seen
throughout this book, a major reason we misunderstand New
Testament passages like these is that we don't pay attention to our Old
Testament that gives them context. So if we go back to the Isaiah passage Jesus is quoting, what do we find? It actually confirms strongly
the paradigm we've looked at throughout this book.

The passage Jesus quotes actually comes at the end of the entire
book of Isaiah, its closing passage. In many ways, the passage draws
together all that's come before in the prophet's work to a climactic con-
cluding finale. And it revolves around the redemption of Jerusalem:
God will come to redeem his holy city, to kick out the rebels within
his people and put an end to the destructive Gentile powers that lord
over his people. God will defeat them in battle and kick them outside
his city.

It's important to recognize that in this Isaiah passage Jesus quotes
the rebels outside the city are *dead*. People walk outside the city to
"look on the dead bodies of those who rebelled against me."[6] This is
the context for the undying worm and unquenchable fire. The worms
are not torturing the bodies of living people; they are feasting on
the decomposing bodies of dead rebels. The fire is not burning folks
alive; it is cremating the bodies of dead people (a common practice in
many places throughout history, and still in many societies like India
today). In its Old Testament context, this passage is not depicting a
torture chamber for the living but a graveyard for dead rebels.

And it is "outside the city"—the logical place dead bodies went in ancient cities.

The primary point of this Isaiah passage, and its resonance for Jesus' audience, is God's victory in Jerusalem. The idea of torturing resurrected bodies would have been foreign to Isaiah and his audience. Resurrection was not, as we have seen, a prominent staple of Old Testament theology prior to the resurrection of Christ. Isaiah's main point is that God will establish his kingdom and banish those destructive powers that have rebelled against him outside his holy city.

This main point is consistent with the overarching Hebrew narrative of the Old Testament. Similar to our observance of the lake of fire in chapter 17, the Old Testament context makes all the difference in the world. Once we place Jesus' reference back into the Old Testament passage he is quoting, his point makes perfect sense and is consistent with everything we've observed thus far.

DARKNESS

QUESTION: We've explored the imagery of fire extensively, but Jesus also uses darkness to describe life outside God's kingdom. What is the significance of this image?

RESPONSE: Fire and darkness are both "anti-creation" images. Sin is a fire that wants to burn down the world; darkness is the absence left when it's gone. They both stand against God's good creation.

If fire is a metaphor for "destruction," darkness is a metaphor for "absence." Darkness is the absence of light: turn off the lights, and find yourself in the darkness. Blow out the evening candles, and sit in the dark, invisible to the world around you. Hide in a cave from the sun, and grope your way through the shadows. Darkness is absence.

Light is the foundation of creation. In the Old Testament, God's first act is to say "Let there be light," separate the light from the darkness and soon after fill the sky with sun, moon and stars.[7] Light is the canvas upon which God is about to paint his creation. Before this, however, "darkness was over the surface of the deep"[8]—darkness is the nothingness, the absence, the nihilistic void into which God is about to speak creation into being.

As we've seen, sin wants to unravel the world, to separate creation from its Creator and drag it back down into the nihilistic void from which it came—into the darkness. Sin is "anti-creation."

But sin's darkness is more than "anti-creation;" on a deeper level it is "anti-Creator." God himself is light. John proclaims: "God is light; in him there is no darkness at all."[9] The psalmist cries out, "Let the light of your face shine upon us."[10] Like the sun, God is associated with light, warmth and goodness: he radiates light, facilitates life and causes things to grow and flourish in his presence.

Sin, however, loves the darkness. It desires distance from God. The Light of the World pursues us generously: "God so loved the world that he gave his one and only Son," as John rejoices in perhaps the most famous verse of Scripture. But our problem, as John goes on to remind us, is not that we aren't good enough, not that we haven't jumped through all the right religious hoops, not that we don't have all the right information—but rather that we "*loved* darkness rather than light."[11]

We love the darkness: we crave it; we want it. We want a world without God. We desire freedom from him. We prefer to live life on our own. God pursues, we like the absence. We crave the darkness. That's why darkness is such a fitting metaphor: it speaks to the absence of God's presence, goodness, joy, and light.

Darkness is more than the absence of God's kingdom.

It is the absence of God the King.

For those who prefer it that way.

WEEPING AND GNASHING OF TEETH

QUESTION: Jesus also frequently refers to "weeping and gnashing of teeth."[12] What is the significance of this phrase?

RESPONSE: When I first heard this phrase, I remember thinking people were weeping because angels were whipping them or gnashing their teeth because God was beating them up—again, images of torture. But diving into the biblical story, I realized it was an image of loss. Folks were fussing because they lost the best place in line. They were weeping because their toys had been taken away. They were gnashing their teeth because God had won and their side lost—they were jealous that God was receiving the glory while they were kicked outside the kingdom.

We've seen pictures of this frequently: the rich man who ignored Lazarus, and now weeps in the rubble of his riches because of the things he lost in the fire (chapter 5). The kings and merchants of Revelation, who weep and wail when the empire of Babylon is destroyed (chapter 17). The prodigal son's older brother, who pouts and gnashes his teeth outside the party: not because the father is beating him up (the father "went out and pleaded with him"[13] to come in and join the party), but because he refuses to let go of his pride and receive the grace that marks the life of the kingdom (chapter 11).

If *fire* speaks to sin's destructive power and *darkness* to the ensuing absence downstream, then *weeping and gnashing of teeth* speaks to the loss entailed when God's kingdom arrives in fullness.

TARTARUS

QUESTION: In 2 Peter 2:4, Peter uses the word *Tartarus*, usually translated as "hell" in our English Bibles. You have dealt with *Gehenna*, *Sheol*, and *Hades*—the three primary words in Scripture translated as "hell"—what is the significance of this final word, *Tartarus*?

RESPONSE: Yes, a couple of things about *Tartarus* are noteworthy. First, this is the only place in Scripture where this word appears, so it's probably not wise to build an entire theology around an obscure word that appears only once in the Bible.

Second, the subjects of this verse are not people, but angels: "God did not spare angels when they sinned, but sent them to Tartarus." So whatever Peter has in mind here with the word *Tartarus*, he depicts it as a place for angels, not people.

Third, it is depicted as a current holding place, not a final destination. Peter tells us God "sent" (past tense) these rebel angels to Tartarus, "putting them in chains of darkness to be held for judgment."[14] Similar to the Old Testament's depiction of dead people being held in the darkness of Sheol, Peter depicts rebellious angels being held in the darkness of Tartarus. But this is not their final destination: the reason they are presently held there is to await the coming (future) judgment.

So in this sense, Tartarus is more like the Old Testament concept of Sheol (or "the grave") than the New Testament concept of Gehenna. It is depicted as a dark, underground holding tank for angels, similar to the way Sheol is depicted as a dark, underground grave for dead people. Both are a current holding place, not a future destination—only one is for people, the other for angels.

Finally, the ancient Greeks' location for Tartarus supports this. In Greek mythology, Tartarus was a place even lower than Hades in the underworld. It was "below the grave," so to speak. As we have seen, Jews of the first century used *Hades* to translate their Hebrew word *Sheol*. I would suggest that, similarly here, Peter is using *Tartarus* to conceptualize a place *lower than Sheol*, deeper in the earth than the grave. Perhaps as these rebellious angels fell from higher in the heavens, they were seen to have fallen deeper into the earth.[15] While dead people are held in the grave of Sheol, rebellious angels are held even deeper in the belly of the earth, in the dark abyss of Tartarus. Awaiting judgment.

So Tartarus is a bit mysterious. Whatever its significance, it does not support the caricature of a place where people are tortured forever. Rather, it shows up only once in Scripture and refers, apparently, to a temporary holding tank in the belly of the earth for rebellious angels awaiting the final judgment.

EVENT AND STATE

QUESTION: In the Conclusion, you say that chronologically these topics actually go in reverse order from the order dealt with in this book:
first holy war, then judgment, then hell. How would you distinguish
these three "movements"?

RESPONSE: I've found it helpful to think of holy war and judgment as
events and hell as a *state*. So, first comes the event of holy war: where
God judges our empires and social structures for their destructive
rebellion against his good kingdom. Next comes the event of judgment: where God gathers the nations before his throne to establish his
justice in the world. Now both of these events are, of course, *judgment*
in an important sense. But I am using "holy war" to describe God's
corporate judgment on the empires and social structures of our world,
and reserving "judgment"—in its more classical sense—to describe
God's *individual* judgment of persons.

While holy war and judgment are *events*, hell is more of a *state*
that follows on the heels of these events. So after God has destroyed
Babylon in the event of holy war, hell is the aftermath state of "the
rubble of Babylon." And after God's event of judgment on our unrepentant sin, hell is the state of being handed over to our unrepentant
sin. Holy war and judgment are *events* that interrupt the history of
our sin-struck, war-torn world (like punctuated "dots" on a historical
timeline); hell is the *state* that follows on the heels of these events.

I find 2 Thessalonians 1:5–10 powerful in the way it seamlessly
draws all three of these movements together in the same breath. First,
"the Lord Jesus is revealed from heaven in blazing fire with his powerful angels" (apocalyptic holy war language). Second, "he will punish
those who do not know God and do not obey the gospel of our Lord
Jesus" (personal judgment language). And finally, "they will be punished with everlasting destruction and shut out from the presence of
the Lord and from the glory of his might" (being handed over to the
state of hell language). The catalyst for all this is "the day he comes to

be glorified in his holy people and to be marveled at among all those who have believed" (draws all three movements together into Jesus' redemptive coming).

POPULARITY OF THE CARICATURES

QUESTION: Why do you think the caricatures have become so popular?

RESPONSE: Hmm . . . I believe there are a wide variety of reasons, so there are a lot of factors I could give. But one I think is interesting: I've come to believe there's a part of us that *wants* the caricatures to be true. If the caricatures are true, it gives us a reason to write God off: to believe we're the good guys and he's the one with issues. We want our independence, so I think there's a part of us that uses the caricatures to feel justified in our desire for distance, autonomy, and independence from God. So that we can feel justified in our sin.

And at the end of the day, we are really the ones—not God—who have constructed the caricatures and given them their validity. But God is good. Better-than-we-could-ask-or-imagine-good. Way better than the caricatures we've created. So I think at some level our caricatures are not just something oppressive we need to be freed from, but something constructed we need to repent of, an idol we've made that we need to remove our clutching grasp from—in order to receive the redemptive embrace of the God who is gloriously good.

GRATEFUL

I'm beyond grateful to:

Imago Dei Community: for running after Jesus together and occasionally slowing down to let me catch up.

Rick McKinley, Luke Hendrix, Jeff Marsh, Paul Metzger, Robert Proudfoot, Abraham Himsimting, and Brandon Song: my mentors. Jesus has shaped me through your presence.

Jake Hendrix at House of Providence (Vancouver, WA) and Kyle Costello at Missio Dei (Salt Lake City, UT): for being crazy enough to risk my preaching a series on this stuff early on!

Jon Collins (the *amazing* video!), Adam Hendrix (web genius), Sarah Thebarge (early editor extraordinaire), Ben Thomas (my one-man PR team!), Scott Erickson (art and inspiration), Sebastian Rogers (words aren't enough), and Jeremy and Brenda Jones (what a writing retreat!).

Don Jacobson and Blair Jacobson: for being so much more than agents, but mentors and friends.

Matt Baugher, Adria Haley, Julie Allen, Emily Sweeney, Stephanie Newton, and the amazing team at Thomas Nelson Publishers: for taking a risk on a new, young ink slinger.

For friendship, encouragement, and listening to my ramblings: Mom and Dad and the fam, Glenn and Sonya and Will, Paul Ramey, Heather Thomas, Steve Wytcherley, Luke Goble, Stan Patyrak, Tony Kriz, Dan Son, Nate Grubbs, Ben Wachsmuth, Paul Richter, Michael Badriaki, Steve and Beth Plymale, Steve and Celestia Tracy, Melanie Brown, Taylor Hawkins, Mike Pacchione, Wes Willis, John Heintzman, Van Wheeler, Daniel Christopher, and Ben Sand.

Crema, Heart, and Little T, where much of this book was written: for refreshment, ambience, and cups served with kindness.

Above all, my wife, Holly Beth: for believing in this project before I did (and occasionally kicking me out of the house to write it!); my daughter, Aiden Ivey: for dancing in the kitchen together when I needed a break (and picking out the book cover!); our foster son, Torin (we're so glad you're in our family!); and our newest little guy Jacob Valdez (welcome to the world!). You guys are the best . . .

And above that: Father, Son, and Spirit, *Soli Deo Gloria*.

ABOUT THE AUTHOR

Joshua Ryan Butler serves as pastor of local and global outreach at Imago Dei Community, a church in the heart of Portland, Oregon. Joshua oversees the church's city ministries in areas like foster care, human trafficking, and homelessness; and he develops international partnerships in areas like clean water, HIV-support, and church planting. Joshua is also a worship leader who enjoys writing music for the life of the church. Joshua's wife, Holly, daughter Aiden, and son Jacob enjoy spending time with their friends over great meals and being a foster family for vulnerable children.

NOTES

Chapter 1

1. Ephesians 1:3.
2. The reconciliation of heaven and earth is a major theme in the writing of prominent New Testatment scholar N. T. Wright. See particularly his *Surprised by Hope: Rethinking Heaven, the Resurrection and the Mission of the Church* (New York: HarperOne, 2008).
3. While the NIV and most translations return zero results, it is worth noting a few translations will return a minimal amount of results. For example, the King James Version returns five results (Job 11:8; Psalm 139:8; Amos 9:2; Matthew 11:23; Luke 10:15) where heaven and hell appear together. The discrepancy arises because the English word "hell" is being used here to translate the terms *Sheol* and *Hades* (terms we will look at more in upcoming chapters), which in these verses are not referring to future eschatological categories (the focus of our current discussion in this chapter and what most people have in mind in a discussion of this nature on hell) so much as present spatial categories (translated in most versions as "the grave," "the depths," etc.) and thus do not affect the overall point being made in this experiment. In these versions as well, it is still note-worthy how very few times heaven and hell appear together versus how frequently heaven and earth appear together. For example, in the KJV heaven and earth appear together in 219 verses, compared to the five verses where heaven and hell appear together.
4. Here again, the exact results will depend on which translation you are using. For example, running this experiment on Bible Gateway (www .biblegateway.com) with the NIV translation returned 195 verses, while the NASB returned 194, the NLT 205, and the KJV, as mentioned in the previous endnote, 219.
5. Genesis 1:1.
6. Genesis 1:26.
7. Psalm 8:4, 6. The psalmist wonders aloud at this great privilege and responsibility, "What is man that you are mindful of him, the son of man that you care for him? . . . You made him ruler over the works of your hands; you put everything under his feet." Authority, dominion, and

stewardship are all words that have been used to describe this central facet of our place in the story: God created us to reign together with him over his world.

8. Genesis 3:17–19.
9. Genesis 6:11 KJV.
10. Genesis 3:8.
11. Luke 15:11–32.
12. Colossians 1:19–20.
13. Revelation 11:15.
14. 1 Corinthians 15:24–28; Ephesians 1:9–10, 19–23.
15. Habakkuk 2:14.
16. Romans 8:18–21.
17. Matthew 28:18.
18. Ephesians 1:10.
19. Revelation 21:2.
20. Revelation 21:3.

Chapter 2

1. International Justice Mission website, www.ijm.org/node/62, accessed August 7, 2013.
2. Matthew 5:27–30.
3. Wikiquote, s.v. "Walt Kelly," http://en.wikiquote.org/wiki/Walt_Kelly; Wikipedia, s.v. "Pogo (comic strip)," http://en.wikipedia.org/wiki/Pogo _(comic_strip), accessed October 3, 2013.
4. See, for example, "Rwanda: How the genocide happened," BBC (April 1, 2004), which gives an estimate of 800,000.
5. While exact figures are hard to calculate, the Cambodian Genocide Program of Yale University estimates 1.7 million people lost their lives, or 21 percent of the country's population (www.yale.edu/cgp; accessed November 15, 2013). Many studies suggest higher estimates over 2 million people, or approximately 25 percent of the country's population (Bruce Sharp surveys some of the more significant studies in "Counting Hell: The Death Toll of the Khmer Rouge Regime in Cambodia" [www.mekong.net /cambodia/deaths.htm; accessed November 15, 2013]).
6. Matthew 5:21–22.
7. Aleksandr Solzhenitsyn, *The Gulag Archipelago 1918–1956* (1958; New York: HarperCollins, 2002).
8. Isaiah 9:18.
9. Hosea 7:4, 6–7.
10. James 3:5–6.
11. See Matthew 5:22–30; 10:28; 18:9; 23:15–33; Mark 9:43–47; Luke 12:5.
12. Genesis 1:31.
13. You can learn more about Tom's organization, EPIK, at their website: www.epikproject.org.

14. Living Water International (www.water.cc) is a great organization that is tackling this problem head-on.

15. International Justice Mission (www.ijm.org) is dealing powerfully with this issue around the world. These statistics can be found on their website.

16. Since the end of World War II, there have been more than 250 major wars across the globe; statistics from: www.worldrevolution.org/projects /globalissuesoverview/overview2/PeaceNew.htm (accessed August 7, 2013). African Leadership and Reconciliation Ministries (alarm-inc.org) is an inspiring organization courageously tackling reconciliation work in post-conflict regions of East Africa.

Chapter 3

1. *Gehenna* shows up twelve times in the New Testament: Matthew 5:22, 29, 30; 10:28; 18:9; 23:15, 33; Mark 9:43, 45, 47; Luke 12:5; James 3:6. Other New Testament words that are sometimes translated into English as "hell" but show up less frequently are *Hades* (which we will explore in chapter 5) and *Tartarus* (see Appendix).

2. *Gehenna* is the Greek translation for the Valley of Hinnom (*Ge-* means "valley," and *-henna* is a transliteration of the Hebrew *Hinnom*). In the Old Testament, the Valley of Hinnom shows up in Joshua 15:8; 18:16; 2 Kings 23:10; 2 Chronicles 28:3; 33:6; Nehemiah 11:30; Jeremiah 7:31–32; 19:2–6; 32:35. In some of these Old Testament verses, it is referred to as "the Valley of Ben Hinnom": *ben* is the Hebrew word for "son," so this is simply a Hebrew way of referring to the same place by its family name, "the Valley of the Son of Hinnom."

3. Jeremiah 19:4.

4. These characterizations of *shalom* are depicted poignantly in the blessings, as well as their negative inversions in the curses, of Deuteronomy 11. If Israel is faithfully obedient to God, God's *shalom* will dwell with his people. But if she stubbornly rebels against him, God's *shalom* will depart. Solomon's dedication of the temple in 1 Kings 8:22–61 also strongly invokes this imagery. *Shalom* is a multifaceted Hebrew concept that involved Israel's relationship with God: God dwelling in the center of the land—in the temple—in power and intimacy with his people. It involved Israel's relationship with each other: the justice and righteousness of God characterizing her normal life as a people. It involved Israel's relationship with the land: the intimate presence of God causing the land to flourish and bring forth its produce in abundance. It involved Israel's relationship with other nations: the power of God protecting the peace of his city from the surrounding empires' imperial ambitions and inviting the nations into his glorious kingdom.

5. 2 Chronicles 33:1–9.

6. J. R. R. Tolkien unpacks this idea of the gospel as the fairy tale come true in his essay "On Fairy-Stories," published in C. S. Lewis, ed., *Essays Presented to Charles Williams* (Oxford: Oxford University Press, 1947).

7. C. S. Lewis, *The Voyage of the Dawn Treader* (New York: HarperCollins, 1952, 1980).

8. Ibid., 60.
9. Revelation 21:25.
10. Revelation 21:24, 26.
11. Revelation 21:27.
12. Revelation 21:8.
13. Zechariah 2:4–5.
14. Isaiah 11:9.

Interlude: The Game-Changer

1. Genesis 37:35 ESV.
2. Psalm 6:5 ESV.
3. Job 3:19 ESV.
4. Psalm 88:4, 6, 12 ESV.
5. For example, Matthew 16:18, where Jesus references the "gates of Hades." In Jesus' day, Jews used *Hades* to translate their Hebrew word *Sheol* into Greek.
6. Genesis 3:19.
7. 1 Corinthians 15:20–23.
8. 1 Corinthians 15:22; see also Romans 5:12–21.
9. Inspired by the John Mark McMillan song "Death in His Grave," from *The Medicine* (Integrity, 2010).
10. From John Donne's classic poem "Holy Sonnet X: Death be not proud."

Chapter 4

1. C. S. Lewis, *The Pilgrim's Regress: An Allegorical Apology for Christianity, Reason and Romanticism* (New York: Inspirational Press, 1933, 1943), 137.
2. Ibid.
3. Ibid., 138.
4. Genesis 2:23; 3:12, 16; 4:8, 24; 6:13.
5. Genesis 6:6 tells us that when God saw the violence that filled the earth, "his heart was deeply troubled." This is the backdrop to the Flood: we fill the earth with violence, so God fills the earth with water. The earth that God brought up from the chaotic waters of Genesis 1:2 is "unraveled" by our violence, so to speak, back in distance from God to the chaos from which it came.
6. Augustine, *In Psalm.* 95, n. 15 (PL 37, 1236). Henri de Lubac cites this passage of Augustine amidst a profound broader discussion of this theme in the patristic fathers in *Catholicism: Christ and the Common Destiny of Man*, trans. Lancelot C. Sheppard and Sister Elizabeth Englund, OCD (San Francisco: Ignatius Press, 1947, 1988), 34.
7. See, for example, Augustine's discussions in *Confessions, VII* and *The City of God, XI–XII.*
8. These analogies are intentional: food, sex, and authority are given by God in the creation account of Genesis 1 as good things to bless those he loves ("they will be yours for food"—v. 29; "be fruitful and increase in number"—v. 22; "so that they may rule"—v. 26).

9. Technically, there is a more minor sense in which "evil" shows up as a noun in the dictionary, but when used as a noun, it is designating the character, intention, conduct, or force of that which is adjectivally qualified as evil. So it is not so much an aside from evil's adjectival quality, as it is the personification of it.

10. In searching for this popular quote's original source, the American Chesterton Society reports, "This story has been repeated so often about Chesterton that we suspect it is true. Also, it seems it is never told about anyone other than Chesterton. What we have not found, however, is any documentary evidence for it. It may indeed be from *The Times*, as the story is usually told, but no one has taken the trouble to go through the back issues and find a copy of the actual letter. It has also been attributed to other papers, but again, no proof. It is also entirely possibly that it actually happened with another author, but has been attributed to Chesterton because it is typical of both his humility and his wit and because it is associated with the title of a book he wrote in 1910, *What's Wrong with the World*." (From: http://www.chesterton.org/discover-chesterton/frequently -asked-questions/wrong-with-world/; accessed November 12, 2013).

11. Revelation 21:25, 24, 26.

12. Revelation 21:8. Revelation includes eight vices on its list that will not be allowed inside God's city; yet more important than the specific vices mentioned is likely their number. In Revelation, where numbers are significant and seven is a number that signifies completion, this list of eight vices is likely a symbolic way of suggesting that the *totality* of sin (*all* sin and *then* one) will no longer be allowed inside the city.

13. Romans 5:8 KJV.

14. Lewis, *The Pilgrim's Regress*, 137.

15. Revelation 21:27.

16. Isaiah 11:9; 65:25.

Chapter 5

1. See chapter 17. I've placed the discussion of Revelation's lake of fire in the section "The Hope of Holy War" because, as we shall see, it is a *holy war* image. The context there will help us reclaim a healthy and constructive understanding of the image.

2. Luke 16:19–21.

3. Luke 16:14.

4. In the surrounding context of Luke, Jesus' clash with the leaders of God's people is a prominent theme. As we shall see in Part 2, "The Surprise of Judgment," this is a primary characteristic of judgment in Jesus' teaching: it comes first to the people of God.

5. Luke 16:20.

6. Luke 16:15.

7. Luke 16:13.

8. The Greek name Lazarus comes from the Hebrew origin *Eleazar*,

which means "God has helped." William Barclay, *The Parables of Jesus* (Westminster John Knox Press, 1999), 92–98.

9. Luke 16:22–26.

10. James Strong, *Strong's Exhaustive Concordance of the Bible*, upd. and exp. ed. (Peabody, MA: Hendrickson, 2007; 2008), G931 (p. 1613).

11. Luke 16:27, 29.

12. Luke 16:30.

13. Luke 16:31.

14. This compilation of C. S. Lewis quotes comes from multiple sources: *Mere Christianity* (New York: Macmillan, 1964), 59; *The Great Divorce* (New York: Macmillan, 1963), 71–72; *The Problem of Pain* (New York: Macmillan, 1961), 116; "The Trouble with X," in *God in the Dock: Essays on Theology and Ethics* (Grand Rapids: Eerdmans, 1970), 155; compiled similarly in Timothy Keller's *The Reason for God: Belief in an Age of Skepticism* (New York: Dutton Adult, 2008), 78–79.

15. Keller, *The Reason for God*, 77–78.

16. Judah's five full-brothers from Leah were Reuben, Simeon, Levi, Issachar and Zebulun. One could also interpret the rich man as the tribe of Levi, the priestly class who oversaw the Temple (who was also from Leah and had "five brothers" in the other tribes). This interpretation would not affect the overall emphasis here; it would simply focus it more on the Temple. I find this interpretation less likely, however, as Jesus' primary antagonists in Luke are the Pharisees (who are not necessarily Levites) and Jerusalem's leadership as a whole.

17. See, for example, Matthew 15:26–27 and Mark 7:27–28.

18. See N. T. Wright's powerful discussion of this theme in *Jesus and the Victory of God* (Minneapolis, Fortress Press, 1996), 320–368. In the Gospel of Luke, Jesus' confrontation with Jerusalem's leadership and prediction of the city's coming destruction are seen most explicitly in Jesus' lament over Jerusalem's coming destruction (13:31–35 and 19:41–44) and Warning of the Destruction of the Temple and Signs of the End Times (21:5–38). Scholars generally agree that Jesus' famous "Cleansing of the Temple" scene is actually a prophetic act in which Jesus intentionally and symbolically foreshadows the coming *destruction* (not cleansing) of the Temple. (Wright, *Jesus and the Victory of God*, pp. 413–428). Beyond these more explicit passages, however, this coming downfall of Jerusalem and its leadership is also an implicit subtext underlying the majority of Jesus' parables in Luke [for example, The Parable of the Rich Fool (Luke 12:13–21), The Parable of the Returning Master (12:35–48), The Parable of the Fig Tree (13:6–9), The Parable of the Seat of Honor (14:7–14), The Parable of the Great Banquet (14:15–24), the older brother in The Parable of the Lost Son (15:11–32), The Parable of the Shrewd Manager (16:1–15), The Parable of the Pharisee and the Tax Collector (18:9–14), The Parable of the Ten Minas (19:11–27) and The Parable of the Tenants (20:9–19)]. From the moment "Jesus resolutely set out for Jerusalem . . ." in Luke 9:51, he is on a crash course with Jerusalem's leadership until he finally reaches

his trial and death near the end of Luke's gospel. The primacy of this over-arching narrative context in Luke *powerfully* reinforces the interpretation that the rich man in Hades is a picture of Jerusalem's coming destruction and the downfall of its leadership.

19. Compare this to my conclusion in chapter 17 on the significance of Revelation's "lake of fire" image, that it is "the rubble of Babylon," the smoldering debris of the once great and now demolished city. This con-nection between Jerusalem aflame here in Luke's Gospel and Babylon's smoldering rubble in Revelation becomes all the more striking if one accepts N. T. Wright's conclusion on why Jesus rails so heavily against Jerusalem in the Gospels, because in Jesus' day, "Jerusalem, under its present regime, had become Babylon." (*Jesus and the Victory of God*, op. cit., p. 323).

20. Though strange to us, the image of a city going down to Hades was familiar Jewish symbolism. Jesus uses this image earlier in Luke's gospel regarding the fate of Capernaum: "Capernaum, will you be lifted up to the heavens? No, you will go down to Hades." (10:15) See also Isaiah's depiction of Babylon going down to the grave, Sheol, the Old Testament equivalent of Hades (Isaiah 14:4–15).

21. If this interpretation of Jerusalem aflame is correct, and I believe it is, then this appears to me the *primary* significance behind Jesus' use of the flame imagery in this parable. Even if not, however, the conclusion has already been established on other grounds in this chapter that Jesus is not here depicting torture in this parable. (For a similar discussion of Jesus using flame imagery to depict Jerusalem's destruction, see chapter 9 where Jesus' parable of the Wedding Banquet uses the image of a king "burning down their city," interpreted there as God's judgment on Jerusalem through the Gentile powers).

22. Jesus' raising of his friend Lazarus from the dead is recounted in John 11:1–44.

23. N. T. Wright, *The Resurrection of the Son of God* (Minneapolis: Fortress, 2003), 85–206. In Jesus' day, Jews translated their Hebrew word for the grave, *Sheol*, which we've seen before, into Greek with the word *Hades*. As we've seen, the Old Testament concept of the grave was simply where we all go when we die. For the Greeks, Hades could be a place of fiery torment, and Jesus may be critically drawing upon some of these resonances. But for the Hebrews, it was simply the closest Greek word they had for the grave. And the Hebrew concept was, as we've seen, very different from the "under-ground torture chamber"—everybody went there and it was not a place of conscious punishment as much as simply of death.

24. Acts 23:8.

25. Matthew 16:18.

26. Revelation 20:14.

Chapter 6

1. C. S. Lewis, *The Great Divorce: A Dream* (New York: HarperCollins, 1946, 1973), 75.

2. This is a paraphrase of Augustine's classic thesis in *The City of God*, bk. 14, chap. 28.
3. Revelation 11:15 NKJV.
4. Winston Churchill, speech, House of Commons, November 11, 1947, in *Winston S. Churchill: His Complete Speeches, 1897–1963*, ed. Robert Rhodes James, vol. 7, p. 7566 (London, Facts on File: 1974).
5. Lewis, *The Great Divorce*, 11.
6. Ibid.
7. Ibid.
8. Ibid., 129.
9. Matt Jenson outlines this idea's roots in Augustine and traces some of its later historical development in *The Gravity of Sin: Augustine, Luther, and Barth on* Homo Incurvitas In Se (London: T&T Clark, 2006).
10. Lewis, *The Great Divorce*, 138.
11. Ibid.

Interlude: Ancient or New?

1. A great resource on the history of Christian political thought that displays this theme lucidly, with a vast array of significant excerpts from throughout the patristic and medieval eras, is Oliver and Joan Lockwood O'Donovan, eds., *From Irenaeus to Grotius: A Sourcebook in Christian Political Thought* (Grand Rapids: Eerdmans, 1999).
2. This is not to say that Augustine does not have passages that at times resemble the caricature. Like most theologians and thinkers through the centuries, key insights are not always worked through to their systematic implications or are often combined with other assumptions, insights, or influences.

Chapter 7

1. Matthew 18:6.
2. Matthew 23:25–28.
3. Matthew 23:15.
4. Matthew 23:33–36.
5. James 3:1.
6. Revelation 2–3.
7. Revelation 2:5, 16, 22; 3:16.
8. Matthew 21:31–32; Luke 15:1–31.
9. Matthew 22:1–14; Luke 14:15–23.
10. Matthew 8:5–13; Luke 13:22–30; Revelation 21:24–27.
11. Matthew 25:31–46; Luke 16:19–31.
12. Matthew 19:30; 20:16; Mark 10:31; Luke 13:30.
13. Matthew 7:21–23; 25:31–46.
14. Matthew 8:5–13; 25:31–46; Luke 13:22–30.
15. Lesslie Newbigin, *The Gospel in a Pluralist Society* (Grand Rapids: Eerdmans, 1989), 177.

16. 1 Corinthians 4:5.
17. Romans 2:16.
18. 1 Samuel 16:7.
19. Genesis 4:10.
20. Psalm 99:4 NLT.
21. Vine Deloria Jr. offers a classic treatise on issues like these from a Native perspective in *Custer Died for Your Sins: An Indian Manifesto* (New York: MacMillan, 1969). *Cultural Survival Quarterly* (www.culturalsurvival.org /publications/cultural-survival-quarterly) is a respected journal focusing on indigenous rights like these, both domestically and internationally.
22. Romans 8:22, 19, 21.
23. Matthew 28:18.
24. Acts 17:31.

Chapter 8

1. For example, Acts 17:24–31.
2. For example, John 1:1–19; Colossians 1:15–21; Hebrews 1:1–3.
3. Revelation 5:9; 7:9–10; 21:22–27.
4. Matthew 8:5–13.
5. Matthew 8:10.
6. Matthew 8:11–12.
7. Luke 13:29.
8. 1 Peter 4:17 NLT.
9. Genesis 1:28 KJV.
10. Genesis 1:28.
11. Genesis 1:31; this theme is also evidenced by the extensive attention given to the genealogy of the nations in Genesis 5 and 10.
12. Acts 17:26.
13. Genesis 6:13.
14. Henri de Lubac explores this theme in patristic thought in his classic work *Catholicism: Christ and the Common Destiny of Man*, trans. Lancelot C. Sheppard and Sister Elizabeth Englund (San Francisco: Ignatius Press, 1988), 29–34.
15. Genesis 12:3.
16. Genesis 12:3; 18:18; 22:18; 26:4.
17. This theme will be explored more extensively in chapter 14, "Evicted from Eden."
18. Isaiah 60:3.
19. Psalm 9:11.
20. Exodus 19:6.
21. Ezekiel 5:5–6; italics added.
22. Ezekiel 8–11; yes, my use of the phrase "outside the city" here is an allusion to our discussion in chapter 3. In chapter 17, we will look more closely at the interrelation of Babylon and Gehenna's futures.
23. Wikipedia, s.v. "Outline of war," http://en.wikipedia.org/wiki/List_of_ wars#Wars_by_date, accessed August 8, 2013.

24. Revelation 22:2.
25. Revelation 21:24.
26. Acts 17:31.
27. Revelation 13:8.
28. John 1:29.
29. Check out Sarah Thebarge's incredible story about battling cancer and befriending a family of Somalian refugees in her book *The Invisible Girls: A Memoir* (New York: Jericho, 2013).

Chapter 9

1. Matthew 22:5–7.
2. On Babylon as God's servant, see for example Jeremiah 25:9; 27:6; 43:10; and 2 Kings 24:2.
3. Mark 15:39; Hebrews 13:12.
4. Edwards is often considered America's greatest philosophical theologian; see, for example, Robert Jenson's treatment in *American Theologian: A Recommendation of Jonathan Edwards* (Oxford: Oxford University Press, 1988). *The Stanford Encyclopedia of Philosophy* affirms Edwards as "widely acknowledged to be America's most important and original philosophical theologian" (http://plato.stanford.edu/entries/edwards; accessed August 8, 2013). Amy Plantinga-Pauw provides insightful observations on Edwards's powerful Trinitarian theology and some of the pastoral crises that gave rise to tensions in his thought in *The Supreme Harmony of All: The Trinitarian Theology of Jonathan Edwards* (Grand Rapids: Eerdmans, 2002).
5. Matthew 22:8–10.
6. Luke 14:21–23.
7. Christopher Wright powerfully explores the centrality of God's mission throughout the biblical narrative in *The Mission of God: Unlocking the Bible's Grand Narrative* (Downer's Grove, IL: Intervarsity, 2006).
8. Matthew 22:11–13.
9. Matthew 21:32.
10. Revelation 7:14.
11. Romans 5:5; Ephesians 1:13–14 (the Greek word used here for "deposit," *arrabon*, was also sometimes used for an engagement ring).
12. Matthew 16:25; cf. Mark 8:35; Luke 9:24.

Chapter 10

1. Matthew 25:31–32.
2. Psalm 99:4 NLT.
3. Isaiah 42:1; Matthew 12:18.
4. Isaiah 5:26.
5. Psalm 65:5.
6. Matthew 25:34–40.
7. Genesis 12:3.

8. Matthew 25:37–39.

9. Matthew 25:44.

10. Matthew 25:34; see also Ephesians 1:4.

11. Matthew 7:22–23.

12. I'm grateful to Bill Clem for this analogy; from his sermon "Old Gospel, New Life: Week 2" at Imago Dei Community on April 14, 2013 (downloadable at www.imagodeicommunity.com).

13. 1 Corinthians 13:1–3.

14. John 10:16.

15. Matthew 25:34, 41.

16. Psalm 99:4 NLT.

17. Isaiah 61:8.

18. Nicholas Wolterstorff, *Justice: Rights and Wrongs* (Princeton: Princeton University Press, 2008), 82.

19. Romans 3:23.

20. Rick McKinley powerfully unpacks this phrase *loved sinners* in his sermon "The Community of the Crucified King: Week 1" at Imago Dei Community on February 17, 2013 (downloadable at www.imagodeicommunity.com).

21. Inspired by Tim Keller's quote, "So we can say that we are more wicked than we ever dared believe, but more loved and accepted in Christ than we ever dared hope—at the very same time." From *Paul's Letter to the Galatians: Living in Line with the Truth of the Gospel* (New York: Redeemer Presbyterian Church, 2003), 2.

Chapter 11

1. Luke 15:24.

2. Luke 15:28–32.

3. In some traditions, nirvana is emphasized less as a teleological goal of liberation and more as a state of mind that can be experienced in the here and now today. Even here, however, it is envisioned as a soteriological goal abstracted away from creation, rather than a redemptive movement toward creation with a soteriological scope that encompasses the material world.

4. Udana 6.1.

5. P. V. Kane, *History of the Dharmasastras*, Vol. 4, 38.

6. In the words of Murray Milner Jr. "The status one will acquire in the next life is determined by a person's current and past behavior, by conformity (or lack of it) to the moral and cosmic law, i.e., *dharma*. So, in principle, status in subsequent lives is based solely on merit and achievement. This is, of course, the famous law of *karma*. In both sacred texts and popular religious thought, the matter is considerably more complicated than this, but the basic notion is clear." From "Hindu Eschatology and the Indian Caste System: An Example of Structural Reversal," *The Journal of Asian Studies*, 52, no. 2 (May 1993): 298–319.

7. For example, *The Laws of Manu*, trans. G. Buhler (Delhi: Motilal

Banarsidass, 1964), XII, 9. [Original English edition, Oxford: The Clarendon Press, 1886].

8. While some scholars contest whether the caste system is integral to Hinduism, I personally find that its monistic tendencies and framework of moral causality fail to adequately guard against the exploitation of those with less access to power, and can thus provide spiritual justification for systems of oppression. Additionally, I believe most traditional Hindus would themselves find the West's divide between a society's "religion" and its "politics" to be an artificial and foreign construct.

9. Matthew 28:18.

10. Daniel W. Brown, "Clash of Cultures or Clash of Theologies? A Critique of Some Contemporary Evangelical Responses to Islam," *Cultural Encounters: A Journal for the Theology of Culture* 1, no. 1 (2006): 83–84.

11. Kenneth Cragg, *Muhammad and the Christian: A Question of Response* (Maryknoll: Orbis Books, 1984). I'm grateful to Dr. Paul Louis Metzger for pointing me to Cragg's work in a personal conversation; many of the insights in this section are drawn from the chapter on Islam in Dr. Metzger's excellent book: *Connecting Christ: How to Discuss Jesus in a World of Diverse Paths* (Nashville: Thomas Nelson, 2012), 80–95, 288.

12. Cragg, *Muhammad and the Christian*, 45.

13. Revelation 5:6, 12; 13:8; 21:22–27; 22:1–5.

14. For a scholarly study of the West's transition from a normative belief in God to normative unbelief, see Charles Taylor's acclaimed work, *A Secular Age* (Cambridge: Harvard University Press, 2007).

15. Bob Dylan, "Gotta Serve Somebody," from the album *Slow Train Coming*, released August 20, 1979, by Columbia Records.

16. For a theological critique of consumerism, see William Cavanaugh's excellent *Being Consumed: Economics and Christian Desire* (Grand Rapids: Eerdmans, 2008). For a fascinating analysis of the mall as a secular liturgy, see James K. A. Smith, *Desiring the Kingdom: Worship, Worldview and Cultural Formation* (Grand Rapids: Baker, 2009), 89–103. For a theological critique of consumerism, see William Cavanaugh's excellent *Being Consumed: Economics and Christian Desire* (Grand Rapids: Eerdmans, 2008). For a fascinating analysis of the mall as a secular liturgy, see James K. A. Smith, *Desiring the Kingdom: Worship, Worldview and Cultural Formation* (Grand Rapids: Baker, 2009), 89–103.

17. For an illuminating survey of this literature and insightful critique of modernity's use of the term "religion," see William T. Cavanaugh's *The Myth of Religious Violence: Secular Ideology and the Roots of Modern Conflict* (Oxford: Oxford University Press, 2009).

18. See, for example, Alister McGrath's *The Twilight of Atheism: The Rise and Fall of Disbelief in the Modern World* (Oxford: Oxford University Press, 2003), 230.

19. Lesslie Newbigin, *The Gospel in a Pluralist Society* (Grand Rapids: Eerdmans, 1989), 159.

Interlude: Love Has a Name

1. This idea is central to Newbigin's classic, *The Gospel in a Pluralist Society* (Grand Rapids: Eerdmans, 1989), particularly in the early chapters.

Chapter 12

1. N. T. Wright uses "colonial" language to helpfully describe the early churches in the Roman Empire: "the scattered and often muddled cells of women, men, and children loyal to Jesus as Lord form colonial outposts of the empire [of God's kingdom] that is to be: subversive little groups when seen from Caesar's point of view, but when seen Jewishly an advance foretaste of the time when the earth shall be filled with the glory of the God of Abraham and the nations will join Israel in singing God's praises." ("Paul's Gospel and Caesar's empire," available at http://ntwrightpage.com/Wright_Paul_Caesar_Empire.pdf; accessed November 16, 2013, 11).

2. Lesslie Newbigin, *The Household of God: Lectures on the Nature of the Church* (Eugene, OR: Wipf & Stock, 2008), 103.

3. I'm grateful to Ben Tertin for this analogy, which he believes came from Michael Polanyi, though I was unable to locate the original source. Polanyi makes similar observations in *The Tacit Dimension* (Chicago: University of Chicago Press, 1966, 2009), and Lesslie Newbigin uses a similar analogy in *The Gospel in a Pluralist Society* (Grand Rapids: Eerdmans, 1989), 43.

4. Lesslie Newbigin, *The Gospel in a Pluralist Society* (Grand Rapids, Eerdmans, 1989), 88.

5. Matthew 12:33–37; Luke 6:43–45; cf. Galatians 5:22–23.

6. John 15:1–17; cf. John 13:35.

7. 1 John 4:16–17, 7–8; emphasis added.

8. Mark 1:15; cf. Acts 2:36–38; 20:21.

9. 2 Peter 1:4 ESV.

10. Romans 10:15; cf. Isaiah 52:7; Nahum 1:15.

11. John 20:21.

12. 1 Corinthians 5:12–13.

13. Matthew 13:24–30, 36–43.

14. Matthew 3:2; 4:17; see also Mark 1:15.

15. Matthew 25:13.

Chapter 13

1. Some scholars debate whether *holy war* is the best descriptor for Israel's wars in the Old Testament, since the term is not specifically used there. I use the term intentionally in this section to draw a sharp rhetorical contrast between Israel's encounter with Canaan and our mainstream associations with "holy war" today. I am referring specifically to the "wars of Yahweh" in the Old Testament as distinct from the "profane wars" of Israel's history. For a summary of some of the historical scholarship and issues involved in these distinctions, see Ben C. Ollenburger's

introduction "Gerhard von Rad's Theory of Holy War" in Gerhard von Rad, *Holy War in Ancient Israel,* trans. Marva J. Dawn (Eugene: Wipf & Stock, 1991).

2. Rudyard Kipling, "The White Man's Burden," *McClure's Magazine* (February 1899), 12.

3. See Exodus 16–17.

4. Psalm 20:7.

5. Judges 6:15.

6. Judges 7:12.

7. See Judges 7:1–5.

8. Psalm 46:10.

9. Exodus 14:13–14.

10. Gerhard von Rad explores how central this theme from Exodus 14–15 is for holy war throughout the Old Testament in his classic work, *Holy War in Ancient Israel* (Eugene, OR: Wipf & Stock, 1991).

11. Ben C. Ollenburger, in his introduction to Gerhard von Rad's *Holy War in Ancient Israel,* op.cit.,5.

12. Deuteronomy 9:4–6.

13. Deuteronomy 7:7.

14. Genesis 10.

15. Exodus 1.

16. Ezekiel 16:1–6.

17. Joshua 10 recounts Israel's armies pursuing the Amorites as far as Azekah, and Joshua 15 outlines the allotment of this land to Judah.

18. 1 Samuel 17:43–44.

19. 1 Samuel 17:45–47.

Chapter 14

1. Deuteronomy 20:16–17; 7:2, paraphrased.

2. Richard Dawkins, *The God Delusion* (Boston: Houghton Mifflin, 2006), 242–48.

3. Richard S. Hess, "The Jericho and Ai of the Book of Joshua," in *Critical Issues in Early Israelite History,* ed. Richard S. Hess, Gerald A. Klingbeil, and Paul J. Ray Jr. (Winona Lake, IN: Eisenbrauns, 2008), 41–42, 46.

4. Paul Copan, *Is God a Moral Monster? Making Sense of the Old Testament God* (Grand Rapids: Baker Books, 2011), 176.

5. In the words of Christopher J. H. Wright, "The key military centers—the small fortified cities of the petty Canaanite kingdoms—were wiped out. But clearly not all the people, or anything like all the people, had in actual fact been destroyed by Joshua." *The God I Don't Understand: Reflections on Tough Questions of Faith* (Grand Rapids: Zondervan, 2008), 88.

6. Copan, 176.

7. Richard Hess, *Joshua,* Tyndale Old Testament Commentary 6 (Downers Grove, IL: InterVarsity, 1996), 91–92; D.J. Wiseman, "Rahab of Jericho," *Tyndale Bulletin* 14 (1964): 8–11. Paul Copan also cites the Code of

Hammurabi and laws of Eshunna regarding innkeepers in *Is God a Moral Monster?*, op.cit., 177, 249 (endnote 21).

8. This phrase shows up in the following passages: Joshua 8:25; 1 Samuel 15:3; 1 Samuel 22:19; Nehemiah 8:2; 2 Samuel 6:19; 2 Chronicles 16:3; and similar rhetoric shows up in Deuteronomy 2:34; 3:6. See Richard S. Hess, "Jericho and Ai," *op cit.*, where Hess clarifies the phrase as a "stereotypical expression for the destruction of all human life in the fort, presumably composed entirely of combatants" (p.46) and "without predisposing the reader to assume anything further about their ages or even their genders. It is synonymous with 'all, everyone.'" (p.39) Israel's encounter with the Midianites under Moses before entering the Promised Land (Numbers 31) is an exception, where women and children are specifically designated. The context and circumstances here are different, however, given the background in Numbers 25–30. This is discussed by Paul Copan in *Is God a Moral Monster?*, op.cit., 179–180.

9. John Goldingay makes this point in *Old Testament Theology: Israel's Life*, vol. 3 (Downer's Grove, IL: InterVarsity, 2009), 570.

10. Hess, "Jericho and Ai," *op.cit.* 46. Hess demonstrates how this translation of *'elep* helps resolve other problems in the Old Testament that arise with problematically large numbers when it is translated as 1,000 (such as in Numbers 1:46). In Joshua 8:25, further support that the *'elep* reference refers to 12 units rather than 12,000 men comes from earlier in Joshua, where Israel sends only 3 *'elep* to take Ai, because "only a few people live there," and their defeat is described as a "rout" even though only 36 men are killed. (7:3–5) Also, Ai's casualties in this passage appear to be lumped together with reinforcement support from the larger neighboring city of Bethel (Joshua 8:9, 12, 17); see Hess' discussion of Bethel and Ai's relationship in "Jericho and Ai," *op.cit.*, 45.

11. Copan, 172.

12. Joshua 11:4. On the defensive nature of the battles: in chapter 10, though the southern kings are going up *directly* against Gibeon, the attack is provoked because Gibeon has allied itself with Israel, putting Israel in the position of needing to honor and defend the alliance (so it is *indirectly* an attack upon Israel). In chapter 11, the northern kings are organizing *directly* against Israel. Both passages are thus depicted as defensive battles. In the words of Richard Hess, "In both cases, they begin as the coalitions assemble against Israel or its ally and therefore force the people of God into battle (Josh 10:3-5, 11:1-5)," in *War in the Bible and Terrorism in the Twenty-First Century* (Winona Lake, IN: Eisenbrauns, 2008), 30.

13. See for example the following passages: Joshua 15:63; 16:10; 17:12–13; Judges 1:19, 21, 27–35.

14. Christopher J. H. Wright, *The God I Don't Understand*, op.cit., 88.

15. It is also worth noting that in this passage, Joshua is described as having done this "just as Moses the servant of the LORD commanded" (11:12, and similarly in verses 15 and 20). This means Israel understood the original instructions under Moses in Deuteronomy to be exaggerated warfare rhetoric (not just the later carrying out of them under Joshua).

16. Joshua 10:20.
17. Another example like this can be found in 1 Samuel 15, where it is said that Saul "totally destroyed" the Amalekites, but before long the Amalekite armies are back again in 1 Samuel 30, powerful as ever.
18. Copan, 170–71.
19. See, for example, Isaiah 5; Jeremiah 12; Matthew 21:12–13, 21–33; Mark 11:15–17; 13:32–37; John 2:13–17.
20. Joshua 17:18.
21. Genesis 15:12–16; emphasis added.
22. Leviticus 18:25.

Interlude: Raising the Bar

1. Paul Copan, *Is God a Moral Monster? Making Sense of the Old Testament God* (Grand Rapids: Baker Books, 2011), 167–68.
2. Walter Russell Mead, *Special Providence: American Foreign Policy and How It Changed the World* (London: Routledge, 2002), 219; emphasis added.
3. Ibid., 218.
4. Ibid., 219; emphasis added.
5. Ibid.
6. Gerhard von Rad, *Holy War in Ancient Israel* (Eugene, OR: Wipf & Stock, 1991), 72.
7. Alister McGrath, *The Twilight of Atheism: The Rise and Fall of Disbelief in the Modern World* (Oxford: Oxford University Press, 2004), 230.
8. I believe the reason for this is that when transcendence is gone, so is the restraint it imposes, and sheer human power rushes in to fill the vacuum. Richard John Neuhaus elaborates insightfully on this concept throughout his classic work, *The Naked Public Square: Religion and Democracy in America* (Grand Rapids: Eerdmans, 1984).
9. David Bentley Hart, *Atheist Delusions: The Christian Revolution and Its Fashionable Enemies* (New Haven, CT: Yale University Press, 2009), 106.

Chapter 15

1. 1 Corinthians 15:24.
2. Revelation 17:1–18; 19:11–21.
3. See Robert Frank, "Richest 1 Percent Control 39 Percent of World's Wealth: Study," *Huffington Post*, May 31, 2013, www.huffingtonpost.com/2013/05/31/richest-1-percent-control-wealth_n_3367432.html.
4. Revelation 18:11–13.
5. Immanuel Wallerstein, *The Modern World-System: Capitalist Agriculture and the Origins of the European World-Economy in the Sixteenth Century* (New York: Academic Press, 1976), 15.
6. Details in the following account are derived from: Owens Wiwa, lecture (Harvard Square, Boston, MA, summer 1999); Owens Wiwa, "Nigeria,

The Exploitation of Ogoni People and Land by Shell Oil" (lecture, University of Oregon Law School, Eugene, OR, January 23, 1999); Human Rights Watch/Africa, *Nigeria: The Ogoni Crisis: A Case-Study of Military Repression in Southeastern Nigeria* 7, no. 5 (New York: Human Rights Watch, 1995); Greenpeace International, *Shell-Shocked: The Environmental and Social Costs of Living with Shell in Nigeria* (Amsterdam: Greenpeace International, July 1994); Center for Constitutional Rights and EarthRights International, *The Case Against Shell* (blog), June 8, 2009, "Factsheet on the Ogoni Struggle," accessed October 9, 2013, www .wiwavshell.org; and www.ratical.org/corporations/OgoniFactS.html.

7. The popular 2006 movie *Blood Diamond* (Warner Bros., 2006) has helped bring widespread international attention to the issue.

8. The 2010 documentary *The Dark Side of Chocolate* can be viewed for free at: http://topdocumentaryfilms.com/dark-side-chocolate/.

9. The Guatemalan conflict's historical backdrop is covered in Susanne Jonas's *The Battle for Guatemala: Rebels, Death Squads and US Power* (Boulder: Westview Press, 1991); and a powerful Mayan testimony can be found in Nobel Peace Prize winner Rigoberta Menchu's autobiography, *I, Rigoberta Menchu: An Indian Woman in Guatemala* (London: Verso, 1984).

10. Oxfam International's influential 2003 report on this impact of NAFTA was originally posted at www.oxfam.org/en/news/pressreleases2003/ pr030827_corn_dumping.htm; the page has since been moved or deleted.

11. Genesis 11:4.

12. Paul M. Kennedy, *The Rise and Fall of the Great Powers: Economic Change and Military Conflict from 1500 to 2000* (New York: Random House, 1987), 4.

13. J. M. Blaut, *The Colonizer's Model of the World: Geographical Diffusionism and Eurocentric History* (New York: Guilford Press, 1993), 91.

14. Ibid., 189.

15. A. Adu Boahen, *Topics in West African History* (London: Longman's, 1966), 133.

16. Blaut, *The Colonizer's Model of the World*, 206.

17. Charles Taylor, *A Secular Age* (Cambridge: Harvard University Press, 2007), 3, 13–14, 25.

18. Hebrews 11:10.

19. Psalm 137:1, 4, 6.

20. Philip Jenkins, *The Next Christendom: The Coming of Global Christianity* (Oxford: Oxford University Press, 2002).

21. Tim Gardam, "Christians in China: Is the country in spiritual crisis?" *BBC News Magazine*, September 11, 2011, www.bbc.co.uk/news/magazine-14838749.

22. Jenkins, *The Next Christendom*, 2.

23. Ibid.

24. Revelation 18:24.

25. Revelation 18:5.

26. Ibid.

27. Revelation 8:3–5.

28. Jeremiah 51:9.

Chapter 16

1. Miroslav Volf, *Exclusion and Embrace: A Theological Exploration of Identity, Otherness, and Reconciliation* (Nashville: Abingdon Press, 1996), 304.

2. For example, Gerhard von Rad's classic *Holy War in Ancient Israel*, of central influence in the last two chapters on Old Testament holy war, has been championed extensively by John Howard Yoder, a leading pacifist theologian, and a vast array of other pacifist authors. See, for example, Judith E Sanderson's "War, Peace, and Justice in the Hebrew Bible: A Representative Bibliography," included in Gerhard von Rad, *Holy War in Ancient Israel* (Eugene: Wipf & Stock, 1991), 135–66.

3. Matthew 5:39; 18:22 KJV.

4. Exodus 20; 32.

5. Matthew 28:18; cf. Acts 2:33; Revelation 5:6.

6. Isaiah 9:6.

7. Romans 13:1, 4.

8. This is not to say soldiers cannot fight a just war. As outlined earlier in this chapter, I do believe there are legitimate criteria that can establish a war as (at least proximately) just. But I am distinguishing here between just war and holy war: the former being a type initiated and undertaken by us, the latter being initiated by God and in which God himself is the primary one doing the fighting. And in relation to judges and police officers, it's worth repeating that we are speaking here analogously: there is obviously a massive difference between Babylon's judges and police officers wielding "the sword," and God rising up himself to punish Babylon (in a manner similar to what we saw in chapters 13 and 14).

9. Volf, *Exclusion and Embrace*, 275–306. See particularly Volf's insightful conclusion that "The violence of the Rider on the white horse, I suggest, is the symbolic portrayal of the final exclusion of everything that refuses to be redeemed by God's suffering love" (p. 299).

10. Psalm 99:9; 1 John 4:8.

11. Genesis 18:16–33, paraphrased.

12. See, for example, Jesus' forewarnings of coming judgment on entire towns in Matthew 11:20–24; Luke 10:12–15.

Chapter 17

1. See Genesis 14; Ezekiel 16:49–50; Jeremiah 50:40.

2. Ezekiel 16:49–50.

3. Genesis 18:21.

4. Exodus 3:7–10.

5. Genesis 19:13.

6. Genesis 19:28.

7. Revelation 19:3; see also Isaiah 34:10 for a similar allusion to the smoldering empire.

8. Jeremiah 50:40; 51:58. In the immediate context, Jeremiah is envisioning Babylon's destruction by another empire (see 50:3, 9, 41–42 and 51:1–2,

27–28, 55–56), so the fire in these passages is not "from heaven." However, Jeremiah sees this judgment on Babylon nonetheless accomplished by God, through the Medo-Persian armies; Revelation draws upon this ethos to depict God's final judgment by fire on eschatological Babylon.

9. Jeremiah 7:31.
10. Isaiah 30:33.
11. Isaiah 30:30.
12. Isaiah 30:32.
13. Daniel 7:23.
14. Daniel 7:14.
15. Daniel 7:11.
16. Revelation 20:9.
17. Rodney Stark, *The Triumph of Christianity: How the Jesus Movement Became the World's Largest Religion* (New York: HarperOne, 2011), 137.

Interlude: The Spirit of Empire

1. Matthew 4:9.
2. Revelation 12:9 NASB.
3. Daniel 7:23.
4. Richard Bauckham, *The Theology of the Book of Revelation* (Cambridge: Cambridge University Press, 1993), 31.
5. Luke 10:18.
6. Isaiah 14:4–6, 9, 11–15. Notice the "Tower of Babel" imagery in this passage: Babylon attempts to "ascend to heaven," to "sit enthroned" above God, to make a name for herself "like the Most High." Babylon's roots are at the Tower of Babel, and Isaiah draws upon this imagery.

Chapter 18

1. Revelation 21:2.
2. The city's dimensions are best understood as a symbolic reference to the people of God. They are given in 12's: 12,000 stadia (width) x 12,000 stadia (length) x 12,000 stadia (height), with walls 12 cubits x 12 cubits thick. Twelve is the number of the people of God (Israel's tribes and Jesus' apostles): and indeed, the twelve gates are named after the twelve tribes of Israel and the twelve foundations after the twelve apostles. This is likely a symbolic way of saying this massive city is *comprised of* the people of God and has room for all God's people who will come.
3. Revelation 21:2.
4. Revelation 21:3.
5. Revelation 21:24–26.
6. Revelation 5:9; 7:9.
7. Revelation 22:2.
8. Revelation 7:14.
9. Revelation 21:4.
10. Revelation 21:24.

11. Revelation 21:4.
12. Ibid.
13. Revelation 22:1–5; see also 21:22–23.
14. Revelation 21:12–14.
15. 1 Peter 2:5; cf. Ephesians 2:19–22.
16. Hebrews 11:10.
17. 2 Peter 3:7, 10.
18. 1 Corinthians 15:28.
19. Luke 24; John 20–21.
20. Ibid.
21. Luke 24:13–49.
22. See 1 Corinthians 15:35–56.

Conclusion

1. God's promise to *raze Babylon* is a major theme in the Old Testament prophets (see, for example, Isaiah 47 and Jeremiah 50–51). God's promise to Ezekiel to *raise the dead*, "I am going to open your graves and bring you up from them" (Ezekiel 37:12) is, in its immediate context, most specifically referring to the end of Israel's exile ("I will bring you back to the land of Israel," v. 12) but, in light of the resurrection of Christ and the New Testament witness, draws our eyes toward the literal resurrection to come. God's promise to *redeem the world* is also a major theme of the Old Testament prophets (see, for example, Isaiah 65:17ff on the new heavens and new earth, and Ezekiel 40–48 on the restoration of the temple—a temple that was, for Israel, the redemptive center of the earth).

Appendix

1. John 18:36.
2. John 19:11; in its immediate context, Jesus appears to be speaking here of the Jewish leaders as those "from above" who have given Pilate authority to execute him (see v. 11). But the allusion in John's gospel appears clearly to be a *double entendre* (similar to John 11:50–51), implicating the Jewish leaders' sinful intentions alongside God's simultaneous redemptive intentions, in the handing over of Christ to the Roman authorities.
3. Matthew 20:25–26.
4. James 3:5–6.
5. See, for example, Michelle Alexander and Cornel West, *The New Jim Crow: Mass Incarceration in the Age of Colorblindness* (New York: The New Press, 2010).
6. Isaiah 66:24.
7. Genesis 1:3–4.
8. Genesis 1:2.
9. 1 John 1:5.
10. Psalm 4:6.
11. John 3:16-19; emphasis added.

12. Matthew 8:12; 13:42, 50; 22:13; 24:51; 25:30; Luke 13:28.
13. Luke 15:28.
14. See also Jude 1:6, which does not use the word *Tartarus,* but has the same concept of angels "kept in darkness, bound with everlasting chains for judgment on the great Day."
15. See, for example, Isaiah 14:4–23 (particularly verse 15: "But you are brought down to the realm of the dead, to the depths of the pit."), a passage Jesus identifies with the fall of Satan (Luke 10:18).